One Down, Four Up
My Bikes, My Life

Motorcycles - The Gift that Keeps on Giving

Nigel M Sainsbury

Publisher - Nigel Sainsbury Consulting LLC - Fairfax, VA
ISBN: 978-0-578-47170-9
Available formats: eBook | Paperback distribution
2019
Printed in USA

Disclaimer - This book is a work of nonfiction. All individuals actually exist. No names have been changed, no characters created or events made up. However, the stories reflect only the author's recollection of events. For authenticity, the opinions expressed were held at the time of the event but do not necessarily reflect the authors opinion of the same event today.

Front cover:
My 2004, BMW R1200 GS, Marlborough, New Zealand (2011).

Dedication

This book is dedicated to everyone who rides or has ever ridden a motorcycle. For those who don't ride, couldn't care less or has a natural fear of motorcycles, then this book is dedicated to you also, as it will be an interesting and enlightening read.

Acknowledgements

British inventor Edward Butler who in 1884 invented the first 3-wheeled petrol vehicle called the "Butler Petrol Cycle". Having three wheels, it was effectively the first motorcycle and motorcar.

Semi-retirement for giving me the time and headspace to research all the bikes I have owned whilst sifting through boxes of old photographs, allowing me to recall and document all these two-wheeled memories.

All the people I have been privileged to meet and get to know just by sharing a common passion for motorcycles.

Finally, special thanks to my wife Carol for believing in me.

Table of Contents

Foreword

I have known Nigel for over 35 years and have ridden and owned many motorcycles myself, but I have never met anyone like Nigel who connects with their machine and shows such a passion for motorcycling and everything associated with it. Nigel's love of motorbikes has been with him since he was able to keep a couple of rotating wheels between his legs and grab some handlebars. His early pushbike experience naturally progressed to mopeds and then onto larger engine and different types of motorcycles. Nigel explains in detail his choice of bikes, some of the technical and brand details, and the memories associated with owning some 24 motorcycles over his almost 60 years including his numerous hospital sleepovers from his motorcycling mishaps. It is Nigel's reflection from his accidents and his misdemeanours that elevates this book above all other books on motorcycles. Nigel's attitude to such incidents is to treat them all as life learning opportunities rather than motorcycling disasters. What would cause most people to take up another pastime, Nigel just looks to improve and be better. Even if you don't like motorcycles, this book is a joy to read. It's a history book, technical manual and autobiography rolled into one. Nigel hangs it all together with some great story telling and if you are a motorcyclist yourself, this book will invariably trigger your own memories and adventures from being on two wheels. It transported me back to the 1960s and my BSA Bantam days. In summary, this book is a light-hearted view on life using motorcycles either as a lead into an interesting story or just as a backdrop to a funny tale.

- *Bob Morgan, Motorcyclist and Nigel's Friend*

Preface

Having been inspired to write my autobiography for my children, I recognized that my life has been peppered with stories of motorcycles. In fact, on average I have had a different motorcycle for every two years of my life since I turned 13. It made sense then that if I were to write a second book, it would be on the memories and experiences associated with these bikes. Not just recall the memories of ownership, but to reflect on the reasons why I had chosen the bike, the influences that were around at that time and a little about the brand history. A motorcycle is like a piece of clothing, it is an extension of the person riding it. Therefore, the motorcycle is a practical way by which we can make a public fashion statement. Over my almost 60 years, I have made many fashion statements with motorcycles and they have become an inherent part of my DNA. If you ride, you will relate to many of the stories in this book and they will likely remind you of your own memories associated with motorcycles. If you hate motorcycles and read this book, it just might reaffirm your thoughts of them being dangerous and motivate you to start a movement to ban them altogether. For those who couldn't care less about motorcycles, I trust you will find this book entertaining and informative. For anyone else, just replace the word motorcycle with your favourite pastime and enjoy the read. - *Nigel Sainsbury*

Me, Cwmfelinfach, Wales, 1962

Chapter 1
Two Wheel Addiction

How do you know if you are going to love or just have a passion for doing something in life? Perhaps try it out first, then decide? Well, that is one sure way to find out. However, some people may not even need to do the activity first, they instinctively know they will enjoy it because either they have seen it being done on TV or have witnessed someone doing it for real. Alternatively, they may know someone who has told an interesting story about the activity and they themselves can't wait to experience the same thing. My interest in motorcycles was a combination of all the above, from as far back as I can remember. I had a love of motorcycles even before I had ridden one.

It all started way back in the late 60s growing up in the small coal mining village of Cwmfelinfach (Comb-fell-in-vac), South East Wales. This small coal mining village was typical of the day and sat almost equidistant between the villages of Ynysddu (un-ess-d) to the north and Wattsville to the south. The local infant (primary) school was in Cwmfelinfach and the secondary modern school (High School) was in Ynysddu. All my close friends lived in one of these three villages. The distance between Ynysddu and Wattsville was four miles (six kilometres) so the furthest I had to travel from home to a mate's house was two miles (three kilometres) in either direction. The only transport available was Shank's Pony, pushbike or the local bus. The bus would cost you money and involved a lot of waiting. As kids we never had any money and we certainly didn't want to wait for anything, so it was Shanks' Pony or pushbike to get you around.

If you didn't like walking, riding a bike as a kid was essential if you wanted to hang out with friends. Everybody had a bike and it was by far the quickest and easiest way to get from A to B. No one had their parents to run them around, primarily because not many families could afford cars. Pushbikes gave you the freedom to move around individually or as a group. In the early 70s pushbikes started to get quite stylish. The introduction of the Raleigh *'Chopper'* in the UK was the first time (in my memory) that pushbikes were being styled on motorcycles. The Chopper had a small front wheel and larger wheel at the back, a long seat with a backrest and *'ape hanger'* type handlebars - just like a chopper motorcycle. It also had a neat gear change lever located in a centre console. It was a very cool bike. Sadly, I never had one. It was an expense my parents could ill afford. I had to manage with hand-me-downs from my brother until I was a teenager and then mum and dad got me a dark green three speed Sturmey Archer *'normal'* 26 inch wheel bike for Christmas in 1973. Mum bought it out of *'Kays Catalogue'* a UK mail order catalogue that mum was an agent for. A sort of 1970s Amazon.com. It was not a cool bike by any means, but I didn't care. It was new, and it was mine.

I must have ridden hundreds of miles on that bike in the three years I had it. I rode it every day. I loved it. I saved up my newspaper delivery round money and bought a Huret combined speedo and odometer for the bike - also out of mums Kays catalogue. I was the only kid with a speedo on my bike. Not even the Chopper's had speedos. So, I made sure all my mates knew about it. Not long after I had fitted the speedo, my friend Bryn and I cycled a round trip up through the Brecon Beacons National Park. I got home very late in the day much to the dismay of my parents who hadn't seen me since the previous night. When I told dad where Bryn and I had been, he didn't believe me at first and I had to explain some details of the trip for him to buy into my story. We had travelled over 80 miles (128 kilometres) - and it wasn't an easy 80 miles either on a three-speed bike. I was absolutely knackered but felt that I had nailed this all-day distance riding thing. The next challenge for me was to see how fast I could go. The speedo indicator needle could swing a full 180 degrees to an indicated 40 mph. Even in third gear and peddling like an Olympic athlete downhill, I could only manage just over 30 mph. It quickly became an obsession to reach 40 mph or more. I realised that I needed to do something special to get the red indicator needle to hit that magical 40 mph.

Behind our street, was a single-lane hilly road called 'Twyn Gwyn Road', it was not a great road with overgrown bushes and shrubs on either side and a miniature grassland fighting to break through the cracked and slightly raised tarmac in the middle of it. However, the worn wheel tracks either side was fine for riding your bike, but you had to pick your track at the start of your run and stick with it as crossing over the central divide was fraught with danger. Apart from not knowing what was buried beneath all the vegetation, the road snaked into a few nasty curves. Not a problem on their own, but if anything was coming up the hill in the other direction and you were travelling down at speed, you had few safe options. I had done this run several times on my own and just couldn't get to that magical 40 mph. I was good at physics in school and knew from my education that with a bit more weight on the bike to give me more momentum, and with a slightly longer run, I was sure it was possible to reach 40 mph plus.

I convinced my mate Tommy, nicknamed *'Tucker'* to be human ballast on my first and only run. Tucker was perched on the handle bars, legs dangling over the front wheel. I was sat on the bike with my arms around him, gripping the handlebars. It was the best configuration we had come up with for a speed trial. We had tried riding with Tucker sat side saddled across the crossbar, but he struggled to keep his arse balanced on the one-inch tubular steel frame and was rocking from side to side with only my outstretched arms stopping him from falling off. The constantly changing weight distribution in this configuration made the bike very unstable at any speed. The handlebars were much easier to sit on and his body weight on the front end of the bike acted like a steering damper which was very useful at speed, but not so much for the slowing down phase.

We wore protective goggles and face masks; the same ones your dad wears when he is drilling and sanding metal or wood in his shed. We didn't have real motorcycle equipment of course, but we knew that the wind at that speed may make our eyes water, and the wearing of masks and goggles also made us look cool. In our minds we looked like real racers. We had no head gear or gloves and were wearing old jeans and tee shirts. So clearly, we had all the other safety equipment we needed. Over the half mile or so we rode at speed, we got the little red Huret indicator needle to eventually hit the 40 mph stop and it stayed there for a few seconds just before we needed to slow down to navigate the curves.

I really didn't give enough consideration to the slowing down stage of the run and Tucker had put his faith in me knowing I was good at physics. However, it became a prime focus of both our attentions pretty quickly as we were approaching the first of the curves. With both brakes applied hard, our momentum was far greater that the energy transfer through the friction of the four small rubber brake blocks trying to slow the rotation of the wheels. The front wheel rim got so hot that it was wearing down the brake blocks quicker than the rate we were slowing. I remember smelling melting rubber and seeing tiny globules of black stuff in my periphery vision being ejected from the now rapidly vibrating front brake calliper. Although I was pulling as hard as I could on both brake levers, it didn't seem enough. I now fully understood the term *'white knuckle ride'*.

My eyes were fixated on the rapidly approaching curve, which at speed, just looked like a blind bend. It didn't help that Tucker was blocking half my vision. I could only see to the right or to the left around him at any one time, never the whole road. With our future uncertain, we did the only thing kids do in such situations - we started to laugh. Without saying a word to each other we instinctively sensed that this was not going to end well. I was doing as much as I could and Tucker - well, he could do nothing other than continue to laugh. We were both in the hands of *'Lady Luck'* and she was definitely looking down on us that day. We managed to navigate through the curves without meeting any vehicles coming up the hill and arrived at the bottom of the run unarmed with both of us still on the bike. The only casualty being my two front brake blocks which were completely buggered. Both were a fraction of their thickness from just a few minutes earlier. What had not been ejected as friction waste had successfully welded itself to the front wheel rim. Bloody incredible really. Although we were lucky, we were also teenagers and bullet proof. Taking risks and ignoring hazards was all part of the excitement. Except that teenagers don't really know much about risks let alone how to manage them until they confront one head on - and that's when luck has a hand to play.

This episode reinforced a few things. Firstly, it proved that my physics calculations were correct; more weight = more momentum = more speed. Secondly, I could tell my mates with confidence that my average 3-speed bike could do 40 mph plus, and I had Tucker as my witness. Thirdly, it gave me an adrenalin rush. Experiencing speed on two wheels was enormous fun and it was incredibly addictive. My pushbike had become more than just a means of transport, it was a fantastic way to spend my free time. The bi-product of cycling was that it kept me pretty fit too allowing me to hold my position in the school rugby team and partake in other athletic activities.

Coupled with my interest in two wheels was my interest in all things mechanical. I loved to take things apart and put them back together again - particularly working engines. I had several small model steam engines, model aircraft glow plug reciprocating engines and loads of Meccano sets. Helping dad fix the car and getting my hands dirty was something I just really enjoyed, so changing brake blocks on a pushbike after a high-speed test run was a breeze.

It was not long after the 'Huret Speed Trial' with Tucker that I had my first experience with real motorcycles, or rather mopeds. It was a 1959 NSU Quickly. An odd name for a moped that was anything but quick.

The term 'moped' means different things to different people depending on which country you come from. The term combines the words 'motor' and 'pedal' which in essence means a bike fitted with a motor allowing it to be powered by either the motor, pedals or both. Engine assisted drives have been fitted to bikes since early 1900s, but it wasn't until the Vienna

Convention on Road Traffic in 1968 that defined a moped as being any two-wheeled or three-wheeled vehicle that is fitted with an internal combustion engine having a cylinder capacity not exceeding 50 cc (Cubic Centimetres). Technically, you don't need pedals under this definition so not surprisingly there was still confusion about the term moped from several countries who were signatories of the Vienna Convention. A small 50 cc scooter with foot pegs could classify as a moped. In the 1970s the UK Government nailed it when they defined a moped as a motorcycle that had an engine size of 50 cc or less and could be powered by the engine or, if you were mad enough, the pedals which had to be fitted as an alternative means of propulsion.

The NSU Quickly was a moped made by NSU Motorenwerke AG, a German manufacturer founded in 1873 in Neckarsulm (NSU) a city about 30 miles (48 kilometres) north of Stuttgart. NSU disappeared in 1969 when it was bought out by Volkswagen. The NSU Quickly was a 49 cc single cylinder, 2-stroke engine producing a neck breaking 1.4 Brake Horse Power (bhp) at 4,600 Revolutions Per Minute (rpm) whilst delivering an earth shattering 25 mph through a two-speed gearbox. It was slower than my pushbike.

I had spotted this mechanical thing rotting away in the overgrown foliage of our neighbour's garden. I didn't know what it was at first, but I could see that it had handlebars, a seat and what looked like some kind of fuel tank. I slowly acquainted myself with this neglected machine over a period of a few weeks, dropping hints to our neighbour that I had a real interest in the thing that was lying in his garden. I plucked up the courage one day and asked him outright if I could have a closer look at what was feeding his plants. To my surprise, he said that if I cleared away all the wild shrubbery from that area,

7

I could have the thing for free. A couple of hard grafting teenage hours later and it was mine. Easy.

After cleaning the decals on the tank and frame I discovered the bike was an NSU Quickly. I had never heard of the make before. The bike had not been run for several years and seemed to be rusting everywhere. However, once I had removed all the vegetation and washed it all down it looked pretty good and the thing was intact - much of the rust was just garden muck blended into the natural rustic fleshy creamy colour of the original paintwork. Not a colour I would have picked for a brand new one, but this was free. Beggars can't be choosers. The good thing about mopeds is that you can pedal them just like a push bike - it's exhausting work so why would you? You are better off with a pushbike. However, the pedals on the NSU were also the means of starting it. There was no kick start. I didn't know it at the time, but this was pretty typical of mopeds of the day and the pedals could also be used at any time to assist the engine when it was running out of puff, like going up an incline. Hills were a real challenge as the bike was so underpowered.

The pedalling ratio on the NSU was quite low so you had to pedal quite fast just to maintain a speed that kept you from falling off. However, once the engine was running you simply stopped pedalling and let the engine do the work. If you wanted to show off, you could make a rapid start from standstill by pedalling like mad for the first 20 feet (6 metres) or so thus assisting the engine and off-loading the clutch. It was a cool toy to have as a 13-year-old and it was a sort of upgrade from my pushbike. Although without the engine working, my pushbike was proven to be faster and much easier to ride.

The 'back lane' connected all the front gardens in our street and the rear grounds of the street in front of us. It was an unlit, unsealed dirt track over half a mile long, but only about 10 feet (3 metres) wide. It was only ever used by the few neighbours who had cars, the coal delivery lorry (truck) and dustmen (trash collection). However, the back lane was a playground for us kids. It could be a football pitch, running track, hiding place and anything else our imagination believed it to be. In this case, it was the Nurburgring, a test track for the NSU Quickly. It got a little tiring pedalling this machine up and down the back lane, so I decided to do something about it. With a little bit of supervision/help from dad, I set about stripping the thing down and rebuilding it.

I had no money for engine parts and didn't have a clue how I could get them even if I did. So, I set about rebuilding the engine with the same original items and made mating gaskets cut from an old Kellogg's Corn Flakes cereal box. A skill I would not use again until 2016 in Tennessee, USA (see Chapter 13). With some fettling of the carb and ignition circuits and with fuel syphoned out of our neighbour's car mixed with old engine oil as two stroke oil, I got the engine running. I surprised a few folk, including myself. What was not surprising was the little 49 cc motor didn't run very long with Kellogg's head and base gasket sets. However, I did manage to make several high-speed passes, touching speeds which must have been in excess of 15 mph, before the cardboard cereal box gaskets finally gave up. They just didn't make cereal boxes to last in those days. The process of strip, gasket making and rebuild was repeated many times over the coming weeks as I got proficient on the NSU two stroke engine, carburation, and ignition system. I also learnt that two stroke engines can run backwards. I found this out by mistake while pushing it backwards in gear. Impressive when your moped has reverse and has the potential to go as fast backwards as it can forward.

I remember running the moped at night and the front dynamo light illuminating about five inches in front of me with its blinding 6 volt 20-watt bulb that seemed to burn a dark orange colour. It was completely useless, I couldn't see a thing in front of me. I simply rode up and down the back lane from memory. It seemed like I was doing 100 mph with the wind blowing in my face. In reality, I was probably just going fast enough to remain upright. Nevertheless, those brief moments of success had a twofold effect on me. Initially, they were huge confidence boosters; suddenly I knew what I was doing, I could fix things. The feeling of success for fixing mechanical things would continue and influence my professional career in the future. Secondly, my success with the moped cemented my desire to seek pleasure from the freedom that was afforded to me by being on powered two wheels. Pushbikes were great, but motorcycles took things to a different level and I loved it. I was already hooked, but now I was determined to get into bigger and faster bikes.

With the NSU Quickly as a down payment and some additional newspaper delivery round money, my next venture was not another moped or a motorcycle, rather a cult vehicle of the 60s; a Vespa scooter. Mine was a dark red 1959 Vespa 150 GS. Like the NSU I didn't have a choice on the colour, but red worked. I bought it from a school mate, and it was in much better condition than the NSU Quickly and considerably faster. I attended a *'Mods and Rockers'* meet up in Baltimore, USA in August 2018 and found the exact same model on display. It was in immaculate condition and had clearly aged much better than I had.

Vespa is a brand of scooter manufactured by the Italian company Piaggio who are also associated with other Italian brands like Aprilia, Derbi, Gilera and Moto Guzzi. Like many other engineering companies before and during World War II, Piaggio had made boats, seaplanes, other aircraft and land vehicles, but like many other heavy industries needed to diversify after the war had ended. Piaggio decided to develop

the Vespa (which means *'wasp'* in Italian) scooter in 1946 as a mass-produced affordable means of transport for everyone post war. A similar thing happened in Germany with Volkswagen when they developed a cheap affordable vehicle in the Beetle (commissioned by Hitler) and the French car company Citroen with their 2CV. Although, to be

1961 Vespa 150 GS, Baltimore, USA, 2018

fair, both the Beetle and the 2CV were mass produced for the people in the 30s before the Second World War had even started, but the idea of mass-producing affordable vehicles was the same theme. I tip my hat to the Italians who had made the decision to go with two wheels rather than four as a people's mode of transport post war.

Like the NSU, my Vespa was nowhere near street legal (I was not of legal age to ride anyway) so we (my mates and I) were confined to riding up and down the back lane. The scooter was a huge amount of fun and offered some protection if you took a tumble - which we often did. You could get three people on the Vespa. The NSU would struggle with one. I never had the Vespa very long, just a few months, but it was a great machine to learn clutch control and gear changing. The left-hand clutch lever and hand grip was also the gear changer so when pulling in the lever you then had to twist the grip to select a gear. First gear was all the way up, so you had to rotate your wrist and twist grip as far as you could towards you and then pull in the level and twist downwards as you went through the four-speed gearbox.

To get the engine started, the Vespa had a kick start not pedals. The kickstart or rather the *'push down foot lever'* was a little different to a motorcycle kick start. The main difference being that your foot pressure is applied to a straight lever in a clockwise motion 90 degrees to the ground. On a motorcycle it's an anti-clockwise motion to a two-piece knuckle kick start lever at 180 degrees from the ground. The Vespa was easier to start before you got on it, whereas a motorcycle kick starter is easier to operate (or kick) once you are sat on the bike.

Like the NSU, the Vespa was a 2-stroke single cylinder engine, but it displaced three times the volume of the NSU with an eye watering 145.5 cc and produced over five times as much power with a claimed 8.2 hp at 5,000 rpm. It was considerably heavier than the NSU but was capable of doing twice the speed. It was claimed, but not proven in the back lane to do some 62 mph. The brakes were significantly better than the NSU too, they actually worked quite well on the Vespa, but you had to be careful as heavy breaking on the small scooter wheels could cause some interesting handling characteristics. At times it was like steering a powered shopping cart. The vespa had a normal front brake lever on the right-side hand/throttle grip and a foot pedal for a rear brake operated by your right foot. A friend bought the Vespa off me and stripped it down to basics and rode the thing off road up the dingle. The dingle was a large public wooded area located behind our street. Unfortunately, the Vespa is not a dirt bike, so it didn't last very long before it was eventually confined to the scrap heap of scooters a few weeks later. The small wheels and low engine in a scooter are not good configurations for off-road riding.

My venture into the world of scooter riding was brief, and I have never returned. Although iconic to some, scooters were an eye sore and just dangerous to others. I was nonchalant about them but appreciate their usefulness as a commuter. They were certainly quicker than mopeds, offered some protection to your legs when you fell off, but the handling at speed (even on the unsealed back lane) was particularly poor and the gear changing twistgrip with clutch was not intuitive to me. However, owning one was a great experience and merely reinforced my desire to stick with motorcycles that had bigger wheels and gear changes that could be done safely with your feet.

You may have noticed that the NSU power output was measured in 'bhp' and the Vespa in 'hp'. So, what's the difference? James Watt the Scottish inventor who was associated with steam engines during the industrial revolution, came up with the term Horsepower (hp) to compare the work done by the steam engine compared to that of horses. One horsepower was the equivalent of one-horse lifting 33,000 pounds of coal out of a coal mine over one foot in one minute. One hp = 33,000 foot-pound per minute or 550 foot-pounds per second (Imperial unit of measurement). The metric version of horsepower is measured in watts (W) or kilowatts (kW) and is equivalent of a horse physically lifting a force of 75 kilograms over one metre in a second. Therefore, 1 (imperial) hp = 745.7 watts with a metric horsepower coming in slightly less at 735.5 watts. Horsepower measures the power of an engine, its delivered output (like a horse). On a bike it would be measured at the rear wheel. Brake horsepower (bhp) on the other hand measures the power at the crankshaft (the potential of the horse) and does not consider the losses caused by friction, heat and any auxiliary drives like the generator or water pump. Therefore, bhp is more a theoretical value to the user and will be a higher figure than hp for the same engine. Many new motorcycles have both imperial and metric power outputs stated in their advertising paraphernalia, this recognises that different generations and countries identify with different units of measurement.

I had a moped at age 13, a scooter at age 14 and now approaching middle teenagerhood at 15, I was ready for a real motorcycle and the bike I ended up with remains to this day the most successful motorcycle ever made. Bearing in mind that in the Welsh valleys you had limited choice and the source of these bikes was dubious at best. Unlike the NSU, I am not sure to this day where the vespa or my next bike came from. You just didn't ask. Anyway, in 2018 there had been over 100 million of these things made since they started production back in 1958 - yes, 100 million worldwide in 60 years, that's over 4,500 a day, every day since 1958. To get this into perspective that is more that the Model 'T' Ford, VW Beetle and Vespa scooter combined. It also accounts for almost one in every three bikes made by this Japanese motorcycle manufacturer.

I had to deliver many newspapers over several weeks to be able to purchase this bike from a mate. Although classed as a motorcycle, in my opinion it was a hybrid moped/scooter going under the guise of a motorcycle. It was a 1969 Honda C50 and it was in its classic Honda red and white livery, a colour set I would have picked had I had the choice, so it was perfect. As with many events in life for me, a song or piece of music is normally associated with big events. The C50 to me is linked with the UK band Queen who had their mammoth worldwide hit Bohemian Rhapsody in November 1975.

Over the decades this bike has been made in different engine sizes (C50, C70, C90, C100) and although it has been modified over the years, the essentials have stayed pretty much the same. The beauty of this bike is that it fits the short distance commuter and the learner market. It is a breeze to ride and extremely reliable. The step through gear change and semi-automatic clutch allows for easy one-handed riding and the easy kick start (no pedals) and weather protection (like a scooter) all adds to its appeal as a comfortable and easy ride. It has proper sized wheels too, so it handles much better than a scooter and if you remove the baffle in the exhaust, it sounds like a much bigger motorcycle than it is. The generic name for the various derivatives of this motorcycle is the Honda Super Cub.

Me & My 1969 Honda C50, Back lane, Cwmfelinfach, Wales, 1975

The Honda C50 was my first 4 stroker. The small low compression overhead valve engine kicked out a wrist wrenching 4.5 hp at 9,500 rpm, allowing man and machine to reach dizzy speeds of around 43 mph. This was the same speed my pushbike could go downhill with Tucker on the handlebars. The low compression engine was standard and had two major benefits for the global market. First, it allowed for low grade fuel to be used in countries that didn't have high octane petrol, and second, it made the engine very easy to kick start, even a child could start and ride the bike. Interestingly, electric starters although very common on most bikes and scooters today (2019), the C50 is still made with the kick start option for some markets. Keeping things simple has probably been the key to its massive success. However, the 2019 version of the Super Cub for sale in the Unites States is quite different and has gone bigger and very high tech. The engine is now a massive 124.9 cc, it has ABS, a four-speed gearbox, a fuel injected engine, keyless ignition and sports a disc brake up front. The obvious thing missing is a kick starter. A redundant piece of equipment on an electric bike, not so much on a small machine like the Super Cub when you have a flat battery.

Like Piaggio, Honda motorcycles rose from the ashes of World War II. However, the Honda brand had been established prior to the war by its founder Soichiro Honda. Mr Honda had grown up with a fascination for cars and bikes and had started his business producing piston rings for Toyota vehicles. He helped the war effort by automating the production of military aircraft propellers, then post World War Two he set up the Honda Technical Research Institute in 1946 and two years later produced his first motorised bicycle with an engine that had been designed by Honda. Then in 1949 Honda built their first complete motorcycle (engine and frame) and called it the D-Type; D=Dream. Just 15 years later, Honda had grown to become the largest manufacturer of motorcycles in the world. Amazing what one person can achieve in such a short space of time. Quite a story in itself

There were a few oddities about the Honda C50 that I have not experienced on other bikes. Firstly, you could do wheelies from a stand still without even trying. With the engine running you could select first gear, and if you kept the pressure on the gear change lever with your foot, it had the same effect of holding in the semi-automatic clutch. Then, if you increased the engines revs significantly and let your foot pressure off the gear change lever, the bike would lunge forward like a startled banshee as the 4.5 horses kicked in. If you were holding on correctly it looked impressive. If you didn't have a firm grip on the handlebars, the bike would simply shoot out from between your legs and you would look like a complete idiot. I had mastered both. The second odd thing was during initial slowing with the front brake, the front end would feel as if it was rising up. On most bikes, the front-end dips during braking, but the leading link suspension on this bike didn't work like that. Not a problem once you got used to it, but it feels very odd at first. The third oddity was that if you lost the key or just didn't have one, all you had to do was remove the single screw that held the ignition block to the side of the frame - with no battery and a broken earth through the ignition block, the bike would start. Not a great anti-theft device, but then that's probably how I ended up with the bike in the first place.

Around this time my brother had bought his first bike, a street legal Honda SS 50. This was in fact a moped and had pedals not footrests, like the NSU you would never want to pedal the thing over any distance, and they were not required on the Honda for starting the engine, it had a kick start for that. I thought it odd that SS was short for 'Super Sports'. You don't normally associate powering a super sports bike with pedals, but when you are 16 and can say you are riding a super sports bike, who cares if it has pedals for footrests. I would ride my brother's SS 50 at every opportunity, without him knowing of course. It had a proper clutch too, just like the Vespa but with a foot gear change. Dad would also take me out on this bike as a legal pillion. He enjoyed taking me out and was always encouraging me to get into motorcycling once I had reached the legal age of 16, like I needed encouraging. My mother was not so keen on me being into motorcycles, she thought they were dangerous. Indeed, it is fair to say she was dead against me having one at all and her 'bikes are dangerous' philosophy would be reinforced to her in less than three years from my getting my first street legal motorcycle or rather moped.

My brother's Honda SS 50 was no bigger (in terms of cc) than the NSU or my Honda C50, but it was much better looking, had a four-speed gearbox, a scrambler type high exhaust pipe and just seemed a faster bike overall hitting speeds well into the high 40s. Two-up downhill, 50+ mph was an achievable goal from this 2.5 hp at 8,000 rpm ripper of a machine. Strangely, it was not as powerful as my C50 for some reason, but when you are talking single figure horses, it doesn't really make a huge amount of difference.

My dad also loved motorcycles and had several bikes of his own in his youth, but family life became more a priority once I had arrived on the scene in 1960. I don't remember dad ever owning a motorcycle when I was growing up, but my brother recalls dad having a BSA or some other classic British motorcycle brand when he was small.

Through riding my brother's SS 50, I learnt how to use a clutch in concert with the foot gear change, a configuration that was new to me and one that would set me up for all my motorcycling days. However, I had to be careful, so to avoid being caught I would usually ride the SS 50 at night. Unlike the NSU which had an incompetent glow worm as a headlight, the 6-volt headlight bulb of the Honda was pretty good in comparison. I would ride up and down the back lane and when I was feeling adventurous, ride it 'around the block'. The block was nothing more than the back lane combined with the sealed road that connected both ends of the back lane around our street. A trip around the block was probably the best part of a mile. Good times!

Chapter 2
Legal Age to Ride

My Dad, Lucky (the dog) & My 1976 Yamaha FS1E, Cross Keys, Wales, 1976

Prior to 1971 in the UK you could ride a motorcycle up to 250cc at age 16. However, government legislation changed in 1971 and a new *'Sixteener Law'* was introduced restricting the engine size to 50 cc from 250 cc until the rider had turned 17. Not sure whether this legislation was to reduce the amount of bike accidents involving teenagers or to force potential young bikers off the road completely. What it was successful in doing was knocking another nail in the coffin of the small engine British motorcycle industry and at the same time spurring on Japanese bike manufactures like Honda, Yamaha and Suzuki to get inventive and develop high performance sports mopeds for the 16-year-olds. The Japanese were never ones to shy away from a challenge and duly stepped up to the plate with some serious machines that were not only very attractive to the new 16-year-old buyers but would hook these teenagers into their brand. I know this, because that is exactly what happened to me and many of my teenage friends.

I finished secondary school in July 1976 (having turned 16 on 7th June) and entered grownup employment within a couple of weeks. I started as a casual labourer for a heavy industrial engineering firm who did things like replace steam turbines in power stations. I got paid in cash, on a weekly basis (with overtime bonuses) which meant that within just a few weeks, I had saved enough money for a deposit for my first brand new legal motorcycle; a Yamaha FS1-E, colloquially called the 'Fizzie' which of course under the new legislation was a moped.

I picked the Yamaha brand for two reasons. Firstly, everyone was talking about them and secondly, Yamaha had the nearest dealership to where we lived. There was no internet to research bikes and their specs in the mid-70s. Magazines were available but were expensive and you would rather spend your glossy mag money on adult stuff like Playboy or Fiesta rather than one on motorcycles; I was 16-years-old for goodness sake! In any case, it was far easier and much nicer to go to the dealership, see the bikes in the flesh and let the salesman talk you into buying one. Dad and I colluded together, and he signed the hire purchase agreement as my guarantor without speaking to mum first. Mum was a little pissed about that, but she knew she was fighting a losing battle. I was always going to get a bike, it was just a matter of time. On the positive side, mum had started to appreciate the benefit in my having some independence to get around, so it was not all bad news for her.

In October 1976, I secured a more permanent job in a supermarket called ASDA (Associated Dairies) stacking shelves in the sauces and pickles aisle. The ASDA job paid a little less than the labouring job, but it was more secure ensuring that I could always make the hire purchase payments on the Fizzie; much to the delight of mum and dad. I was always going to join the Royal Air Force (RAF) and had already started the recruitment process in August 1976 but had to wait until January 1977 when I would turn 16 1/2, the legal age to join the Armed Forces with parental consent. I did wonder whether mum would withdraw her consent card when dad and I first colluded to get the Fizzie.

Yamaha are synonymous with a whole range of products like motorcycles, watercraft (jet skis), boats, generators and of course musical instruments. Indeed, the Yamaha Cooperation and the Yamaha Motor Company brand symbol is made up of three interlocking tuning forks set 120 degrees apart in a circle recognizing their musical instrument heritage. Yamaha started in 1887 producing pianos and reed organs, but it wasn't until after the Second World War that Yamaha started to get into motorcycles. Yamaha made the decision to repurposed much of its war effort manufacturing equipment towards the development and manufacturing of motorcycles. In 1955 the Yamaha Motor Company became an independent company splitting away from the Yamaha Cooperation. The first motorcycle Yamaha produced was a 125 cc, single cylinder two-stroke bike inventively called the YA-1. Which just happened to be quite a successful motorcycle in the three years it was in production. It was no fluke that the YA-1 looked remarkably like the German DKW RT125 and the BSA Bantam.

The Yamaha FS1-E (E = English version) was the most popular choice for a 16-year-old in 1976 (the Honda SS 50 was second). The Fizzie was a super cool 49 cc two-stroke, four speed moped, capable of reaching speeds in excess of 45 mph and possibly 50 mph on a good day. The speedo went up all the way to 80 mph whilst the Honda SS 50 speedo only went up to a pathetic 60 mph. Clearly the Yamaha was the faster machine. Psychologically, I am sure that would have swung a few 16-year old's in favour of the Yamaha. The Yamaha was certainly quicker on acceleration but that came at a cost to fuel consumption. The FS1E would return about 95 mpg whilst the Honda would seem to run on a tank full of petrol forever, returning around 120 mpg.

The other cost to running the FS1E was the need to pre-mix the petrol with two-stroke oil when refuelling. This was a complete pain in the arse. If you got the mixture wrong and didn't put enough oil in the petrol you were in danger of seizing the engine. Conversely, if you put too much in, a thicker than normal blue haze of smoke would swirl around the back end of the bike and you had diminished performance - which was not a great outcome on a bike that had single figure horses on tap. I always erred on the side of safety and put an extra splash of oil in the tank when I filled up. No such hassle with the four stroke Honda.

Most other two stroke bikes of the era had a separate oil tank that delivered the correct amount of oil through an oil injection system and there was always a debate at the time about what was best; pre-mix or separate oil injection systems. The answer is quite straight forward. Oil injection systems are much better. The only advantage of a pre-mix system is that it has no separate oil system to maintain making the fuel system simple. The disadvantage is that fuel is delivered to the engine at the same fuel/oil ratio throughout the rpm range. At idle and low engine speeds a two stroke is not working hard and doesn't need as much lubricating oil. Also, at low rpms the engine tends to run a little dirtier and leaner because of the oil and the reduced fuel/air mixture (oil dilutes the fuel) this can cause the engine to run hotter (lean mixture) and the spark plug to foul making for a very smoky exhaust - especially if you are overzealous with the pre-mix during refuelling. Therefore, the pre-mix ratio (normally 20:1) on the Fizzie catered for the worst-case scenario. Oddly, not putting enough oil in the fuel makes the fuel/air ratio richer so the engine runs colder. You really can't win with a pre-mix. A separate oil injection system takes care of all that. You just need to make sure you have enough two-stroke oil in the oil tank every time you fill up.

The Fizzie is credited with hooking a complete generation of upcoming kids like me onto motorcycles. Not that I needed much hooking. When it was first introduced in the UK in 1973 it became the bestselling bike in just three months.

Like the Honda SS 50, the Fizzie also had pedals as footrests. The pedals were a legal requirement for the bike to be classed as a moped. The pedals could also be used to propel the bike if you were crazy enough to try it, but they could not be used with the engine running. Unlike the old slower mopeds of the 50s and 60s, which you had to pedal to start the engine and could use in concert with the engine, these new super-duper mopeds were fitted with a standard kick starter, so the pedals really were just footrests. To engage the pedals was fiddly and a pain in the arse, after all they were never meant to be used for real, they were just satisfying a legal requirement. If the bike broke down, it was much easier to just push it.

My Fizzie was the last year the bike was fitted with a front drum brake. The later FS1E -DX had a front disc brake. I never felt that a moped needed a disc brake to stop, but the front disc did make the bike look cool and aligned it with the much bigger bikes which were also being produced with hydraulic disc brakes around this time. The bike also had an unusual gearbox. All four gears were down. Usually it's one down and the rest are up which puts neutral between first and second gear. That is by design as it makes for easier slowing down and selection of the correct gear when pulling off from standstill. The Fizzie was different.

The Fizzie kicked out a whopping 4.8 bhp at 7,000 rpm with a claimed top speed of 48 mph. Although you never knew what the engine rpm was as the bike never had a tachometer fitted. You could easily get caught speeding through our village which had a 30 mph speed limit if you really wanted too, but I never did feel the need to challenge the local constabulary's speed monitoring equipment until a few years later. As it was my first brand new bike, I also had the choice of colour. This was a first for me. I chose Baja brown it was the coolest colour and made the bike look much bigger than it was (in my opinion). I loved my Fizzie and it was an incredible feeling at 16 to be free and independent. I could go anywhere, anytime and I didn't need anyone's permission.

August 1977, was an interesting time in the UK as all mopeds sold from that date forward had to be restricted to 30 mph. The government realized that by reducing the engine capacity from 250 cc to 50 cc in the 1971 legislation, didn't really have the effect it had hoped for, so it decided to slow these 50 cc lightweight teenager rockets down a bit. I was lucky, my 1976 model was not restricted. There were several other moped makers around at the time like Gilera, Puch, Garelli and Fantic and many of these even after the August 1977 legislation, could easily be derestricted by the owners. I am not sure how heavily they policed the practice of de-restricting a restricted bike but in 1976 there were plenty of these machines blaring around. I wouldn't even bother trying to keep up with these screamers even though they would often provoke Fizzie owners like me into racing them.

The Garelli and Fantic were particularly fast bikes. The Fantic engine kicked out a breath taking 9 bhp and could do an indicated 65 mph, but it never had pedals, so it failed to make the Sixteener Law, but there were still plenty of these 50 cc rockets around and of course you could ride them at age 17 and up anyway. If you have ever ridden a moped, you will know that 40 mph feels fast. A derestricted lightweight rocket in the hands of a 16-year-old could be quite dangerous. I was satisfied with my Fizzie and knew that it was merely a stepping stone to the world of real motorcycles that I could access legally just one year later, when I turned 17.

I was so excited the day dad and I signed the agreement for the Fizzie I could hardly sleep the day before I picked it up. It may have only been a moped, but it was a superbike to me and it came with a free Yamaha sports jacket. I kept that jacket well after my Fizzie days and subconsciously that jacket made me loyal to the Yamaha brand every time I wore it. Being a street legal bike the Fizzie gave me independence and some real kudos with my mates, both these aspects were important as a teenager and I was the first of my kind to get a Fizzie. Mum was coming on board with the idea too, realising that I no longer needed dad or public transport to take me back and forth my work in ASDA which was about six miles (10 kilometres) away. Also, I could come home under my own steam on the weekends once I had moved away with the RAF to bring mum my laundry.

It was a beautiful day when I picked up the Fizzie. It was at 5:45pm on Tuesday 12th October 1976, registration number *OTG 538 R*. The British Government have fun every twenty years or so and mess around with the number plates on vehicles. From 1963 until 1983 they had employed a system of three letters, one to three numbers followed by a letter. The second two letters were the area identifier and indicate where the vehicle was first registered (**TG** on my Fizzie represented Newport, Wales). The last letter, 'R' was the age identifier or year and represented the date when the vehicle was first registered - so suffix 'R' = 1976. However, the year letter in this crazy scheme was not made compulsory until 1965. So, a vehicle could have been registered during 1963 and 1964 without a year letter. Anyway, it all changed again in 1983 when they swapped around the three letters at the front for the single letter at the back. Had I bought my Fizzie in 1983 it would have been **A 538 OTG**. Although suffix 'R' represented 1976 'S' was 1977, 'T' was 1978 and 'V' 1979. There were a couple of letters that were excluded as a suffix. The letters 'I', 'O', 'Q,' 'U' and 'Z' were not used in Great Britain (Wales, England and Scotland) The letters I and Z were used but were reserved for Northern Ireland registrations. The Q was used to register vehicles that had a date of manufacture that was dubious or just unknown. It was common for Q to be on kit or self-build cars if most of the parts could not be attributable to one vehicle. The Q plate was not transferable to any other vehicle once it had been allocated. The letters O and U were not used because they looked too much like Q, Zero and V. There was always a logic in there somewhere. You just gotta love the British licencing Centre for making up these ideas.

I was euphoric when I picked up the Fizzie, it was a special moment in my adult life, and it was not lost on me. However, the feeling of euphoria was short lived. I had travelled less than five miles (eight kilometres) from the bike showroom before I approached my first set of traffic lights. Taking it easy I decided to go through the gears gently, only to realize that I could not find the gear change lever with my foot.

A quick glance down my left side, just to make sure my feet were in the correct place, I realized that the gear lever had fallen off the bike. I was stuck at traffic lights on a brand-new bike in top gear and unable to move off. I had to park the bike on the side of the road and then walk back to the bike shop hoping to find the gear lever on the way. I had only walked about a quarter of a mile when I saw the lever glistening in the sunlight on the side of the road. Sprinting back to the bike and using the on-board tool kit that comes with the bike, I was soon back on the road. It was here that I tried using the pedals for the first and only time I had the bike. Holding in the clutch and pedalling brought back memories of my time peddling the NSU Quickly. Like the NSU I had to pedal like crazy just to keep the bike moving forward with enough momentum to remain upright. It was far easier to park the bike and walk - which is exactly what I did.

I think I rode my Fizzie every day I had it. I would ride anywhere and everywhere and in all conditions. Rain, snow and ice. I was finishing a late shift at ASDA just before Christmas 1976 and there was snow and ice on the roads. On this night, everyone on my shift was given a large frozen chicken as a Christmas present from the ASDA management. I took great care to strap this chicken to the rear seat of the Fizzie with bungee cords before slowly and diligently making my way home. I was thinking to myself as I pulled off what a lovely surprise the chicken would be for mum; it would save her buying one for Christmas. I had travelled about 100 feet (30 metres) in the car park before I hit my first patch of ice and the inevitable happened. Travelling at no more than 20 mph the front wheel decided that it wanted to go in a different direction to the course I had set it on. The whole bike agreed with the front wheel and just slipped graciously away from me in slow motion sliding elegantly across the car park under its own steam. Realising my fate, I unceremoniously let go of the handlebars pushing my hands out to the right in a desperate and successful attempt to prevent my face from kissing the car park tarmac. This was my first fall on my beautiful Fizzie. I would experience a few more '*offs*' over the coming months and years, a couple of which would be ten times worse than this little mishap, but this was a horrible feeling, nonetheless.

As the bike and I parted company, the chicken whacked the ground with gusto and the bungee cords securing it to the seat acted like a medieval catapult and slung the chicken across the car park tarmac. As the chicken was still frozen and had a slight spin on from the bungee catapult, it literally skipped across the icy patches like one of Barnes Wallis, dam busting, bouncing bombs finally coming to rest in the gutter some distance away from me and the bike. I was unhurt apart from my pride and a few bruises, but the Fizzie suffered a few paint scrapes and a bent brake lever. I never told mum about the incident because she would just worry the shit about me. I do remember on Christmas Day her questioning why there seemed to be tiny stones, almost gravel like, in the flesh of the chicken. Clearly, I was not the only one that got a little gravel rash that night.

Once I had joined the RAF in January 1977, I left the Fizzie at home with dad for the first six weeks of my basic training, preferring to use the train for the few times I could make it home. Basic recruit training was conducted at RAF Swinderby, Lincolnshire about 200 miles (320 kilometres) away and would take well over six hours on a moped. However, my professional training was at RAF Halton, Aylesbury, near London a mere 150 miles (240 kilometres) away, so I considered that to be well within a commutable distance for a weekend.

I had arrived at Halton in March 1977 so only had to commute on the Fizzie for three months before I would turn 17 in the June, then I could get a real motorcycle. A few months commuting on a moped was not that bad; I thought. Well, imagine strapping yourself to a washing machine with an uneven load on a fast spin for four hours at a time, only then will you have some idea about what it was like commuting on the Fizzie. Four hours was the quickest I could do the 150 miles and, depending on the weather (less so on the traffic) it would often take me five. I would be on full throttle for over 95% of the journey, backing off only on reaching the back lane at our new home in Cross Keys, South Wales.

Although it was an extremely risky practice, I used to slipstream lorries (trucks) to get an extra few mph out of the screaming 50 cc engine to make the journey quicker - every little bit helped. Slipstreaming takes practice and it's a bit of a riding skill too, it's a very small sweet spot behind a large vehicle where the vehicle shape and forward momentum causes a small area of turbulent low-pressure air to form behind it. The low pressure is actually drag to the lorry, but if you are following close enough, you can literally feel it sucking you into this low-pressure zone. You can't see it, but you can certainly feel it on a moped. It is like being in the eye of a storm. It's quiet and peaceful once in there, but there is chaos all around you. Get to close and the turbulent air buffets you from side to side and you are in danger of running into the rear of the lorry. Too far back and the dirty air just bashes you around and leaves you fighting for control of the bike. The skill is breaking through the dirty air layer as quickly as you can and then holding yourself in the limited sweet spot.

On a moped you have a very small window of opportunity to slipstream, its normally when the lorry is accelerating through 20-30 mph because you just don't have the power to keep up with the lorry and break through the dirty air once it gets above 40 mph. That little 49 cc piston would be working flat out at around 7,000 rpm and once in the slipstream sweet spot it was the most prominent noise you could hear. There was no tachometer on the Fizzie, but you could guess by the vibration through the handlebars and pedals that the engine was being rung out as much as possible. By the time I got home, my whole body would be shaking having been subjected to the constant vibration. Tapping my fingers on a solid base felt like my hands were a set of tuning forks. I don't think it was doing my body a whole lot of good, and I was extremely fatigued after the ride home. Clearly, mopeds were not designed for long distances. Although the Fizzie was my first love in terms of legal motorcycles, after a year of travelling thousands of miles at 50 mph or less, I was ready to move up to the grown-up's learners' league. On turning 17 on 7th June 1977, I could ride any motorcycle with an engine size not exceeding 250 cc and allow myself the privilege of riding at the maximum national speed limit on any road or motorway. I didn't know it at the time, but I would have a few issues trying to remain within these government imposed speed restrictions.

Chapter 3
Two Strokers

My brother had already progressed from his Honda SS 50 to a Yamaha DT 125 well before I had even got started with my Fizzie. I loved riding his bike not just because it was bigger and faster, but the fact I could ride it off road. The Yamaha DT series of bikes were classified as *'Enduro'* bikes which simply meant they had the ability to go off road or cross-country. Cross country was a posh term for off road, but these bikes had all the street legal items like headlights, indicators, horn and brake lights. They were the modern-day dual sports bikes of the 1970s. I would ride my brother's DT 125 at every opportunity up in the woods (again without his permission).

Unfortunately, one day I took a tumble when I clipped a tree and slid down an embankment ending up on the banks of the local Sirhowy river. I never let go of the bike, which was a big mistake. I pulled the bike down the embankment with me and once I had stopped sliding at the water's edge, the bike's momentum kept the bike sliding, finally coming to rest with its hot exhaust resting on my right calf muscle. I was wearing waterproof rubber leggings that day and the hot exhaust welded the leggings to my skin. A scar I still carry today along with the memory of the pungent smell of burning rubber on human flesh. Although not a wonderful experience of riding off road, I was hooked on this type of motorcycling. I loved the idea of having a bike that I could ride both on and off the road.

My teenage mind was made up, I was going to get a Yamaha DT when I turned 17 years old.

Sadly, my brother had his DT 125 stolen by a joyrider and then dumped. It was a significant event for my brother and he never really went back to motorcycles much after that. I got a spanking new Yamaha DT 175. Other than the ability to ride off road, there were a couple of other reasons I choose the Yamaha DT 175. Firstly, it was like my brother's bike only bigger. This was important to me. It was the first time I had something bigger and better than he had. Boasting rights are a sibling thing. After all the growing up 'big brother' stuff and 'hand-me-downs', motorcycles made us equals in my eyes. Secondly, it was a Yamaha. I had become tribal to the brand. The free Yamaha sports jacket I got with my Fizzie played a small part in this decision. I wore that jacket everywhere, I loved it, so sticking with the Yamaha brand was a no brainer and allowed me to get maximum use out of the jacket.

Back in the mid and late 70s, my dad, brother and I would often go to the Newport Speedway track at Somerton Park on a Friday night (which was also the home ground of Newport County football team) and watch the Newport Wasps speedway team. One of the famous riders at that time was an Australian called Phil Crump and after the event, if I was on my bike, I would pretend to be 'Crumpy' and enjoy doing speedway racing starts at every red traffic light heading out of town. If I popped a wheelie that just added kudos. The DT 175 was many things to me at different times, but at a red light on a Friday night, I was Crumpy on a Jawa 500 in the final race of the speedway world championships. A good start at the lights was me getting away from the competition and winning the world championships. In that moment I was living the dream.

Yamaha made several DT models ranging from 50 cc up to 400 cc. They were all single cylinder air cooled two-strokes. To me the DT 175 was a perfect entry level motorcycle kicking out around 15 horses at 7,500 rpm; three times the power of the Fizzie. The DT was also fitted with a tachometer, so I could see when I was approaching maximum engine power. It also had 100 mph indicated on the speedo, but thankfully the bike would top out at around 75 mph. This was plenty fast enough on a lightweight two-stroker with knobbly tyres. I could have gone for the 250 cc version (maximum legal size on a learner's license) but that was physically much bigger, a little heavier and of course more expensive. Also, I didn't feel the need to get the maximum legal size of engine as a learner because I never intended being a learner for long.

In the bike showroom just before my 17th birthday, they had a grey and blue Yamaha DT 175 on full display. As soon as I seen it, I loved the colour and it was perfectly suited to the bike. I agreed to trade my Fizzie as a down payment. I also applied to take my bike licence test that same week, even before I took possession of the bike. I was pretty serious about my motorcycles by then and I knew there would be a few months wait for my test, but I was wasting no time. The commute from RAF Halton to home did not reduce as much as I thought it would on a much bigger and more powerful bike. However, it was a far more pleasurable ride home and a much safer one too. I no longer needed to slip stream large lorries to make good time. I could reach the maximum speed limit on any road; this was just a pipe dream on the Fizzie.

However, both the DT 175 and the Fizzie still had the piss poor 6 Volt lighting system. Ok during the day, but at night you could see Jack Shit, it was a struggle to see more than a few feet ahead. Reduced visibility has the effect of believing you are moving much, much faster than you are. Having said that, the headlight was still bright enough to attract wildlife. On riding

Me & My Yamaha DT175, Cross Keys, Wales, 1977

home one weekend from RAF Brawdy, West Wales, a very large owl came out of the darkness whilst I was riding through the Brecon Beacons. With its wings at full stretch and talons facing forward it came straight at me clipping my right shoulder. I immediately tilted my head to the right

and closed my eyes when I saw it, if I hadn't, I am sure it would have taken me out. It frightened the shit out of me, and it happened so quickly. It went from a small unidentified shadow in the distance to a full-on in my face obstacle within a second. The whole incident happened quicker than I could determine what it was. It was only a few seconds afterwards that I determined it was a bird. Nothing like an owl strike to sharpen your riding senses at night.

In contrast, to a real beast that seen me at night, targeted me and then hit me, the same weekend I bought the bike and with less than 100 miles (160 kilometres) on the clock, I was in daylight, not seen and hit by an inanimate beast. A car. Coincidentally, I was sat on my bike waiting at a red light, the same traffic lights I would practice my speedway starts just a few weeks later.

In hindsight, I should have ridden straight through the changing lights, but being a sensible motorist on a brand-new motorcycle, I decided to make a cautionary stop. Unfortunately, the idiot behind me had already made the decision to be first from the lights and as there was no room for both of us at the stop line, he simply shunted me out the way. The bike literally launched itself vertically from between my legs, front wheel getting airborne before the whole bike came crashing down into a heap on its left side with the engine still running. I was knocked off balance as the rear indicators ripped through my thighs forcing me to fall forward in a show of sympathy with the bike. I couldn't believe it. My adrenaline rush was trying to sort out the priority of whether I needed to deal with the shock of seeing my new bike on the floor or express my anger at the fricking idiot that just rear ended me. Luckily, the driver of the car was immediately apologetic and helped me and the bike get reacquainted. A few scratches on the bike, a bent clutch lever and a broken indicator lens was the only damage. I was pissed but surprisingly unhurt. This would be the first and only tumble I would have on this bike.

The DT 175 was a reliable bike and served me well. It was nice to have a two-stroke that didn't need me to mix the oil in the petrol tank. All the DT models had a separate auto lube system which metered the amount of two stroke oil feeding the engine at any given rpm. You just needed to make sure the oil tank was kept topped up as there was no warning light on the dashboard, but it did have a small indicator window in the righthand side panel, so you could visually check every time you filled up. A full oil tank would last three to four fuel stops.

I took my bike test in Aylesbury, London on Wednesday 31st August 1977 at 11:30am. I know this to be true because I still have the hand-written appointment card they send you through the post as a memento. The test was just three months after getting my DT 175. One of the more challenging aspects of the test was the slow speed handling check. I had to follow the examiner on my bike as he walked along the pavement. I was not allowed to put my feet down, snake the bike or allow myself to drift into the centre of the lane. After about 30 seconds of walking he stopped, turned to me and said, *'please try and keep up Mr Sainsbury'*. I knew then that I had a great chance of passing my test as this was quite a common test failure. Riding in a straight line at walking pace is not as easy as it sounds. However, on a low geared enduro bike it wasn't hard either. The Yamaha was very stable at low speed and first gear was so low it was slower than walking speed with the clutch engaged; it was a breeze. Hearing those two immortal words *'you've passed'* was not lost on me. I was ecstatic, at 17 years old I could now ride any bike I wanted. I was no longer limited to engine size. However, before I could progress to a bigger and more expensive motorcycle, I had to earn some serious money to pay off the hire purchase agreement. I was still less than half owner of the DT 175; the finance company owned the other half.

As the DT 175 was a real bike, this meant that I could also use the motorways which were (and still are) prohibited for mopeds. More importantly, the DT 175 allowed me to please mum every weekend by giving her all my laundry to do. I could strap my bag on the back of the bike without incurring any speed penalties. I was restricted on the moped by the seat size and the additional weight really did make a difference. Mum would wash, dry and iron all my clothes for my return on Sunday afternoon, including my underpants and socks. Because that is what mums do for their boys when they live away from home. When my undergarments were worn out, she would simply buy me new ones and replace them over a wash cycle because that's also what Mums do for their boys. It was certainly one less thing for me to think about. I would be married and in my mid-twenties before I realised, I had to buy underpants. It was like finding out that there was no Santa Claus.

I had been posted to RAF Brawdy, in West Wales in October 1977 and winter was clearly on its way. Although Brawdy was only about 120 miles (200 kilometres) away, a little closer than RAF Halton, the journey home took me through the Brecon Beacons National Park. The Beacons are a beautiful part of South Wales, but when the weather is bad, the road through the National Park can be treacherous, and there were not many crash barriers to stop you going off the road and down the side of the mountain. Even though the DT 175 was an off-road bike, I really didn't want to take a forced diversion down the side of a hill. Here I was, getting myself ready to head home after work on a cold November Friday evening. Sleet had started to fall less than an hour after I had set off and I reached the Brecon Beacons much later than normal. I knew the weather was going to be cold, but I didn't expect it to be freezing cold - literally. I had put on several layers of clothing and had my waxed jacket and trousers on. Waxed apparel (colloquially known as Belstaffs, which was the name of the clothing manufacturer) was the motorcyclists' clothing of choice in the 1970s, it was effective in keeping out the rain, but bloody useless in keeping out the cold.

The sleet had turned into snow as I entered the Brecon Beacons National Park. Then, it turned to shit on me very quickly. The A470 road that takes you through the Beacons takes you quite close to the peak, Pen-y-Fan which is just shy of around 3,000 feet (914 metres) above sea level. The snow was falling hard and had completely covered the road. The temperature had dipped so low that the bike was struggling to keep going. The engine had stalled several times due to my going so slow in the conditions and it being so cold. Full choke was required to get the engine started again; even after just a few seconds of it being stopped. The little single cylinder 175 cc air-cooled engine wasn't generating enough heat to keep itself warm. Even when it was running, I found myself pulling the choke out several times along the way to try and stop the engine from stalling.

My speed was just a little quicker than walking pace and I had to keep both feet down using them as stabilizers to stop myself falling off. My concentration was equally split between feeling for the left side of the road with my foot and watching where I was going. Then, just when you think it can't get any worse; it does. The snow got heavier, the wind picked up which made the temperature dip even further and my progress was slowed even more, and I was still going uphill. I had not yet reached the peak of Pen-y-Fan. I was a confident rider even then and was comfortable riding in adverse weather conditions, but this was a few notches up on the bad weather scale and I had started to get really, really, worried.

I was wearing an open-faced crash helmet with a fixed visor and a scarf around my neck, mouth and nose. However, the small areas of exposed skin had already began to tingle with the bitterly cold wind and each icy snow flake that had made its way under the visor inflicted a tiny stabbing pain on top of the tingling on my face. It was intense. The snow that didn't hit my exposed face either made it to my eyes or merely attached itself to the inside of the visor. Either way my vision was being obscured. Breathing out warm air through my scarf didn't help much either, as all that did was fog up the visor. Wiping the visor both inside and out with my frozen glove just made what I could see blurry. I couldn't win either way and the road ahead was becoming less defined by the minute. There were hardly any cars around for light, so I was riding in almost *'white out'* conditions and I was shaking so badly I could hardly focus my eyes through the snow baked visor. My fingers and toes had been numb for some time and I felt that I was slowly losing movement in my hands. I don't think heated handgrips had even been invented then and even if they had been, they would have gone on strike under these conditions. I was physically and mentally tired and getting totally exasperated with the weather. I had absolutely no idea what the time was. No watch, no phone. I wondered if I was ever going to make it home. I just wanted this journey to end.

Unbeknown to me, dad had watched the weather forecast and had decided to come and look for me even before my

expected home time – I was so glad he did. I made it to the peak and had started going downhill slightly when dad found me. He spotted me– it would not have been hard, there were no other idiots out on motorcycles that night. I was so, so pleased to see him. We sat together in

My Yamaha FS1E & DT175, Cross Keys, Wales, 1977

the car for a while as I defrosted and then warmed up before getting back on the bike for the final stretch home. We stopped once more on the way home just to make sure I was ok and not freezing up. I was completely exhausted when we eventually made it home.

A good ride home from Brawdy would take me just under three hours. This trip took over six. If ever there was going to be a scenario where I had decided to stop riding bikes in favour of cars, this would have been it. However, it did nothing of the sort. Clearly, I needed a bigger bike and better clothing, but more importantly, I needed to learn to do my own laundry. Forcing myself to go home in severe weather just to get my laundry done was dumb. I have never experienced anything like that since because I won't let myself get so focused on the destination without considering other factors that literally have the potential to stop me in my tracks. The DT 175 was a true trusted steed. It got me home. I am not sure I would have made it safely on a normal road bike. Knobbly tyres, low gearing and light weight were the key attributes on a bike in these conditions.

Two stroke engines are much lighter and, with some clever control over the exhaust port with a properly designed expansion chamber, have the potential to produce considerably more power than a four-stroke engine of the same cubic capacity. A two stroke fires on every revolution of the engine (two strokes of the piston) as opposed to every second revolution in a four-stroke engine (four strokes of the piston). Two strokers also produce much more noise than their four stoke brethren as they need a free-flowing exhaust to allow the combustion chamber gases to evacuate quickly and get ready for the next firing. As a two stroker burns oil, they can smoke like chimneys and are considered by some to be environmental disasters. However, the smell of a two-stroke engine is very distinctive. Smelling a two-stroke is as enjoyable to me as chocolate is to my taste - and I am a chocoholic. Because they fire every stroke, two strokers are not particularly fuel efficient, what they are though, is easy to maintain and bloody awesome fun. I loved my two-strokers. Once you get the two-stroke engine into the sweet spot of its power band, the acceleration can be phenomenal even with small sized engines.

I could not afford another brand-new bike, but still wanted to step up to a bigger machine from the DT 175 after I had passed my test. I enjoyed the fun of riding off road but was starting to think about a sportier bike for the road. After all, I was 17 and a 17-year-old thinks differently to a 16-year-old teenager. I could always come back to the enduro/dual sports bikes later in life and indeed I would - big time. Then out of the blue came an opportunity when my brother's mate Keith Walker decided that he wanted rid of his metallic blue Yamaha RD 400. This bike just looked awesome and of course it was very fast (compared to the DT175). The RD 400 was a legend in the mid/late seventies. The ability to pop wheelies in the first two gears and then take its rider to well over 100 mph was the hallmark of the RD 400. Its top speed was stated to be around 106 mph. I can confirm that it was certainly capable of doing over 100 mph - and quickly too, a standing 1/4 mile could be covered in just 14 seconds (if you could keep the front wheel down). The RD 400 kicked out a whopping 44 bhp at 7,000 rpm and boy, you could feel every one of those horses kicking in when you accelerated hard, but such rewards came at a cost. I rarely got more than 35 mpg out of the bike, but then again you didn't own a RD 400 to save money on petrol.

The engine was a twin cylinder 398 cc two-stroke. Keith's bike ticked all my boxes for stepping up from the DT 175. It was a Yamaha, a two-stroker, faster, bigger and affordable and it also had an aftermarket nose fairing so offered me some protection for commuting. What more could I ask for? It turned out that the Yamaha RD 400, of all my inventory over the years, would be the legal bike that I would own for the least amount of time, it was also the one bike I thought could kill me. My road riding skills went up exponentially during the time I had this *'lighter than air'* stroker. It really was a quantum leap up from a DT 175 enduro. I had the bike for around 6 months, but boy did I make some great memories in those six months. Of all the bikes I have owned, this was one of only three bikes I never took a photograph of for some reason. The development of two-stroke engines progressed during the 1970s and my RD 400 was one of the last air-cooled models before it was superseded by the RD 350 LC (Liquid Cooled). The RD 350 LC would also make it as a classic and for the same reasons as its predecessor.

The RD400 demanded respect, if you didn't treat it right, you would get a brief warning that you were abusing it, and if you didn't back off, it would punish you. Luckily, I learnt fast, and operated just below its limits. I had a few tank slappers (warnings) and other near misses but managed to keep the bike shiny side up. However, I was acutely aware that the tolerance band between warnings and punishment was very narrow. When the engine reached the start of its crazy power band at around 4,500 rpm, if you twisted the throttle quickly it was like being rear ended by a fast-moving train and the front end would literally take off and you would be grinning from cheek to cheek trying to keep the front down.

I never took a speed tumble on this bike, so my punishment was confined to adrenaline rushes and scary moments. Most of which have been burned into my long-term memory as lessons learnt. The RD 400 could scare you easily and quickly. Remembering, I had no real experience of riding road bikes or bikes with large capacity engines and I was still only 17 years old with no formal motorcycle training. There were two real memorable moments on the RD 400, both of which epitomises the fact that you had to treat this machine with respect.

I took dad out for a ride one day just to show off its performance and on our way back home I got the front wheel up as we were approaching the apex of the hill coming into our village of Cwmfelinfach. With the power still rolling on and the front lifting, the bike got airborne just for a brief second as we started down the other side of the apex. I knew this to be the case as the revs peaked once the rear wheel had left the road and then reduced immediately on touchdown. I could hear dad shouting obscenities at me as we pulled up outside our house and then he slapped me across the head when he got off. He must have been shitting himself, he had never slapped me around the head before - ever. I knew exactly what I was doing and was in complete control but didn't tell dad thinking I would surprise him - guess what? It had the desired effect – he was surprised! I think that was one occasion where he gave me some immediate feedback, albeit in jumbled up swear words, if he were alive today, we would laugh together recalling that moment. Sadly, that would be the last time he would ride pillion with me and the last memory I have of dad and motorcycles before his untimely passing in August 1978.

The second story was a little untidy and embarrassing more than anything. Returning home from the movies one night, I did a quicker than normal start on the hill outside Haverfordwest cinema in West Wales with my mate on the back. The front wheel got airborne almost immediately, which was well within my capabilities, but a few seconds later came crashing down on the pavement as I failed to negotiate the kerb. The result was a zero speed topple, making me and my mate look like a pair of amateur stunt artists (or complete dicks) as we recovered the bike off the floor in front of everyone leaving the cinema. Had I pulled the stunt off properly and missed the pavement kerbstone, it would have looked quite impressive. I was not trying to impress, and the wheelie was unintentional, but the combination of my heavier than average mate on the back, facing an upward slope and not wanting to stall on the pull off with a cold engine, made for an aggressive start and the bike duly punished me. However, under the right conditions, like accelerating up a progressive hill, I could pull and hold the wheelie for some considerable time even with a passenger on the back, much to the dismay of my passengers. Even though I was punished on this occasion, I like to think that the bike and I had a mutual understanding and respect for each other.

The RD 400 was the only two-stroke twin I had owned and the last two-stroke bike I would have in the UK. However, I always admired the Suzuki GT750 water cooled 'Kettle' or 'Water Buffalo' as it was affectionately called and the Kawasaki H2, Mach IV - KH750 the big 74 hp brother to the KH500 'Widow Maker'. Both the Suzuki and the Kawasaki were two-stroke triples. These three-cylinder engines sounded (and smelled) just awesome and in my opinion, both these machines were the best of the large capacity strokers. It is perhaps just as well I never managed to own either of these bikes. The Yamaha RD 400 took some taming and demanded respect, I am not sure that as a 17-year-old I could have tamed the H2, Mach IV, one of the fastest production bikes in the world and a big brother to a bike with a reputation of being called the Widow Maker.

Chapter 4
Middleweight Four Stroke Twins

The Yamaha RD 400 was a terrific bike, period. I had learnt a huge amount about riding fast motorcycles and had honed my road skills in the short time I owned it, but I was craving something different, something bigger and a bit more fuel efficient that would be good for longer distances. The RD 400 was a much sought-after second-hand bike and I got a good deal on a trade in. I was still loyal to the Yamaha brand as my Yamaha sports jacket was still functional and would easily out last another new bike. I really fancied the new 1978, XS 500 in bright red.

My Yamaha XS 500, RAF Brawdy, Wales, 1978

The Yamaha XS 500 ticked all my progressive boxes. I liked that it was similar in design to the RD 400 in that it was a twin with similar plastic trim. I wanted to keep with the twin cylinder concept a bit longer. Apart from the twins being a bit cheaper, they didn't look as much as a handful as the air cooled four-cylinder bikes of the same size. I just wasn't quite ready for those beasts at 18. The engine was a 498 cc four stroke - so no more two stroke oil and hopefully less fuel stops. The salesman convinced me to get one based on technical details. The XS 500 was fitted with a new high-performance engine that had an eight-valve head, double overhead camshaft, 180-degree crank, two Constant Velocity (CV) carburettors and an electric start. The CV carbs were great for fuel economy as regardless of how quickly you whacked open the throttle, accelerating the engine was dependent on engine vacuum in the intake. Ultimately, that translated into a bike with roughly the same amount of power (it actually kicked out 48 horses at 8,500 rpm compared to the 44 horses at 7,000 rpm of the RD 400). The XS 500 was considerably heavier at 458 lbs compared to 364 lbs for the RD400. Also, being a four stroke, it had a lot more moving parts in the engine. It also had an electric start but had one less

My Modified Yamaha XS500, RAF Brawdy, Wales, 1978

gear in the gearbox. This bike was one down, four up. In 1978 this was an extremely smooth twin cylinder engine and was surprisingly light on engine vibration due to the fitting of a clever crankshaft counterweight system. The counterweights sat behind the crankshaft and effectively balanced out the natural vibration caused by the 180 degree firing sequence of the twin cylinder motor. Overall, it was a pretty responsive middleweight twin but no real match for the character of the RD 400.

The good news was that the front wheel stayed in contact with the ground even on hard acceleration and I could get a good 20 mpg more out of the 4-stroke twin. My mate had a Suzuki GT 500, a two-stroke twin. I could never keep up with him accelerating, but I could always pass him at a petrol station because he would always have to stop to fill up. His was a gas guzzler. One of the cool things I did to this bike was to fit Dunstall reverse cone, straight through mega exhausts pipes, which on a middle size four stroke twin like the XS 500, made the bike sound bloody awesome. I could also get a flame out the back of the exhaust by hitting the kill switch off and back on quickly with a fist full of throttle. Not a smart way to make the engine back fire and draw attention to yourself, but it looked and sounded impressive at night at when you are 18 years old that's what you do. Note to self; never buy a second-hand bike from a teenager.

The XS 500 would also be a bike of unsuccessful experiments for me. It was the first large four stroke engine bike I tried to service myself. My very first attempt at adjusting the overhead cam chain cost me 400GBP. I snapped the adjuster (overtightened it) and it fell into the engine requiring a professional top end strip of the engine. I also fitted the bike with a rear sissy bar, huge brake lights, a rear rack, a self-made dashboard panel and air horns. The sissy bar spoilt the looks of the bike, the brake lights blinded everyone behind me, and I fitted the air horns without an electrical relay in the circuit which resulted in an electrical weld of the handlebar switch and the horn getting stuck on, nothing that another 100GBP couldn't fix.

I suffered my second bird strike on the XS 500, this time in broad daylight on a beautiful day and doing around 50 mph. A small bird (I have no clue what species of bird it was) with dark feathers went straight into my Griffin full face crash helmet. My visor was up, and the bird hit the right side of my face wedging itself between the side of my head and the inside of my crash helmet. It just missed my right eye. I never even seen it coming until its beak hit me and then I suffered some immediate pain as its beak and claws tore the skin off the side of my face. It continued into the dead end which was the back of my crash helmet. There were feathers and blood everywhere and I could immediately smell the bird's natural fragrance as it filled the air space within the helmet. I am assuming it was a natural fragrance and not an almighty bird fart let loose from its impact into my face. The whole event was over in just a few seconds. I think the bird panicked more than I did and was wriggling like a worm on a fish hook before I managed to pull it out of my face. I maintained control of the bike and stopped without any drama and wondered what the hell had just happened. My riding mate, like all good biking mates, just pissed himself laughing.

The rate of acceleration on the XS 500 was not as snappy as the RD 400 over the rev range, but it did seem to have a bit more grunt/torque at the top end. I think it was more the noise than anything as the torque figures for both bikes were roughly the same. The XS engine did rev a little higher (redline 9,500 rpm compared to the RD 400 of 8,500 rpm). I did have these awesome Dunstall exhaust pipes fitted which would have allowed the engine to breathe more easily adding one or two horses to the stable and a few pounds of additional torque. I also knew that the XS 500 could reach its top speed of 105 mph.

How did I know? Because I got official validation from the South Wales Traffic Police.

I was keen to show off my new Yamaha XS 500 at every opportunity I could. I rode it to the local disco near RAF Brawdy called the Roch Gate Motel on Sunday 10th September 1978. I parked the bike near the front entrance of the motel, so everyone could see it. Unfortunately, someone had decided that they also liked my bike and wanted a souvenir from it and stole both the wing mirrors. Bastards. I was absolutely gutted and pissed that someone had messed with my new bike. Of course, no one had seen anything, and surveillance cameras didn't exist at these places in 1978.

The following Tuesday, 12th September 1978 I was heading home on leave and at 7:30 pm, I got stopped by the police about 15 miles (24 kilometres) from home (mum's house). It was a lovely evening and the A470 road was the last bit of fast dual carriageway before heading into the smaller village 'B' class roads. The road had light traffic at that time of night and the bike had been 'broken in' so it was a perfect opportunity to open the gas taps and to see what this baby could do. A quick glance behind me (remembering no wing mirrors) gave me the all clear to go for it. I had done about a mile or so on the road and the bike was purring along nicely. I stayed in the outside lane and the traffic that was on the road must have seen me coming because they were moving over to let me by, way ahead of my getting anywhere close to them. Great news, but I was about to discover that it was not me they were pulling over for. As I seemed to have free rein in the outside lane, I managed to maintain momentum and go even faster on the straight bits.

With my head down behind the handlebars for the last half mile before my exit I managed to squeeze the last few miles an hour out of the bike. On reaching my exit, some five miles (eight kilometres) after I joined the A470, I sat up and started to brake, thinking to myself that I must have hit the ton (100 mph) three or four times during that sprint. I was feeling rather pleased with myself and the bike. Then in the last 300 feet (100 metres) or so of the slip road, a police car with flashing lights and sirens shot passed me and skidded to a halt some 65 feet (20 metres) in front of me. Suddenly, I thought shit....... now I knew why all the cars had been pulling over to let me by. Perhaps there was a slim chance that the nice police officer just wanted to compliment me on my riding skills. Ummm. Perhaps not.

I gave the nice policeman a severe listening too. He told me how he kept a big black plastic sack in the boot of the squad car to scrape people like me up off the road; that was the nicest thing he said. I thought better of it than to ask to see the black sack in his car. He was bloody furious. I think he had trouble catching me but was too embarrassed to admit it. Once again, I thought it best not to ask the question, he seemed very excitable. However, what he did do was validate my top speed. Over the four miles (six kilometres) that he had been following me, he clocked me at speeds between 90 and 106 mph. I was well pleased with that – but once again kept that thought to myself.

The sad but true story of the wing mirrors being stolen just 48 hours previously seemed to carry no weight at all in mitigation, which was a big disappointment considering it was the truth. I never thought to look behind me once during this five-mile sprint, why would I? Nothing would be going as fast as I was going, and it would be dangerous to try and keep up with me at that speed.

When I got the court summons, the statement of facts stated that when I was stopped and spoken to regarding the speeding offence, my response was *'I must be bloody dull'*. Then when told that I would be reported for speeding in a 70 mph limit I said *'Ok, fair enough'*. Clearly, I was an 18-year-old of very few words. Nothing in the statement of facts about any black plastic sack kept in the boot of police cars. My luck ran out a second time on this bike on Monday 14th January 1980 at 11:20am when I was caught doing 51 mph in a 30 mph limit. Again, it was whilst I was going home to mum. My response as recorded on the statement of facts, when told that I would be reported and cautioned, was *'No thank you'*. This made no sense at all to the traffic cop but to me it meant simply *'Fuck off'*. Clearly, either I needed to stay away from home or change my bike. I had to figure a way to stop accumulating endorsements (adverse points) on my licence. At this rate I only had a couple of years left before I would be banned.

However, I needn't have worried about accumulating more endorsements, that would be the least of my worries in just a few months' time. I have never felt that speeding is dangerous on a bike. However, the conditions must be suitable and providing you are not endangering others, then go for it. Still, trying to see how fast a bike goes on a public road was probably not a great idea. But then being a teenager, who gives a shit.

Apart from being responsible for accumulating points on my licence, the XS 500 was a memorable bike for me as it was the only memory of biking I could share with my mum. My dad had died in August 1978 just before I changed out the RD 400 for the XS 500 and I wanted to take mum out on the new Yamaha, so she could share a motorcycling experience with me just like dad had done riding pillion on my RD 400. She was not keen at first but realised that it was important to me to be able to do this with her.

It was a beautiful day and we went up over the mountain road near to where dad had died (not intentionally). On the way back down into the village, I missed a corner and rather

Me being 'Bullet Proof', RAF Brawdy, 1979

than jink on a bend that had a lot of loose pea gravel, I decided to ride straight through an open (thankfully) farm gate and into a farmer's field. We never crashed, and we were not going that fast, but we did have a bit of a laugh. We had to get off the bike and then mum helped me push the bike backwards through the soft ground back onto the main road. That single event reminded mum of the time she spent riding pillion on dad's motorcycles in their youth, so it was a nice memory for her to share with me. She never found out about my speeding transgressions, but she knew I was no angel either.

I was convinced that I needed a bike that would slow me down. The XS 500 and RD 400 were naked street bikes and easily capable of doing speeds well above the legal speed limit. I was clearly struggling to ride and keep within these speed constraints. I had enjoyed my DT 175 enduro but wasn't quite ready to go back to that kind of motorcycling yet, and I had been mulling the idea of getting a cruiser, a Harley Davidson kind of bike for no other reason than they were different, and I could. I didn't need permission from anyone and at the time I was feeling a bit different and ready for a change.

I was approaching the grand old age of 20, and from my school days, I was always impressed with the elaborate air brush art work some of these cruiser/chopper bikes had. Indeed, I had recently bought an air brush to practise the skill myself. The combination of wanting to change bikes, the recent speeding offence and considering some fancy art work had made my mind up. Although these are weak arguments for changing your bike, when you are a late teenager rational argument are not a natural part of your logic, so you just make a decision and live with it.

Once again, remaining loyal to the brand was important as a teenager and Yamaha had recently introduced their Harley Davidson equivalent bike called the XS 650 Special. The XS 650 had been around since 1969 so it was not a new bike by any means but the 'Special' was the cruiser model introduced in 1978 and stayed in production until 1985. It came in a dark metallic black and looked just awesome. The bike even had an American flag on the side panels to remind the rider it was an American style bike and was crying out for some fancy art work on the fuel tank.

The XS 650 engine has an interesting history and is a classic example of how the Japanese copied (or inherited) other world leaders designs and simply made them better. In this case, the XS 650 engine had its genesis in a German motorcycle company called Horex. In 1951 Horex developed a new 500 cc Overhead Camshaft (OHC) parallel-twin engine and fitted it into a bike they called the Imperator. Horex were bought out in 1960 by Daimler-Benz but the technology of the engine had already gone to Japan around 1955 where a Japanese company called Hosk developed and improved the Horex engine design. Hosk were themselves bought out by another Japanese company named Showa in 1960 who ended up being part of Yamaha the same year. So, Yamaha were now in possession of the original design and its subsequent developments. The engine was bored out to 650 cc and was manufactured with a horizontally split crankcase which was excellent at holding all the engine oil in the sump as opposed to the normal British vertically split crankcases which leaked like sieves. The engine has not really changed since 1968 and even then, was considered one of the most advanced engines (in the way it was manufactured) for its class in large parallel twin motorcycles. I never knew all this stuff then, it just looked like a cool bike for a 19-year-old.

The XS 650 Special had ape hanger type handlebars, stubby exhausts, a fat rear tyre and a slightly lower seat than the XS 500. The bike delivered five more horses then the XS 500 a monstrous 53 of them kicking in around 7,200 rpm, but the machine carried an additional 5 lbs of fat over the XS 500, weighing in at 463 lbs. Even though it was a bigger bike, it felt easier to handle due to the lower seat height and a more relaxed riding position.

Although a breakthrough in engine design and build a decade before, the engine did vibrate. It had a 360° crankshaft which simply meant that the pistons went up and down together (but fired on alternative strokes). A sort of twin cylinder bike that behaves like a two-stroke single. Also, the engine was not counter balanced like the XS 500 engine, but by fitting different bearings to the big end bearings to that of the crankshaft main bearings, they did make an extremely reliable engine. Over the years these bikes (and the engines in particular) have been customised into just about every type of bike you can imagine from chopper and boober to café racer and flat trackers to cruisers.

I was sure that this bike would not get me any more speeding tickets and I was 100% correct on that point. Also, I had decided that I was not going to modify this bike like I had modified the XS 500 - apart from perhaps a fuel tank paint job. It looked pretty cool as it was. However, I would modify it in a way that I never intended within three months of owning it. In the short time I rode this bike I would learn a lot about motorcycling, motorcycle insurance, money and life in its broadest sense. The XS 650 Special would be a *'Special'* bike in many ways.

The XS 650 was the fourth bike I had bought brand new. All of them were bought on Hire Purchase Agreements, a high interest cash loan that that needed servicing every month. It was quite common for people (read single lads with money, no girlfriends or other commitments) to change bikes once the loan amount had reduced to the devalued (actual) value of the bike. In the case of the XS 650, I took out a reduced insurance liability premium, so I could afford the monthly repayments on the bike. I compromised a fully comprehensive insurance policy for a third party, fire and theft one. I was 19 and stupid - bloody stupid. What could go wrong here?

I was going home to mum (again) from RAF Brawdy for a long weekend on the afternoon of Thursday 27th March 1980. I was not feeling great, perhaps even a little flu like. The weather was not brilliant either, a little drizzly at times, and it was cold for spring time. Once again, the waxed Belstaff jacket and trousers were pretty good at keeping shower rain out but were bloody useless at keeping you warm. I was about two thirds the way home and the bike was purring along nicely. I had been following an articulated lorry (truck) for a just a short time and seen an opportunity to overtake. I was travelling on a single carriage highway near a place called Glyn Neath in South Wales. I almost got past the lorry and was just rear of the driver's cab when the whole unit rapidly swerved out to overtake a car in front. I had no chance. There was no indication, no looking, no warning, nothing.

Instinctively, I hit both brakes hard and managed to drop back to the rear boogie of the trailer before the trailer unit hit me on my left side, sticking to my jacket like a fridge magnet. The road was so narrow and the pavement kerb so high that it was impossible to mount the walkway and break away from the lorry. The result was that both the bike and I were trapped between the kerb and the trailer.

My Yamaha XS650, Cwmfelinfach, Wales, 1980

After what seemed like an eternity, physics made the next move. Gravity took control of the bike forcing it to tilt to the right, and aided by the traction of the tyres, began to pull the whole bike and me under the lorry. I no longer had control of the steering and sensed that this moment was not going to end well. I handed over full control of the bike to gravity and we went our separate ways. The bike slipped gracefully under the spinning rubber of the rear bogie of the trailer whilst I literally ejected myself in the opposite direction falling unceremoniously onto the kerb. I didn't have a whole lot of time to think about my next move. I made initial contact with the ground with my back before momentum threw me awkwardly along the pavement like a clumsily thrown bowling ball.

I must have been travelling at around 45-50 mph during the fall. My kinetic energy took me some way down the pavement and my rapidly rotating field of vision of gravel, hedgerow, grey sky repeated itself many times over before I finally came to rest in the dampened hedgerow on the side of the road. From this ground zero vantage point I watched the bike elegantly spin on its side, in the middle of the road whilst listening to the scraping noise of the black top on the exposed metal of the exhaust, fuel tank and handlebars, each part throwing out its own bright orange friction sparks like an uncontained firework, stopping only once the bike had come to rest on the wrong side of the road. The lorry continued to complete its overtaking manoeuvre without a care in the world and disappeared into the distance as if nothing had happened. The whole event was all over in just a matter of seconds, but it would turn out to be life changing seconds for me.

I was to learn later from the police that the lorry/trailer had made it to Scotland, over 700 miles (1,100 kilometres) away before it was tracked down as the other vehicle. From impact with the lorry to lying on the side of the road, could not have been longer than 10 to 15 seconds yet it all seemed to happen in slow motion and remains burnt that way into my long-term memory. You cannot forget a vivid memory like that. The injuries and subsequent disabilities I carry today because of the accident are not (to me) a constant reminder of the accident, they have simply become part of who I am. I had fallen awkwardly on the kerb and landed on my pelvis and back. The impact broke them both, severing the sciatic nerve on my left side in the process.

My pelvis actually snapped, disrupting it forward on my left side doing some internal damage in the process. The subsequent tumble broke my right leg, tore some flesh from my left thigh, broke an undefined number of ribs and did a whole load of other periphery damage. I was taken to Glyn Neath Hospital and that is where I stayed until released on 23rd May. One of the more interesting, almost entertaining moments of this episode was watching the unconventional and rapid arrival of the ambulance. It first swerved to avoid hitting people who were in the middle of the road simply trying to clear up the mess the bike had made, before finally screeching to a stop within a few feet from where I was laying. I swear to God, I thought the ambulance was going to run over me. I recalled my mum's philosophy, on how she believed that bad things always happen in three's. Well, this looked like it could be number two, and for it to happen within an hour of the first bad event, was going to be shit bad luck! Thank goodness I was spared the second bad event that day.

I had only just passed the car that was now behind me, a BMC Mini, prior to my attempting to overtaking the lorry. The driver of the Mini was a doctor. His wife was his passenger and she wanted to stop and help me rather than go after the lorry driver. Both looked after me well before the crazy ambulance guys took over. My crash helmet, a fibreglass Griffin full face (the same one that took a bird on the XS 500), took a real hammering this time as I was skidding down the pavement and without a doubt it saved my pretty face as the chin piece of the helmet had been worn away considerably. I was in no doubt that the helmet had saved my life.

I was also wearing a full complement of clothing; jeans, Belstaff waxed trousers and jacket and even a pair of nylon tights. Tights were great for stuffing with newspaper to keep your knees and legs warm - which I had done. They all helped save my body in some little way. It could have been a lot worse. Armour protection was not that common in bike gear in the 1970s, maybe that would have saved my back. In any case I was alive. I had a guardian angel looking over me that day because the accident should not have been survivable. Not only did I survive, but I had the delightful pleasure of remaining fully conscious throughout. I think my being young played a major part in my survival, a fact I would learn to be partly true during a later hospital visit. The three-month-old XS 650 was declared a write off, and so was I. After they cut away all my clothing, I was spread out on a stainless-steel gurney, naked, cold, shivering and in shock with no pain relief. There were injuries all over my body and the touch of the cold steel gurney on those broken areas was intense. The smell of surgical equipment and the bustling of people moving

My Modified Yamaha XS650, Cwmfelinfach, Wales, 1980

around me was overwhelming to my senses. It was a feeling and image that will stay with me for the rest of my life. If I had been presented with a button to press that said, *'die peacefully and be free of pain'*, I would have pressed it without hesitation.

The adrenaline had worn off and the pain seemed to be emanating from all over my body with each broken area taking turns in telling my brain that it was hurting more than any other part. There was so much wrong with me they completely missed a broken left leg. It was like a paparazzi frenzy as they took what seemed like hundreds of photos (x-rays) as quickly as they could. I felt like a circus freak displaying all my unusual charms to the world. I didn't care one bit that I was naked, I just wanted it to be over and the pain to end. Once the initial gurney frenzy was over, only then did they start to treat me and give me something for the pain. The first thing I remember after the gurney experience was waking up to the noise of a drill going through my left leg tapping the traction pin that was needed for my pelvis and back. They didn't know at that time that the leg they were drilling was in fact the broken one.

I was on some powerful drugs by now, so I couldn't tell them if it was hurting or not, but I do remember on waking seeing flesh and blood twirling around the electric drill like a red onion stuck to a food mixer with a badly fitting lid. Blood was splashing over me, the gurney and the doctor, all this was happening in slow motion. The doctor did not stop drilling even when he realized I was awake. The drug trip was awesome. I was flying high through the air over a castle holding onto a piece of string that was connected to the castle tower. It was a beautiful day and I swear I could feel the sun burning me and the cool breeze blowing on my face. I would wake up fully from this drug induced heaven suspended in a hospital bed with just my head and right foot in contact with the mattress. Blood and something else plugged into my right arm and a sling and some monitors plugged into the left.

I was in intensive care for a few days with bleeps and flashing lights emanating off small green screen monitors demanding medical attention when they made unusual deviations from their regular rhythms. All those thoughts of flu like symptoms had magically disappeared. Five pints of someone else's blood and a few days' rest under some powerful pain killers, I was finally moved out of intensive care and into the normal orthopaedic ward to begin my recovery. Not surprisingly, mum was pretty upset, and I knew that she was just itching to tell me that motorcycles were dangerous, but she said nothing of the sort. She looked frightened to death to see her 19-year-old son suspended and plugged in to a hospital bed. I felt sorry that mum had to see me this way.

Me Not So 'Bullet Proof' & My Modified XS650, Cwmfelinfach. Wales. 1980

During the first few weeks of my hospitalization, I was left wondering what the hell had happened to me, going over the crash and worrying about what the future would now look like. You have a lot of time to think about these kinds of things when you can do little else. My physical pain was at times unbearable and a constant reminder of my situation.

I dreaded being lowered out of the pelvic sling. The pain was so intense throughout my whole body when I was lowered onto the bed, it was impossible to identify what hurt the most. The feeling of your legs spreading out from your body and not having control is as strange as it was painful. However, after about three to four weeks I could feel that things were beginning to heal and settle down. I would focus my thoughts on those small incremental progressions of feeling better and often score my pain at certain times of the day and compare with the day before. Those small improvements acted like a catalyst in my mind for further healing to take place.

Hospitals can be a dreadfully depressing place if you are ill. However, if you are not ill but are just broken, it can be a fun place to hang out. The orthopaedic ward is full of broken people – nobody is ill. The difference between broken and ill is that there is a real community atmosphere in the broken ward and you can have a laugh and joke about life and of course the event that put you in there. Everyone has a story to tell and you know everyone is going to go home eventually. That is not a given in the other surgical or other trauma wards where people really are ill.

The daily lowering out of the pelvic sling for personal cleaning was not something I enjoyed; it was an extremely painful experience. I had a sheep skin cloth rested over my private parts, no underwear, or pyjamas. The washing of my private parts was not the most enjoyable thing at first, I was badly bruised and battered in that area and had a catheter fitted, but the smoothing action of the washing would often result in my getting an erection which, with the increased blood flow, could be quite painful, much to the amusement of the nurses. That was until one day it didn't hurt. I managed to feign pain for some time afterwards. I considered it one of those small luxuries I had for being in hospital, and I was 19 for goodness sake - it was good to know things were returning to normal.

As much as the nurses cared for me, they did neglect my left foot which was propped hard against a foot drop plate to prevent shrinkage of my Achilles' tendon. The traction weights hanging off my knee for my back and pelvis injuries were never adjusted for my weight loss and I was losing around one pound of body weight each day. This meant that the pressure on my foot was increasing and without proper nursing care, I ended up with a massive pressure sore on my left heel that would take months to fix after I had left hospital. In fact, the sore was so big that it needed surgery to close it up fully.

Although I was losing weight daily, I didn't poop for several weeks due to dehydration, shock, pain medication and immobility. This became a major problem. To be fair, the hospital tried many techniques to make me poop. It started with some orange syrup and tablets, progressed to enema's and then an attempt to undertake some manual extraction. Unfortunately, it was not one of the nice delicate female nurses with tiny hands and thin fingers that was assigned to attempt this procedure, but a big hairy arsed male nurse with hands the size of snow shovels and fingers like hotdog buns. I thought my days of intense pain were over until I underwent this procedure. I have never experienced anything like it or since. Using just hot water and latex rubber gloves he tried to extract weeks old poop out of my arse.

After about 20 to 30 minutes of being subjected to this procedure, he had some success. I cried with pain as it hurt so much, so when he said he had some success, I couldn't wait to see what he had pulled out of my colon. Imagine my disappointment when I was expecting to see a house brick or something of equivalent size resting in the bed. I looked around to see a small black, almost perfectly round stone like object on a dry nappy surrounded by dark red droplets of my blood. It was no bigger than the size of a garden pea. I couldn't believe it, I was devastated. I insisted no more manual extraction, I was not designed that way. If they needed to get something out of the mine shaft, they had to come up with some other ideas. As luck would have it, something had shifted because of this induced trauma. The nurses were able to get some other liquid stuff up my bottom to soften the waste that was trapped.

Combined with the syrup and tablets, things were about to change….and they did – big time!

Ken was the patient in the bed opposite me in the ward. A gentleman in his late 60s early 70s who was recovering from a car accident. Ken had been a passenger in a car that his wife was driving, and he had been thrown from the car. His wife was allegedly hysterical at the crash site as she was calling for her husband, but no one could see him, so they thought she was just in shock as she was trapped in the car. Poor Ken was unconscious in the hedgerow. The special thing about Ken was that he only had one leg, the left one. He had lost his right leg in the war I believe, or it could have been due to his wife's poor driving record. It was so funny to hear the story of the ambulance men searching for Ken but finding just his artificial leg. The ambulance men thought his wife was delirious, but she was insistent. They eventually found Ken during the subsequent search.

We all had funny stories to tell in the *'not so ill'* ward including the chap who had lost all his fingers when they dropped a steel plate on the top of a dumpster skip whilst he was hanging on to it. I remember seeing the result of his surgery. He looked like something out of a Frankenstein movie. Healthy looking hands but all his fingers were black and the stitching attaching his fingers to his hands looked like it had been done by the three blind mice. He was remarkably upbeat about the whole thing even though it looked as if only two of his ten fingers would be functional.

It was pretty late in the night when my stomach started to make rumbling noises and I just knew something was about to happen soon, and my guess was that it was not going to be pretty. The ward was in darkness apart from a few random reading lights that had been left on throughout the ward and everyone was asleep. The night shift staff were on duty but there was nobody in the ward office. Ken had recently woken up and was reading, I could see his silhouette moving against the backdrop of his reading lamp. I propped myself up in my sling and whispered across to Ken to call the staff as I was about to let go of something in my stomach. My normal method of getting attention during the day was to call out but I didn't want to do that and wake everybody up. Ken had complications with his injuries and had a special little bell on his bedside table that he could tinkle to attract the staff at night. I thought he could use that bell to get the staff to come to me. Ken immediately took up the challenge recognizing the urgency of the situation as we had been joking that same day about my lack of bowel movements. I heard the soft tone of Ken's voice calling *'nurse, nurse'* followed by the tinkle of his little bedside bell.

The *'whatever'* in my tummy was getting more vocal by the minute and the urgency in my voice for Ken to get the nurse got more desperate. Ken's response was to raise his soft tone a little and to tinkle the bell a little longer than previously. This went on a few more times but no nursing staff appeared. Then without any more warning or input by me, my bottom just let out an almighty burp and released a tidal wave of semi liquid waste. I could feel a void being created in my stomach as it all started to flow out. My colon had turned into a fully automatic belt fed machine gun on steroids, pulsing every few seconds pumping out more of this disgusting black gooey waste. I had no control over what was happening, and the pulses kept coming. There was a volcanic eruption going on inside of me and there was nothing I could do.

The smell was intense, I swear there was a smog that had started to surround my arse. Very quickly my pelvic sling was filling up with this gooey black flowing disgusting mess. In between retching from the smell, I was pleading to Ken to get the nurse. Ken upped his game and began rattling his bell with some gusto. It is worth mentioning here that Ken's bell was smaller than the smallest hotel reception bell you have ever seen, but Ken was trying his best to squeeze maximum decibel's out of it – all to no avail. No nursing staff to be seen. With the pelvic sling full, the flow continued along the path of least resistance which just happened to be the natural dip in my abdomen. It was now heading towards my neck. The rapid evacuation of my colon had caused this dip. I started to panic as I imagined the waste making a complete body loop by re-entering my stomach through my mouth and nose. I was stretching my neck as much as I could both as a preventative measure for re-entry whilst also trying to get my nose away from the intense smell of this tsunami of shit. Ken, sensing my fate from the stench, which had reached his part of the ward, went into panic mode and decided to take things into his own hands. He had decided to go and get the night staff himself.

I remember the scene vividly, Ken's bedsheet flying up passed his bedside light, Ken sitting upright just for a second before disappearing from sight completely, a second later there was one almighty crash. Ken had fallen out of his bed. In the panic, he forgot to attach his false right leg, and in desperation of his own fate hung tightly onto his bedsheet that neatly swept away the bedside light, water jug, fruit bowl and everything else that was on his bedside table - including his bell. The crash of Ken hitting the floor and the smashing of glass and plastic had the desired effect and the nurses came running out of the darkness to sort poor Ken, who, God bless him, tried his best to explain to the nurses that it was me who needed attention and not him. Anyway, we both eventually got sorted that night. I had a late-night complete all over bed bath for the first time since the accident. The emptying of the colon was a significant event in my recovery, I now felt my body was beginning to heal. I still had the catheter fitted but felt that I could start to take control of my arse once more and didn't need to worry about what I was eating.

The orthopaedic ward was on the ground floor of the hospital and, at that time, the hospital was having some maintenance work done on the outside so there were workmen near hospital walls and windows. The window curtains were old and ineffective, so it was easy to see what was going on inside the hospital from the outside. I could now poop in bed by pulling myself up out of the pelvic sling on the overhead bed ring and do my pooping into a dry nappy on the bed. I was not allowed to use a bed pan all the time I was in the pelvic sling because it would put pressure onto my broken pelvis and hips. If my aim was poor and I missed the nappy, I would just flick the poop into the nappy with my right foot. Once I received a round of applause from the workmen who clearly thought this was cool entertainment. That's the thing in hospital, you don't really concern yourself about how you look, you just do what you gotta do.

I was discharged from hospital on 23rd May 1980, so made it home for my 20th birthday on 7th June. I had to wear my sister-in-law's trousers as none of my clothes fitted me anymore. I had lost over 50lb in 57 days. Now the hard work would begin. I was on crutches, wore a foot brace for my left foot drop, nursed a serious pressure sore that needed daily treatment on my left heel and was more than a little depressed. Going from hospital care where there is 24/7 support to home where you had to fend for yourself, is tough. I went back into hospital on 13th July 1980 for plastic surgery to close up the pressure sore on my heel.

The insurance aspect was a huge life lesson for me. Neither the bike nor me were covered in the event of a crash. The accident was effectively a *'hit and run'* as we could not identify the third party. If you can't afford to buy a bike/vehicle outright, make sure you can at least afford fully comprehensive insurance. It is a game changer in these circumstances. Indeed, the insurance battles from the accident would not be settled for nearly six years. The criminal court case was not proven, and all the evidence we had was categorized as circumstantial; time and place stuff. Apart from some scuff marks, there was nothing else the police could produce linking the trailer (which they believed had hit me) to the driver. The defence lawyer was good, maintaining that there were thousands of these lorries and trailers on the road and without hard evidence, we could not prove without reasonable doubt that the police had found the right lorry and driver.

Subsequent advice from a barrister suggested that we only had a 50% chance of winning a civil case and that would cost money up front to pay for council. That of course would never happen these days. They would be falling over themselves to help me for a percentage of the claim. In the end, it was the Motor Insurance Bureau (a neutral non-profit company who compensates people for injuries sustained where insurance did not cover them - like hit and run) that paid me a small compensation for my injuries; that money effectively paid for the bike with some money left over for mum. The good news was I continued to get paid so had some money saved up from being in hospital, but I would not be buying a new bike anytime soon.

It was during my short stint in hospital in July 1980, whilst having my pressure sore closed, that I met a genuinely inspirational person who unwittingly taught me the benefits of positive thought whatever your condition or set of circumstances. I didn't realize the extent of his influence at the time, but I certainly felt that I was a better person from knowing him. His name was Bill.

Although Bill was a little older than me, he was 23 years old, married and recently his wife had given birth to their baby daughter. Bill had crashed into a tree whilst on active duty in Germany on his Triumph motorcycle. The fiberglass fuel tank exploded leaving him with severe burns to his body. His legs had been amputated below the knee and the top half of his legs were withered and useless and so was one of his arms. He continued to have saline baths every day and had lost count how many operations he had been through. But he always had a smile on his face and was always up for a laugh. For the short time I was with him in hospital, we had become good mates, as there were just the two of us in the plastic surgery ward. I only had one opportunity to take Bill out in his wheel chair during my time there, and I fucked it up. In a big, but funny way.

The operation on my heel was straight forward and had been a success but now I needed to get myself a couple of pairs of trainers to fit my newly shaped left foot and newly modified foot calliper. I had to buy two different sizes of shoe to fit my feet, a normal size pair for my right foot and a one to two size larger pair for my left foot. There was a local shoe shop about a half mile away down the hill from the hospital and I convinced the nurses that pushing Bill in the wheel chair would give me stability. Also, I was supposed to be partially non-weight bearing on my heel for a few more days so hanging onto the wheelchair would be helpful. At the same time, it would offer Bill some much needed fresh air. It was summer in the UK and an absolutely beautiful day. Reluctantly, they agreed, but made it clear to me that I needed to be back around 3pm for Bill's bath time. Easy, I estimated we would be back around lunch time, what I failed to factor into the adventure was Bill's plans.

We set off around 9:30am and had my new trainers all sorted by 11am, easy. Bill had hardly been outside much since his accident and had always had a plan in his mind to go for a beer with me before I left hospital. Bill was not allowed to drink in hospital and had not touched a drop since the accident. I initially said no, but then thought one drink won't hurt, right....? Wrong. I think we only had two drinks, well maybe three. Not much I thought. We left the pub around 1pm so had plenty of time to get back before his 3pm bath. What I had failed to factor into this scenario was the warm weather, my tiredness, Bills inability to process alcohol, and the fact that I had to push him back up the hill with a bad foot. Bill was fast asleep not long after we set off from the pub and was slouched in his chair holding on to my new training shoes. I got really close to the hospital ward but was exhausted. I couldn't get Bill and the wheelchair up the steps. I decided to move Bill and leave him in the shade of a tree with the brakes on whilst I go inside and get the staff to come and help me. Unfortunately, I ended up slouched over my bed and fell asleep without telling anyone about poor Bill.

I was woken up by the ward nurse shaking me furiously and ranting on about the trouble I had caused and the fact that the Nursing Officer was on the war path. It appeared that a hospital guest had found Bill under a tree, still asleep in his chair, gripping some new bright yellow training shoes. The guest was wondering how the hell he had got there with only one arm and why he was clutching two pairs of brand-new trainers when he didn't have any legs. Both Bill and I found ourselves grounded because of this episode and Bill insisted that he take the brunt of the blame for the incident. I thought to myself then, if someone like this can accept life as he is, and still enjoy life's little moments and share a laugh, and then take responsibility for something that was not his fault, then I had absolutely nothing to complain about. In life, there is always someone who is worse off than yourself and it doesn't hurt to reflect on your own situation and be thankful for what you have.

Seeing what a motorcycle accident did to Bill, gave me cause for reflection on whether I would continue motorcycling after my accident, so I dabbled with three-wheeler cars for a while. These *'death traps'* were popular in the UK at the time. Not trikes but fully enclosed cars; two wheels at the rear and one at the front. They were not categorized as a car under UK law, but as *'tricycles'* and because they were also under 7 cwt (783 lbs), they could be driven on a full (Class A or B1) motorcycle/tricycle license. Colloquially known as *'Plastic Pigs'* and *'Resin Rockets'* they kept you dry and warm and, on the inside, they looked and drove just like a car. The engines were centrally mounted, and you could change the spark plugs from the driver's or passenger seat. In many ways, these vehicles (let's call them vehicles) were considered more dangerous than motorcycles. They were extremely unstable at speed and in any cross-wind conditions. Cornering could be pretty exhilarating too. In short, they were fun things to drive and I really enjoyed my time owning them. However, they were no match for a motorcycle, but did offer a little more protection and you never had to wear a crash helmet whilst driving them.

Both my plastic pigs, a British Racing Green and a white one were Reliant Regal Supervan III. I have no idea where the *'Super'* prefix came from as they were anything but super. The Regal was in production for some 20 years in various guises and were made in the UK by the Reliant Motor Company in

Tamworth, England. A classic British car - not! My Regal Vans were the light-commercial versions which had a side-hinged rear door which was handy to climb out of if you tipped the car on its side - which I did just once driving it into a shallow ditch but came close to repeat performances on numerous occasions. You could get it up on two wheels without even trying and if you didn't react quickly enough it would punish you. The vehicle was made famous by the popular British television comedy series *'only fools and horses'*.

The 701 cc engine knocked out a massive 29 bhp of which you needed every one of them horses to be on their 'A' game working flat out to get even average performance out of the car. However, there was so little weight in these things that they could accelerate quite quickly compared to normal cars and if you were brave enough you could cruise between 60 and 70 mph if the conditions were favourable i.e. no wind.

My 1972 Reliant Regal Supervan III (Plastic Pig), Cwmfelinfach, Wales, 1980

In 1973, the Regal was replaced by the nicer looking and much posher version three-wheeled Reliant Robin which, to be fair looked more like a car than the Regal. Between 1970 and 1974 Reliant also made a Bond Bug another three-wheeled death trap which earned the reputation for being one of the ugliest cars ever made and, if that wasn't bad enough, you could only get these things in bright orange. The 1970s were an interesting time. Reliant also made a 3000 cc Scimitar car which was one of the fastest cars on the road in the late 70s and early 80s. The Regal (as was the Scimitar) was an all fiberglass body construction which was good for performance, not so good for self-protection and crashworthiness. After dabbling with the three wheeled vans, I didn't feel it necessary to progress to the Robin or get a Bond Bug. It was natural and sensible to progress onto four wheels as I entered my early 20s, but it would not be that long before I would hear the calling back to two wheels.

Of the four legal bikes I had owned to date, the most benign bike of them all, the XS 650 had bitten me the hardest. It had caused me the greatest grief and physical pain of my life and in the shortest amount of time. Also, it was the bike that give me some of the toughest life lessons I have ever learnt - period. However, even after such a terrible accident that left me with scars and a disability that would last the rest of my life, I have never had any regrets owning it. Indeed, it was the bike that literally changed my outlook on life. A lot of people reading this would have perhaps given up two wheels at this stage thinking that this accident had been a warning shot, a lucky escape with their life. I have never once thought of the accident in those terms. The accident was unfortunate for sure, but there are risks associated with any activity that involves machinery, speed and human interaction.

Stopping riding motorcycles was never a serious consideration even after this accident. I simply learnt from it. However, I did experience first-hand and remain conscious today of the grief riding motorcycles can have on loved ones who don't ride or share the same passion for motorcycles. Motorcycling somehow gets into your blood, but perhaps the middleweight twins were not the bikes for me. Maybe I needed to change the brand and/or go a bit bigger ...... So much choice....

Chapter 5
Adaptation & Starting Again

Amongst all the other things I had either cracked, snapped, punctured, bruised, disrupted or just temporally damaged during the accident, the most enduring injury was the severed sciatic nerve on my left side from breaking my back and pelvis. This severed nerve had left me with a permanent left foot drop. As it was my left side, I could no longer change gear in a conventional manner as I had lost the ability to lift my foot up. I am also left footed, so that killed off any hope of me becoming the next Welsh wizard on the football field. However, my right foot was fully operational, so I could still operate a kick starter - which is pretty handy for motorcycling. Driving a car was not a problem either, because you only need your left foot to operate the clutch, a pushing down movement which I could still do.

The thing is, both riding a bike and driving a car are sedentary activities i.e. you are sat on your arse. I could still do that, so all I had to do was adapt my operating techniques to my new set of restricted capabilities. Walking however was not straight forward (literally) for me. I had to relearn how to walk and it was kind of awkward at first as I had to adapt to wearing a cumbersome foot brace which I thought I would have to wear for the rest of my life. Getting back on two wheels (lifting my leg over the saddle) was literally posing me a real-life challenge. Not to mention my inability to change gear with my now gammy left foot. I was also carrying a wasted calf muscle and some muscles in the left side of my arse were not working either. The nerve damage had left me with a weaker left side overall and in combination with the foot drop, I had lost the ability to balance on my left side completely.

Everything else about me worked fine (eventually), but I had to be mindful of these physical limitations – not to stop me riding, just needing sometimes to proceed with caution. I was adamant that my biking days were not over. I can thank my hospital buddy Bill, for the attitudinal stuff. Even losing his legs and an arm, I am convinced that given the opportunity he would have climbed back on a bike without batting an eyelid even after all that he had been through. What I learnt from Bill was that positive things happen with positive thoughts, but it would be an element of luck and timing that would see my physical progress take a step change (pun intended) for the better, just one year later.

In October 1981, I was one of a dozen patients taking part in an orthopaedic medical review conference that was held in a military hospital in the UK. My collective injuries were considered unique in that several consultant surgeons believed that the accident I had suffered, should not have been survivable. Other patients at the conference had other unique orthopaedic issues, but mine was the only RTA (Road Traffic Accident). I felt a little bit like a prize exhibit. *'Here is Nigel Sainsbury our one and only RTA patient'*. However, I was happy to be there as the RAF Surgeon who had been handling my case (and was the host of the conference) thought I would generate some interesting discussion - he was right; I did. The luck part was that this was the first time the RAF had hosted such an event and it just so happened that my accident was one of the more interesting cases in the RAF at that time. All up, a group of around 10 orthopaedic surgeons from all over the UK came around and went through my medical history. Discussions then ensued about my progress, current limitations and future treatment strategies before they moved on as a group to the next patient.

After the doctors had discussed my case and were moving to the next patient, I was getting ready to leave when one of the surgeons in the group asked if I could stay a little longer as he wanted to talk to me. He returned about 30 minutes later, introduced himself again, and began asking me detailed questions about the accident, the trauma I had suffered and the difficulties I had been having with my recovery. His interest was piqued in my case as he had significance experience being the orthopaedic surgeon at the Isle of Man TT (Tourist Trophy) Motorcycle races for the past several years. He told me that he had only seen injuries like mine twice before. Both were motorcycle accidents, and both were during TT races where sadly, both patients had died from their injuries. Not only did he validate what others had said to me, but he had witnessed and treated my type of injuries first hand. He was more than curious how I had survived the accident. He said I should consider myself a *very lucky young man* to have survived such trauma. I didn't feel so lucky at the time of the accident but kept that thought to myself.

He also said that his fellow doctors agreed that there was little to no chance of further neurological improvement for my foot drop. That was the bad news. I thought my sciatic nerve had been growing back slowly as I could feel a tingly pain every so often on my left side which I thought was nerve growth. Apparently not. However, they did agree that I would be a good patient for an operation that could correct my foot drop. His final words to me were along the lines of; *someone must have been looking out for you on that day*. Those comments resonated with me and I immediately thought of my father looking over me from someplace in the afterlife and wondered if indeed there was some substance to his words. I told mum what he had said, and she took some solace that maybe dad had, somehow, influenced the accident outcome. The story made her smile. It made me smile too and was quite comforting in its own way. If it was dad, he clearly thought I had more motorcycling in me and it wasn't my time to call it a day. I was alive, and I wasn't going to let him down by giving up on motorcycles now.

I was just 21-years-old and a prime candidate for a tendon transfer operation to correct my foot drop. In the one year I had been living with this disability, I had needed three different foot braces, so this operation would be a significant life changer for me. The first brace was extremely painful to wear and consisted of a large spring held to my leg via a Velcro strap and a hard-plastic foot plate that would hold my foot at a 90-degree angle to my leg. As I mentioned earlier, I needed a much larger shoe size for my left foot to wear this orthopaedic monstrosity, so I was now in the business of buying two pairs of identical shoes but different sizes. I just needed to meet someone with the same injuries on their right leg who had the same size feet.

When walking, the brace would flex at the ankle allowing my leg and foot to move with my walking action before flicking my foot up towards 90 degrees when I raised my left foot off the ground. I hated wearing the thing, it was heavy, looked hideous and didn't help my gait much at all. However, it was robust and would last much longer than the other two braces I had. The second and third braces were both one-piece moulded plastic braces that were shaped to my leg and foot. They were much more comfortable to wear, but they could not withstand the constant flexing at the ankle and therefore would crack and fail. I lost count how many times I had to repair them. However,

I did manage to pass my driving test whilst wearing one of these monstrosities. I never told the driving instructor I had this disability and he never asked, so that was all good.

After two unsuccessful hospital admission attempts due to illness and surgeon availability, the third admission was a goer and the operation was eventually carried out on 21st December 1981. The surgeon had never done the operation before and asked me if the procedure could be videoed. *'Sure, no problem, providing I can see it too'* I joked. So, it was to be, on Christmas Day 1981, I would be propped up in my hospital bed watching my operation on video tape with a visiting Father Christmas.

The operation consisted of cutting the Achilles' tendon in a Z shape, stretching it, raising the foot so it would be at right angles to the leg at the ankle, then stitching it back together. At the same time, disconnecting the Tibialis Posterior Tendon (the tendon that twists your foot in towards your other foot) at the lower end of the

Me & Santa, Christmas Day, Wroughton Military Hospital, Swindon, UK, 1981

tendon and pulling it out of the top of the foot and then re-attaching it to the instep. Please do not try this operation at home. Although armed with a Leatherman pocket knife, a sharp pair of scissors and a stapler you could probably give it a good go.

The outcome meant that when I pulled my foot inwards, it would pull the foot up. Yep, that's exactly how it works and it's weird – believe me! Even today it seems weird. The actual movement is quite small, but the tendon does hold the foot at right angles which allows me to walk without a foot brace. I had to re-program my brain, so I could walk without falling over. It was not easy at first and took some serious physiotherapy and walking in front of mirrors to make the transition. Some would argue that I have never mastered walking again. I would agree with that statement. I certainly have a unique gait now. Once I had mastered the walking part, it did not take me long to learn how to run and get myself back to fitness. Once I felt fit enough and got my self-confidence back, I was one step closer (pun intended) to getting back on two wheels.

I had gone from two, to three to four wheels in the space of two years. Cars were great, but I was itching to get back onto two wheels. The first opportunity came just a few months later when along with a few mates we booked an 18 to 30-year-old holiday to Spain. Apart from drinking, partying and seeing how long you could go without sleep, one of the more traditional things you did on a single boys' holiday was to hire local mopeds and go exploring the local town and countryside.

In Spain (during the early 80s) mopeds were like pushbikes. Anyone could hire them, no need for crash helmets or any other protective gear, nothing. I am not sure you even needed to have a driver's license to ride them. However, there were many horror stories of people having serious accidents on these mopeds who were not covered by travel insurance. Many of them had never ridden any type of motorized two wheeled vehicle before, and even though they are just small mopeds capable of around 20 to 25 mph max (downhill with a strong wind behind you), they can cause you some grief if you don't respect them. Also, Spain, like most European countries drive on the other side of the road to the UK and it is quite easy to forget that when you are messing about on a motorized bicycle.

I had not been back on a bike since my accident so when the boys suggested we go out for the day on mopeds. I was up for it. I saw the opportunity to go back to my roots, back to my NSU Quickly days. Indeed, the mopeds were very similar to the NSU requiring a *'pedal as fast as you can'* start, whilst twisting the throttle to go. These particular mopeds were single speed too, so no gears to change you just held the throttle open wide and rung it out as much as you could.

My riding skills immediately kicked in and it was not long before I was leading the pack on how to ride these bright yellow Spanish bikes. I am assuming they were yellow, so they could be spotted easily by other motorists who must have hated these things buzzing around town ridden by noisy brits. The picture depicts me showing off my balance skills noting that I am standing on the

Me & Mates, 'Boys on Tour', Spain, 1982

saddle with my right leg and not my left. Had I stood on my left leg, I would have ended up in a heap on the floor in no time. The other noticeable thing about this photo, and it makes me cringe even looking at it now, was that we were all riding with no protective gear at all, nothing. Just a pair of shorts, some flip-flops and body skin. Not a great advert for being sensible riders, but in mitigation most of us were in our early 20s and you don't give a shit when you are that age.

The experience on the mopeds was a great lead in for getting back into motorcycles once again and it would be less than a year later that I would get myself another proper motorcycle. Although I felt that I didn't really need an excuse to get a bike, I had several up my sleeve if anyone asked why? Firstly, I owned a very unreliable sports/rally car, a Ford Escort RS 2000 and needed a back-up form of transport. Secondly, I had moved to South Wales and had a much shorter commute to work so didn't always need a car. Thirdly, I had moved closer to mum (this was not through choice - just career circumstances) and could nip home during the week through the narrow and twisty back roads which was perfect for a motorcycle not so much for a car. However, financially I had been hurt by the life episode of motor insurance on the Yamaha XS 650, so I was thinking that I would shy away from a brand-new bike. All I needed at this time, was a smallish affordable second-hand bike whilst saving up some money for whatever was coming next.

When the sixteener law took effect in 1971, the arse fell out of the 250 cc market. You could get 250 cc bikes of all makes pretty cheap on the second-hand market as they were no longer the learner bikes of choice. I had found a really nice, cheap, red 1976 Honda CJ 250 T. Not a popular bike by any means, classed as a T= tourer for some reason. In Japan is was classed more as a café racer design as it was the successor of the CB 250. The CJ 250 T did have a sporty/touring looking two-into-one exhaust system (which was popular at the time). It was comfortable to ride but was a pretty bland bike overall. What it was though, was a good old workhorse that would serve my practical needs for a bike until I had decided to get a bigger bike of choice. The CJ had a modest 27 horses but for the riding I was doing it was perfect. I could get up to the legal speed limit of 70 mph pretty

easy and it would sit there comfortably and still return around 60 mpg. This bike was so reliable it never once let me down in the two years I had it. I never garaged the bike either thinking nobody was ever going to steal it, so the bike was left out

Me & My 1976 Honda CJ 250 T, Cwmfelinfach, Wales, 1983

uncovered in all weathers. This was my first legal Honda and I was liking the brand.

It was not a fluke that I had chosen the Honda CJ 250 T. I had been looking at several bikes and in particular the gear change lever mechanisms. Although my foot drop had been corrected, I was still unable to put the top of my foot under a gear change lever and change up. Changing down was not a problem, but I needed to master the skill of changing up.

I had come up with three solutions to change gear. The first and preferred method was to modify the gear change lever on the bike. The other two methods were foot operating techniques. Remembering my days from the Honda C 50, the gear change on that bike was a *'step through'* with a semi-automatic clutch. This meant that the gear lever was pivoted at the centre of the lever rather than at just one end. This configuration allowed you to push down on the forward end to change down and also push down on the aft part of the lever to change up. Simplicity itself. On the CJ 250 T there was no obstruction to fitting this centre pivoted step through lever, so I simply removed the original gear change lever and replaced it with a step through lever off a C 50. The gear change spindle diameter was exactly the same size on both bikes, so it fitted perfectly. That was one of the main reasons why the Honda CJ 250 T was such a great post-accident first bike for me.

The other two gear changing techniques involve using other leg muscles that still work on my left side. The first and safer technique is to place my instep under the gear change lever as you would normally do with a good foot, but then twist the foot in an anti-clockwise direction rather than pull it up. The twisting action is done by acting a rotational movement through the knee and upper leg. The sturdiness of the side of the shoe or boot will then (hopefully) provide enough upward force to change gear. However, I can't feel any feedback from the gear change lever using this method, so I have no idea how positive the gear change has been. The good news here is that the bike tells me almost immediately if the gear change has been unsuccessful. The bike will do one of two things, it will either: 1) rev up and not produce any additional forward momentum (missed gear) or, 2) the bike goes forward a short distance and then jumps out of gear into a false neutral resulting in a repeat of 1). This technique can be more than a little frustrating and embarrassing, and its success depends on the footwear I am wearing at the time. If there is too much play in the gear shift lever, then I have little to no chance of making a successful gear change.

The second and less safe technique, is the one I use predominantly today, simply because it's not dependent on my footwear or the bike. I call it the ' hook and pull' technique. I literally hook the back of my heel, under the gear change lever and pull my whole leg up using my quad muscles. Because it's a direct lifting force being applied, I can feel the gear change movement through my leg muscles, so the change is much more positive overall, and I am less prone to a mis-selection. The down side is that my whole foot must extend under the gear change lever with my toes pointing down. Even on a slight left-hand bend, I am prone to catching my foot on the road and scraping it during gear changes, on sharp bends I am afraid of trapping my foot under the bike and there is no good outcome from that scenario. So, prevention being better than a cure, I make sure I am in the right gear before going around even the slightest of left-hand bends. Right hand corners pose no problem.

As with all bikes, you have experiences. The Honda CJ 250 T was no different, but it never did me any harm. Although the bike was reliable, the fact that it was out in all weathers did not do it much good. In winter time, if it was below freezing or close to freezing, the clutch inner cable would freeze to the outer cable preventing me from using the clutch. I had moved into my own house in Barry, South Wales and lived at the bottom of a hill that seemed to hog cold air and freezing temperatures.

If the clutch cable had frozen overnight, I had to boil a kettle of water and pour the hot water over the length of the cable. Once it had started to defrost, I literally had about two minutes to get going before the cable would refreeze. In that two minutes, I had to ride up the steep hill, cross a major road junction and get into the traffic on the main road to work. If the cable refroze after that, which it often did, I could use clutch-less gear changes all the way to work. In fact, there is nothing like a frozen clutch cable to force you to hone your clutch-less gear changing skills and I had become quite adept at it, ably assisted by the step through gear change lever. It's not a terribly difficult skill to master, but if you get it wrong the engine will let you know by making some horrible grating and crunching noises. If the cable remained frozen all the way into work, I would literally stall the bike at my works entrance if I couldn't find neutral. Easy. The Honda didn't mind, and it's a testament to Honda engineering that the bike could put up with such abuse. I guess I could have replaced the clutch cable, but it was perfectly functional for 97% of the time and the other 3% I had a perfectly good workaround solution.

The other event resulted in my thinking that the bike had been stolen when in fact it was just hiding on its side, under a dumpster (skip). My girlfriend's father's driving was legend, but for the wrong reasons. He never really liked driving and only did it because he had to. Literally, the first time I went to his house we had this incident involving the Honda. He had hired a skip to take the waste from a kitchen makeover he was working on. The skip was parked right outside his house on the side of the road. He had positioned a plank of wood as a ramp for his wheelbarrow and he would use this plank to judge his distance from the skip when reversing his car to park. Anything in between him and the plank didn't really exist. Except of course on this occasion my bike did. He drove his car into the bike without even noticing, pushing it under the skip.

When I left the house to go home, I found my lovely Honda resting on its side hiding under the lip of the skip. No real damage other than a bent lever and a few scrapes but no broken glass to my surprise. This told me a couple of things. Firstly, don't mess with my girlfriends' father, he clearly doesn't care for anything that imposes on his own car parking space and, secondly, when on the bike, park it somewhere obvious so people can see it. It was not deliberate of course, he didn't even know that he had hit it. He thought that he may have just touched the plank – touching the plank was not unusual (his words not mine) as by doing so he knew he was as close as he could be to the skip. The bikes value had already been depreciated to zero, so no real harm done.

Chapter 6
Making Choices from Experience
& Influence

I had a very positive experience with the Honda CJ 250 T and I was liking the Honda brand. Although the 250 T was nothing special, it was the right bike at the right price, and at the right time filling a gap in my transport arrangements. I was now ready to return to the bigger middle weight category. I have never been superstitious, so I was confident that I would be alright getting back into this class of motorcycle. I really wasn't that keen to move onto the larger engine and fairing covered sports bike category. The performance was attractive, but the plastic moulded fairings do nothing for the aesthetics for me. Fairings tend to hide the engine, and the riding positions just look uncomfortable over long distances. And then of course, how could the gear changing mechanism be modified for my gammy left foot (although my foot was never a deal breaker in not owning any bike I liked).

To own a bike, I must immediately like the look of it. The ride is almost secondary at that stage. I always believe that I can adjust my riding style to the particulars of the bike. Sounds daft, it's like buying a surround sound system for your house because it looks good and fits in with the other furniture without actually listening to it. Odd I know, but it is all about the look. At this stage of my motorcycling life, I would sum up my favourite bikes as being quick and naked. Not super sporty and plastic. Indeed, my view hasn't changed much over the years. I still appreciate the technical design of a bike, seeing the engine, frame and componentry being connected and somehow blended in between two wheels is pure beauty in my eyes.

I had recently married, and family matters were quite rightly taking priority in my life. I just wanted a bike that I could take pride in, ride it as a commuter or whenever, and have something in the garage to look at when I couldn't go riding. Motorcycles are like that. You don't have to be riding them all the time. They can and should be ornaments and engineering pieces of beauty to admire.

When I bought my new Yamaha XS 500, one of my biker friends *'Windy'* had a Honda CX 500 and over a five-day holiday in July 1978 we went camping to the South of France on his bike. Why the South of France? Well, we were teenagers and wanted to see for ourselves the French topless beaches. Sounds shallow I know, but we were going to go somewhere, so why not down to Marseille? We decided we would do it on the cheap and just take the one bike rather than both bikes. My Yamaha was so new it would have run out of mileage for its initial *'break-in'* service anyway. So, it was not a difficult decision to take Windy's CX 500.

Windy's 1976 Honda CX500, France, 1978

I was impressed by the way the CX 500 handled two up with all the camping equipment and the fact that we didn't have to

90

do any maintenance on it at all. The shaft drive on the CX 500 was brilliant. Not only was it maintenance free, the rear of the bike kept itself nice and clean. Chains can be so messy and are often in constant need of attention regardless of the conditions you are riding in. I thought to myself then, shaft was the way to go on any bike I was intending to keep for a long time or do some serious mileage on.

When we arrived at the Port of Dover, we called into the local post office and bought ourselves a cardboard style one-year passport before crossing over to Calais, France on the channel ferry. Because in 1978 that's how you got to travel through France and into the rest of Europe. The Channel Tunnel (nicknamed the Chunnel) was a pipe dream in 1978. The 31-mile rail tunnel that links Folkestone, in the United Kingdom, with Coquelles, Pas-de-Calais, near Calais in France, and runs some 250 feet (76 metres) beneath the English Channel didn't open until 1994 having started construction in 1988. At the time, it was the most expensive construction project ever undertaken.

Once we had gotten down to the South of France and had a good look around to see the local sites walking the beaches (several times over I might add), we decided that we would head straight back home. We also thought it would be fun to see if we could get back to RAF Brawdy, West Wales in one day - around 800 miles (1,300 kilometres).

We got up very early the next morning and went for it. It took us around 17 hours from somewhere between Marseille and Lyon (including a cross channel ferry journey) back to our barracks at RAF Brawdy. It was an incredible journey. Riding pillion is tiring in a different way to riding yourself. I fell asleep on the back of the bike somewhere west of London. If it wasn't for all the shit and camping stuff that we had strapped onto the bike and wrapped around me, I was sure I would have fallen off. Riding for that long in one go was not the best idea we had, but it was a real adventure for sure. It was the trip that did two things for me. Firstly, it sowed the seed that influenced my thinking about long distance motorcycle adventures. I knew even then that this was just the first of many more adventures to come. Secondly, the CX 500 was a very reliable bike. It never missed a beat all trip.

I was not 100% sure what my next bike would be as I had a family to consider and was on a budget. I had kept a bit of an open mind but was also actively looking for a decent second hand CX 500 as well. My thinking was this next bike was going to last me a few years and I did not want to be spending lots of money on its maintenance.

A family friend had a Yamaha TDM 850 for sale. It was a beautiful bike and very fast but was a bit heavy for me at 485 lbs, had some plastic bits, and a chain final drive. That was it. I really wanted a shaft drive next time and would hang out for a CX 500. I didn't have to wait long. I got my hands on a 1982 Honda CX 500 E (E=Eurosport). It was perfect. It was affordable and looked much better than Windy's CX 500 'A' model - which could have been mistaken for a stubby water-cooled air compressor. I could also hook my heel nicely under the gear change lever. Honda had made some significant improvements for the CX 500 E. Some were obvious like the styling and suspension, some not, like modification to the beefed-up front end and some engine modifications. The original CX 500 was a difficult bike to categorise because it didn't fit into any one genre. A water cooled 500 cc V-Twin with a shaft drive that looked a little odd. The only other water-cooled bike Honda made was the 1000 cc GL Goldwing. Not surprising then that these smaller engine water cooled shaft driven bikes ended up being covered in plastic fairings and then called Silverwings, a smaller more affordable version of the Goldwing. Therefore, the CX 500 ended up being placed in the long-distance tourer basket.

The CX 500 E though was different. This model was hybrid tourer and sports bike (in my opinion). To me it looked the part and ticked all the boxes for what I wanted out of a long-term commitment bike. The metallic white accentuated its long design lines that were complimented with the various chrome elements of the bike. The cockpit looked very modern with a fuel gauge (which was a first for me) and was very cool when it lit up in the dark. The

Me & My 1982 Honda CX 500 Eurosport, St Athan, Wales, 1988

water cooling and the V-Twin engine just made the bike look and sound different to anything else that was on the market in the middle weight category. I like different, because I am different and would choose a similar bike based on the very same criteria in 2012 whilst living in the USA.

The CX 500 E was capable of doing the *'Ton'* kicking out a modest 50 horses at 9,000 rpm whilst returning over 40 mpg. Its competition at the time was the up and coming popular four-cylinder machines. The water cooled strokers like the replacement Yamaha RD 400, the LC 350 were still around and capable of going much faster and quicker. However, I was very happy with my ton-up CX 500 E. The bike had a great upright riding position which suited both short or long distances although the small nose fairing was more cosmetic than functional. The engine sits high up in the frame on the CX, but it was not a beast to handle, even though the bike weighed in at some 458 lbs. You could feel a small counter twist from the shaft when you accelerated which was a strange feeling at first but then a comforting one once you got used to the bike. You could compensate the twisting by leaning harder and proportional to the acceleration. It was also the first bike I had owned that had a single shock rear suspension and this would be an extremely expensive item to replace a couple of years down the line when it sprang a leak.

I had two other memorable issues with my CX. Firstly, the bike had a real problem waking up after its winter hide away, to be fair this was probably more about my not treating and draining the fuel system and winterising the bike correctly than anything else. The other issue was an annoying fuel tank leak caused by internal corrosion on the left-hand seam weld at the base of the tank. That was a real pain in the arse to fix and eventually was the deal maker for the next buyer as the repair was looking more likely to be a replacement fuel tank - that was going to be more expensive than the rear shock absorber.

The CX 500 series of bikes were extremely popular in the UK. It was the preferred choice for dispatch riders due to its reliability, shaft drive and its record for doing high mileages. These included the CX 500s big brother the CX 650, but not so much, the crazy turbo charged 570lb, 140 mph, 100 bhp monster version. However, all these bikes were built for the rider to knock out some serious high mileage days - and in some cases, quickly too.

The CX 500 E was a recognisable and brilliant bike all round. No doubt about it. I loved owning it and for four plus years, it was my trusted steed and it looked after me. It did everything well and people always commented on how good it looked, and so by default it made me look good too. I even used it as an ambulance once when my mate got knocked off his pushbike having been struck by a large wing mirror that was sticking out from a lorry cab. The mirror smacked him in the back at traffic lights and sent him flying off his pushbike. The CX 500 and I was dispatched to pick him up from the hospital and take him home.

If I hadn't had suffered the fuel tank problem and didn't need the money for an ambitious self-build car project, I would have kept the bike much, much longer. In the four years I owned this bike, I never took a tumble. Just like the Yamaha XS 500 I had kept a 100% record. Funny that I seem to judge my performance on riding a particular motorcycle buy my accident rate on that bike. Perhaps the 500 cc middle weights were my sweet spot for motorcycling. Clearly, the benign 650 cc twin category was a challenge. I wondered about how I would perform on larger capacity bikes, would they also pose me a problem? Well, I would discover in 2016 that the 650 cc category might be my '666' - my devil, my darkness, my nemesis!

In the last year I owned the CX 500 E, I was well into my new RAF career as an Engineering Officer, was married, had one son with another son on the way and was about to move the family for a third time. The bike was a great second form of transport whilst I was undergoing training, but with a growing family it was time to think about sharing my time with the rest of the family which meant something different to motorcycles. After all, I could always return to motorcycling as the children grew up. Perhaps, the children would get into motorcycles too? Ha, ha, ha. Wishful thinking of course. I wouldn't have changed my circumstances for the world, I was very happy, but it was time to put motorcycles to one side for a while. On reflection, I guess I was now in the same situation as my dad found himself in the late 50s. Second child Nigel was on the way, and neither time nor money for motorcycles.

For a little while, me and my fellow engineering friend had been smitten to build a kit car each. We talked about it, visited shows and researched the various options, as you do over time, but it was only me that eventually followed through on the crazy idea. As an engineer I have had this insatiable appetite to get my hands dirty with all things technical. So, let's just think about this.....I needed more time to spend with the family, did not need to spend any

My 'Kindred Spirit' Kit Car, RAF Lyneham, England, 1991

more money than was necessary and my solution was to build a kit car? I could not have picked a project that was more out of whack with what I wanted to achieve than this. The CX 500 would provide me with the cash I needed to buy both the kit car and donor vehicle that would provide all the parts not provided by the kit. Having driven and owned a couple of three-wheel death traps just a few years ago, I was keen on building a three-wheeler car but this time with two wheels at the front and one at the back. That seemed a much safer configuration than two driving wheels at the back and one steering wheel in the front like the Reliant Regal Supervan.

The kit car I ended up buying was called a *'Kindred Spirit'* by Hudson Cars, Norwich, England. The car was designed around a Renault 5 donor car but looked nothing like a Renault of course once it was finished. The two-seat tandem (no doors) configuration looked very much like a small racing car crossed with a motorcycle. It was a perfect design for me, and I thought it would be fun to build with the boys growing up. What I failed to appreciate was how much of a money pit these projects can be, and the amount of time you spend building them which is at least double what the manufacturer suggests. How I ever found enough time to build this car at all, remains a mystery to me, but I did it. I finished it and it looked really cool in British Racing Green and Red.

Luckily, I had at my disposal all the facilities and resources I needed at my place of work to build the car. Paint stripping, bead blasting, coatings, paint, general service tools and all sorts of engineering equipment used to maintain aircraft can also be pretty useful to build kit cars. My mate in the other building next door kept me supplied with general nuts, bolts washers etc. I swear to God the car would stand to attention when the national anthem was played, such was the amount of military help and government equipment that went into the build. The final phase of the build was to paint the various fibreglass panels in British Racing Green.

One of the painting specialists offered to get the paint and do the job for me for a small charge, but he needed somewhere to hang the panels dust free for a few days for the paint to cure. Just a few weeks earlier, my team had refurbished an old 1950s caravan that fitted in the back of an aircraft for use by VIPs travelling overseas on military aircraft. We spent a small fortune on its upgrade and as soon as we had finished it, the mission was cancelled. This came of no surprise to anyone, as the caravan even after the refurbishment was still a 1950s caravan. It was a crap idea and it still smelt like a 1950s caravan too. It was no VIP transport in the 1950s so you can only imagine what it was like 40 years later. Reminds me of the metaphor *'You can sprinkle glitter on a turd to make it look good, but it's still a turd'*. Anyway, I gave permission for the painter to hang my panels in the newly refurbished VIP caravan.

Unfortunately, questions were being asked about the money we had spent refurbishing this bloody VIP caravan and a senior officer decided to just pitch up one day to inspect it. Bearing in mind that no one had shown the slightest bit of interest in the caravan until a few months ago and it was simply standing dormant once again now the mission had been cancelled. I guess in hindsight the visit was neither unexpected nor unreasonable, just that no one ever mentioned it to me beforehand. I was away at the time of the visit but my deputy, who was a very mature and street wise supervisor said that even he was *"torn another arse hole'* when the senior officer found the kit car panels hanging in our plush VIP caravan. Not only that, but the painter had touched up a couple of the panels in-situ and there were splatters of British Racing Green paint all over the new caravan trimmings. That coupled with the strong smell of paint thinners resulted in me being reprimanded a few days later when I got back to work.

When asked about the caravan and my car panels, all I could do was apologise, say sorry and declare bad judgement on my behalf. I took full responsibility and promised to sort things out and put it right. My admission of guilt certainly took the heat out of the reprimand. Although, I think he was more pissed that I had never mentioned to him what I was doing, and I felt that he may have given me his approval (with some caveats) if I had asked him first. I didn't really know, and I didn't want to take the chance. After all he was not the most approachable man in the world. Everyone had an opinion on this guy. I guess I thought it was better to ask for forgiveness than to do something against his will.

I should have done more research on building kit cars. Without the support and facilities around me, the build cost and time would have been prohibitive for me and I would never have finished the car. I would never undertake such an ambitious project again. In fact, I sold the car just months after making it legal to drive on the road as the enjoyment of driving this pretty sporty lightweight rocket was not as great as I thought it would be. The challenge and attraction were all in the build and seeing it completed. I guess that's the engineer in me. However, I never lost any actual money on it, which was a miracle when I have spoken to others who have done something similar. Having said that, I did put hundreds of manhours into the strip of the donor, prep of the parts and building of the kit car itself which realistically I was never going to get any money for in the sale price.

So, the car was completed, and we were on the move again as a family. We took the car with us initially then I sold it. I really missed not having a motorcycle, even one to look at. With the money from the sale of the car, guess what I did (with permission from the wife of course). Yes. I bought another motorcycle. This time it would be a brand-new one and I had concocted some pretty good reasons for getting it.

Chapter 7
Four is Bigger than Two

Our move (with the kit car in tow) to Lincolnshire, was only for six months and then we would move the family again. In fact, the next move would be our sixth move in less than five years. The money from the kit car was burning a hole in my pocket and we already knew where we were going to move next but accommodating the family would initially pose a problem due to a lack of available housing. Consequently, we would need a second vehicle, so I could commute on a weekly basis. A one-way trip was 230 miles (370 kilometres). It was the perfect excuse for....... yes, you guessed it, another bike. Excuses are quite handy when you have other life priorities like a growing family.

I was happy with owning second hand bikes, but a long commute and for an undefined period of time required something reliable, something trustworthy, something under warranty if anything was to go wrong. And perhaps this vehicle, let's call it a motorcycle, needed to be a little bigger than 500 cc and have more cylinders. Why? Well, bigger engines and more cylinders are much quicker (gets me home earlier) and they are safer of course. Absolute bullshit really, but a couple of great points to start the family discussion.

It just so happened that in 1992, Yamaha introduced their XJ 600 S Diversion model which went on to become a very popular naked bike. That meant any brand new unsold 1991 XJ 600, Sport Touring bikes - its predecessor, were going cheap as the dealers just wanted rid of them because they were now a discontinued model and they were focussed on selling the new naked Diversion model.

There was one XJ600 left in the Yamaha dealership and it was a beautiful red and silver one. I must be honest, this was a financial choice more than a preferred bike choice. However, I didn't really have a preferred choice of bike in my mind at that time. I was in the early stages of research when I noticed this bike in the showroom. I loved the colour and it really suited the bike. It was brand new, under warranty and was an affordable (kit car money fund) sports tourer commuter with a four-cylinder 600 cc engine. The sports tourer model and four-cylinder engines (vice twins) were firsts for me. The fairing was not all plastic like a full sports bike

My 1991 Yamaha XJ600, RAF Valley, Wales, 1992

but a nice practical nose fairing for touring protection finished off with a small bottom fairing to streamline the bike giving it its sports looks. Yep, this was a great choice and I was going back to my roots, my very first trusted brand of Yamaha.

What most Yamaha Diversion owners didn't realise was that my 1991, XJ 600 was better than the 1992, Diversion model in a couple of ways. Mine had 72 horses locked away that were unleased at 10,000 rpm whilst the Diversion only had 61 horses delivered at 8,500 rpm. That is around a 20% power differential which is significant for the same size engine. Admittedly, the Diversion engine was slightly different to the XJ engine and the bike overall was around 10 lbs lighter at 458 lbs (because it was naked), but the top speed of mine was 123 mph compared to the Diversion which was a paltry 111 mph. I never did a speed run on my XJ 600 like I did on my XS 500, but I knew it would do 100 mph easy enough. And finally, the XJ 600 was considerably cheaper than the new diversion, and in my opinion looked a much better bike too. But I would say that wouldn't I? It's all part of the psychology when considering buying a new bike.

I loved the XJ 600 and owned it for five years. It was such a reliable bike it was boring. Boring in this sense meaning I didn't need to do any work on it. I never modified it either, I just rode it, and rode it and rode it. The Yamaha four-cylinder motor in this bike was bullet proof and so smooth compared to the twins. Although it did rev a bit higher and there was not as much engine breaking as the twins, but it could handle any riding style you threw at it. The XJ 600 would be my first bike that I had a real adventure on since I rode pillion on Windy's, CX 500 back in 1978. A journey that would take me the length of Britain from home to Lands' End, up to John O'Groats' in Scotland then home again. An adventure of almost 1,900 miles (3,000 kilometres) in just three days.

I was lucky to work alongside a Scottish mate, Matt, who was probably a bigger fan of motorcycles than I was. In fact, I am surprised we got any work done at all in our two years of working together. It seemed like we were always talking about bikes. Matt rode a great big 675lb, Kawasaki GTR 1000. A real beast of a bike, renowned for doing huge mileages in between fuel stops with its massive 7.5-US gallon fuel tank. A lot of these late 80s super tourers are still in service today carrying mileages similar to those of the Space Shuttle.

One day in work the subject of a Land's End to John O'Groats (or End to End) run came up over a coffee break. I had done this trip before with my wife in a brand-new Ford Sierra hire car back in April 1987 but had always hankered doing it again on a motorcycle. The journey in the car had taken us 13 hours and one minute over a distance of 876 miles (1,400 kilometres). I had already got the tie, badge and certificate and was a fully paid up Member of the Lands' End to John O'Groats Association; membership number 118. The End to End distance does not seem that bad on its own, but you have to get to the start and then return from the finish, so it is quite an adventure all up. Particularly if it's against the clock. I remember the return journey home from John O'Groats to South Wales seemed to go on forever and was a killer drive. We ended up completing over 2000 miles (3,200 kilometres) in under two days. I was absolutely exhausted and with less than 150 miles (240 kilometres) to run for home, I had started to hallucinate through lack of sleep and was forced to stop for a little while to power nap. It was dangerous and stupid to be driving for so long whilst being so tired. My wife didn't drive at that time either, but she too was exhausted as she stayed awake with me.

We did it, and for the most part it was great fun as well as an awesome sense of achievement. I kept myself awake by asking my wife to feed me something to eat every 15 to 20 minutes for the whole journey. The hire car company didn't believe the mileage when we handed back the car. Luckily it was an unlimited mileage special deal. My experience doing this adventure in a car was tough. I knew that doing it on a motorcycle would take the adventure to another level, but there was no way I was going to do the whole thing without a rest period in there somewhere. And who would feed me every 20 minutes on a bike?

Matt was also keen to do the trip on a motorcycle but wanted to raise money for charity at the same time. His mate Ian was also keen to do the trip on his Honda VFR 750. So that was it then, three of us doing an End to End charity run discussed and sorted during a normal coffee break. Normally these things are discussed and decided over a beer or two when you are tipsy or full on drunk, and then you conveniently forget the discussion in the morning. This was different, we were stone cold sober and had made a decision over the innocent morning coffee – and it wasn't even an Irish coffee. There was no backing out the following day either, we were fired up to do this.

I was not keen to take the same route I took in the car on a motorcycle, the motorways were boring in a car, they would be brutally boring on a motorcycle. The choice of route taxed our tiny minds, but we were united in avoiding motorways. We wanted to make the adventure more interesting by putting our riding and navigational skills to the test, so we decided on planning our route through five RAF stations. A computer route planner (there was no Google Maps in 1995) suggested it would take us 24 hours non-stop. Ummmm...add some time for a coffee at the five RAF stations, refuelling and a minimum three-hour rest break for safety, we reckoned that 30 hours would present a reasonable challenge. We would start the adventure from Land's End (it was closer). We just needed to get there first and rest up the night before.

The three of us had different charities we wanted to help, but we eventually settled for the charity that had benefited the least from local fund-raising events. This ended up being the Sleaford & District Talking Newspapers for the Blind. This charity transfers newspaper and magazine articles onto audio tape for those who the written word cannot reach. A visit to their premises in Sleaford, Lincolnshire, left us impressed by the dedication and devotion of the volunteers who selected and recorded the written material. We were also impressed by their enthusiasm for our bikes and motorcycling in general. To make the most of the money raising event, many local and national organizations were approached for help. We had a relatively high hit rate which when coupled with our own work mate contributions allowed us to make 440GBP for the Charity (worth about 800GBP in 2019).

We had decided to do it over a long weekend starting and finishing from our place of work. So, on Thursday 8th September 1995 after a warm send off from our work colleagues in classic wet and miserable British weather, we set off. The wet and miserable weather continued for much of the way down to Land's End. In fact, it just got worse the further south we went. I had adopted the *'many layers of clothing'* principle which made me look like an overweight Michelin man, but I was warm - whilst we were still moving. However, I got a little over heated and went all shiny and red when we stopped. I had over done the clothing thing, but my philosophy was I could always take shit off. It's hard to put additional stuff on if you don't have it. Bearing in mind, I had not done anything like this since my adventure to the South of France, so I was learning as we went along.

Our hosts at a guest house we stayed in near Lands' End were very motorcycle friendly and showed us volumes of visitor's books which End to End hopefuls had completed. This was just what we needed before starting the adventure north, it motivated us to get going and we were excited to get to the start. Unfortunately, I had over packed (this would be a recurring trend in my motorcycle adventures) and required an extra half an hour to get ready, so we were a little late leaving the guest house. It was just a five-minute ride down the road to the official start which, to be honest is nothing more than a signpost, a hotel and the coast line. It was the bottom of the British Isles. We set off from Lands' End at 09:45 hours.

It is worth mentioning here that the major 'A' roads, minor 'B' roads and 'M' motorways in the UK are part of a zonal system. Assume all roads flow in and out of London. It's not an exact science, but if you overlay a clockface on a map of the UK with the centre point on London and divide it up into six zones in a clockwise direction starting at zone one, then all roads in that zone will start with the zone number. For example, the main 'A' road heading north out of London is the A1, east it's the A2, southeast the A3, west the A4, you get the idea. Any roads off these main trunk roads will carry the zone number plus another digit increasing as you move away from London (up to four digits total). So, if you ever get lost in the UK and don't have a map you know roughly where you are in relation to London simply by knowing the road you are on. Zones seven, eight and nine are used in Scotland.

The road out of Lands' End is the A30, so Lands' End is in the third zone (south west of London). If you were to stay on the A30, then go onto the A303 and then M3 you will end up in London.

Our progress out of Lands' End was a bit slow at first due to the narrow roads which comprise the early part of the A30. However, after 20 miles (32 kilometres), the route improved, and we sped towards our first port of call at RAF St. Mawgan, Newquay, where we got our made-up official forms stamped. The next stop would be RAF Locking, Western-Super-Mare, after which we had to refuel. We had decided beforehand that we would allow 30 Minutes for each refuel (needed about every 160 miles (250 kilometres)). This would allow 10 Minutes for filling up/paying and a further 20 Minutes to rest. Such detailed planning – that's quite typical of engineers and there were three of us - all engineers. One of our greatest concerns was fatigue and the resultant loss of concentration whilst riding, so we hoped these breaks would keep us on our toes. The other result of the enforced breaks was that our minds turned to our stomachs and food. With the only purveyors of grub (slang for food) being the garages we stopped at, we embarked upon the junk food diet comprising of coffee, crisps, and chocolate in the hope that all the 'E' numbers and additives would keep us alert. I should have known this would happen, I could have done with a charcoal insert for my motorcycle suit to absorb all the farts generated as a result of eating all this junk food.

Our route took us through Bristol and the spectacular Avon Gorge, Gloucester and then on to RAF Boddington, Cheltenham, where an enthusiastic Ministry of Defence (MoD) Policeman stamped our forms before sending us on our way. I think we were the only people he had seen in days. Thereafter, it was up through Telford and on to RAF Shawbury, Shrewsbury, where we found that the Orderly Corporal who manned the guardroom was a fellow student with Ian and Matt on their Instructor Course some weeks earlier (it's a small world in the RAF). At this stage, it was starting to get dark and Matt discovered that he had forgotten his torch for route reading at night (remembering no phones or GPS in 1995 - it was all paper maps). After what seemed like a hundred service stations later, we found a place that sold torches and we headed north once more. It was at Warrington that our progress started to deteriorate.

The A49 road we were on consisted of 30 and 40 mph speed limits with traffic lights and roundabouts every couple of yards. It also started to rain again which was killing our morale.

We continued to the A6 heading for our last RAF station at Carlisle. The route took us through Lancaster where we had to stop for food and rest. By then, it was throwing-out time in the pubs in the city centre on a Friday night and we were entertained by the revellers' antics in the pub doorways, pavements and gutters which had become standby public toilets to some. We all agreed that we never behaved like that when we had had a few drinks - yeah, right. We arrived at RAF Carlisle where we received a very warm welcome from the MoD Policemen on shift. We had intended to find somewhere to nap at some point so when we were offered the luxury of a heated room (prisoner cell) at the guardroom we gladly took up the offer and bedded down there. Two hours later, and with bellies full of hot coffee, we headed out towards the Scottish Borders.

We really should have checked the weather because unbeknown to us, we had been following a storm up the country since leaving Land's End. Apparently, many of the main routes in Scotland had been closed and some towns cut off. It was only when we reached the Scottish Boarders that we saw the effects of the storm. Some roads were flooded and strewn with debris from the high winds. Furthermore, the drop-in temperature, dark, patchy fog and the general low ebb felt at 4am in the morning made the going the hardest on the trip. Also, the navigation became complicated as a tortuous route round the M74 had to be negotiated with a torch and wet paper maps. The local wildlife jumping out on us unannounced wasn't helping. First it was rabbits, then larger hares and by the time deer had arrived, we thought we had entered Jurassic Park.

We approached Perth at day break and on time which lifted our spirits. We celebrated with caffeine and food saturated with

E numbers at the next fuel stop. By this time the rigors of navigating the Scottish Borders had shot Matt's nerves to pieces. He had had enough. In between dribbles and twitches, he muttered that he was going on strike and that someone else could lead as it was the A9 (one road) all the way to the finish - 'can't go wrong etc etc....'. So, I boldly stepped up, took control of the lead from Matt and set off in completely the wrong direction taking us through Perth city centre. I could see Matt's liberal use of hand gestures and once I had allowed him to take back the lead, we were on course for Inverness heading in the right direction. Like packing and strapping my motorcycle load, leading and navigation was not one of my motorcycling strengths. I am the type of person Google Maps was designed for.

The A9 north took us past Dunkeld, Pitlochry and the ski resort of Aviemore with its accompanying stunning scenery. We bypassed Inverness, then about 30 miles (70 kilometres) south of Wick our progress was almost stopped by thick fog colloquially known as a 'real pea souper'. From the gloom ahead, we were flagged down by a Dutch tourist who was clearly lost and insisted on asking us how far away he was from the town of Thurso. He thought it was a good idea to have a discussion in the middle of the busy route north. We hastily told him he was about 60 miles (100 kilometres) away, but he was heading in the wrong direction. We then sped off before we were hit by some other crazy lost tourist. The fog started to get worse and we were concerned that we would miss our deadline for arriving at John O'Groats. You whisper to yourself, 'surely, things can't get any worse' because you don't want to be the pessimist, but then of course things get worse.

The white road markings guiding us along had now completely disappeared. We had no reference point to follow other than the darker shade of grey that was the road and not the fog. Our embarrassingly slow (but safe) progress continued as we literally wobbled our way north as we were travelling at walking pace with nothing visible except the odd tractor or sheep overtaking us. Thankfully, the fog finally started to lift, and we completed the final miles to John O'Groats getting there within our 30 hour window. The obligatory photos were taken before we enjoyed a celebratory coffee in the John O'Groats Hotel. Having paid our dues after this short, but very welcome break, we set off for home heading towards Wick, for our Bed & Breakfast guest house and a welcome shower.

We had a pretty cheap Saturday night out in Wick as the few restorative refreshments we consumed had quite a dramatic effect on our tired bodies. This was the first time I had experienced the hardened Scottish tradition and stable diet of deep fried chocolate bars and whiskey. It made me sick just thinking about it, but the Scots love it and can live on anything, including road kills provided they have been processed through a deep fat fryer.

We left Wick well rested and started the ride south. We had bad luck with the weather going north, but at least the bikes were behaving themselves and we were in good shape. Going south, it was role reversal. Weather was good, but the bikes were playing up and we had a few niggly things to deal with. Ian's helmet got broken, my throttle control started slipping and Ian's drive chain on his bike had reached its wear limit and was making quite loud and frightening noises. I got hit by a bit of road thrown up by Matt's back wheel and my luggage almost fell off despite my overzealous use of lashing tape and bungee cords. The weather however, allowed us to enjoy the many views that we had missed going north in the fog. In fact, it even started to get warm, but as we approached home, it started to rain again. We had arrived back as we had left 3 days before – bloody wet! We made the RAF News and local newspapers and were minor celebrities for a day. We were happy and chuffed that we had done it and all in the name of charity. Good times.

I have to say, the trip to the South of France in 1978 was great fun, but this end-to-end adventure was awesome. Combining my passion of motorcycling with a purpose was extremely rewarding and the experience is almost addictive. It was so much fun and there was much discussion afterwards about what we could do next. Unfortunately, life got in the way for the three of us. We really wanted to do more, but it was just too hard for us to plan. However, I now had another adventure under my belt and I knew there was more to come, but it would

Me, Matt, Talking Pages Rep & Ian, RAF Cranwell, England, 1995

be a number of years down the line before it would happen. The XJ 600 was awesome throughout the adventure and just seemed the perfect bike for this kind of motorcycling. It had made me very happy.

When the family eventually moved across country and joined me in North Wales, the XJ 600 got a bit of a rest from the weekly commute. Our new home was just a couple of miles away from where I worked, and I really didn't want to use the Yamaha for the short trip. Also, we were now living right on the coast facing the very windy Irish Sea. The sea breeze (let's call it a breeze, but more like a low-grade gale force wind) was pretty corrosive, something Japanese motorcycles don't really care for. I remember a friend who was pro-British motorcycles telling me that in the 1970s *'Japanese motorcycles only last as long as the payments'.* Not an enduring endorsement of their workmanship and engineering, more a reflection on the piss poor UK weather. Having had all Japanese motorcycles, I understood the point he was making. Some of them started to rust the moment you wheeled them out of the showroom. The combination of poor weather and salt on the roads during winter plays havoc with the most ardent of bike finishes. You really must keep them washed and clean in the UK.

One of the guys I worked with was selling his trusted *'go faster'* (his words not mine) dark red Tomos moped. I had heard of these things and seen pictures in mail order magazines, but never actually seen one in the flesh. The price was right, and it was a legal runner, so I bought it without even looking at it. I had never ever done that before and I shouldn't have done it this time either. However, twice since I have bought bikes without physically seeing them in the flesh (just bought from photographs), but in my defence both those purchases involved huge travelling distances, so I had limited options to see the bike for real beforehand. It's not the best way to buy a bike, and it's a judgement call. The Tomos moped had been used for the last umpty umph years with no issues (apparently) and he was a good guy, so I was confident everything would be fine. It really didn't bother me if it needed a bit of work to keep it going, it was a moped for goodness sake and a means to get to and from work in a corrosive (bad weather) environment. What could go wrong with this?

Call me old fashioned and eccentric, but I love riding mopeds. They have a special place in my heart and serve a real purpose as an affordable means of transport. I enjoy cycling too, but a moped makes a commute that little bit easier and more enjoyable than a pushbike as you don't need a shower from sweating when you eventually get to work. A moped is great over a short distance, between one and five miles (one to eight kilometres) maximum. Less than a mile you could just walk or cycle to work. Over five miles, take the car. My work was just two miles (three kilometres) from the house. Perfect for a moped. However, a Tomos moped is no Yamaha Fizzie or Honda C 50. This is a monster of a moped, and when I say monster, I don't mean big and powerful, I mean ugly. Man, these are real ugly mopeds and reminded me of the NSU Quickly. However, I am a man of my word and could not back out of the deal. I was now the ~~proud~~ owner of a 1982 Tomos moped. I had no idea what the model was, but with some research, I determined it was a Tomos A3. The American version was a called a Tomos 'Bullet'. A most inappropriate name for this moped. If you associate a bullet with speed, then this was a misfire. These mopeds were first introduced into the UK in 1954 and the style had changed very little over the years. Tomos mopeds are made in Slovenia, which to my knowledge, is not a country known for ground breaking engineering design for motorcycles, but they were cheap and sort of worked. I seemed to recall that you could buy these things in some supermarkets in the 70s adding one to you weekly shopping basket would probably not have even doubled your grocery bill.

My Tomos moped was equipped with a couple of value-added accessories - both of which just slowed it down. A rubber bulb horn fitted to the handlebars just added weight but was necessary because the original electric buzzer type horn didn't work. It was important to warn pedestrians that they were likely to be approached in a few minutes by a motorised push bike. It was also laden at the back with a bright red top box in lieu of the front shopping basket which had been removed due to aerodynamic drag. The top box was big enough to hold my lunch and a drink but not much else, and probably doubled the value of the moped when it was first fitted.

My Tomos also had front and rear brakes too, but I never understood why. It never went fast enough to use them. However, it would run on an oily rag and do well over 100 miles (160 kilometres) to the gallon. That was in part because I often worked harder than the little 49 cc engine. You peddled the thing to get it going (like the NSU), and then had to pedal a bit more to maintain forward momentum when the engine had run out of steam (just like the NSU). When facing the incoming Irish Sea breeze, I found myself pedalling all the time. I might as well have used my pushbike. Apparently, it had two gears, but I don't remember it going fast enough to select the second one. I think the top speed was around 20 mph, but that was just a pipe dream on most days.

Overall, the performance of this moped was one notch down from pathetic. I would be lucky to get this thing up to its design top speed on a good weather day. Although I never knew how fast I was going as the speedo was another piece of equipment that didn't work. To break double figures in terms of speed, I often needed assistance from the Irish Sea breeze and at least one minute of full throttle. Although it only happened once, I got overtaken early one morning going into work by a jogger! Bloody unbelievable, but true. I could hardly keep the bike going forward such was the strength of the sea breeze and the lack of horses (or horse) being generated by the little 49 cc engine. On a windy day the people in work would quite rightly laugh at me battling the elements as they could see me coming up the side of the airfield for at least 10 minutes before I arrived, and it was less than a mile away from our office.

Me & My 1982 Tomos Moped, RAF Valley, Wales, 1992

Having said all that about the Tomos, the moped was immense fun for my young boys, Dan and Josh. I could run them around in our back garden with them standing on the frame and holding onto the handlebars with no fear of them hurting themselves, it just didn't go fast enough to have a proper fall. I never sold the Tomos, rather I gifted it to a work mate just before we left. I felt embarrassed asking for money for something that was corroding before my very eyes and had devalued so much I thought I would have to pay someone to take it off my hands.

Chapter 8
Triumph Triples

Riding the same bike after a while is like going to the same café every week and ordering the same meal until one week you decide that you are going to try something different on the menu. Don't get me wrong, the Yamaha XJ 600 was a great meal, but I wanted to try something else. It would be nice to order the same meal (XJ 600) with a side of something (another bike). However, we had a growing family, my daughter had just arrived so there were five of us now, and we were about to move yet again. Apart from money, the one thing that is in very short supply is space. You just can't keep adding to an already growing inventory of kids toys and school stuff. Therefore, when you want to try something else on the menu you must exchange it for the meal choice you have already made. There are no side dishes in this metaphor. And by the way, those were the family rules. I have totally ignored the financial aspect of such change as one metaphor per story is enough. The middle and both ends of this idea was that if I wanted a different motorcycle, I had to sell the XJ 600 to pay for it. Simple. No ifs, or buts - sell it.

If money had never been a consideration, there are a few bikes I had owned up to this point (and a bit later on in life) that I would have kept in a safe storage facility to ride and admire later on in life. I have lost count on how many times I have sold something or just got rid of something that I used to enjoy only to reflect a few years later and say *'I wish I had kept my .....'* (fill in the blank). Of course, we conveniently forget the reason why we did part with this item in the first place, because we only remember the good times we had with it. I was in the military, money was not bad, but it wasn't that good either and we had to move every few years as my career progressed.

Collecting motorcycles and keeping them locked away for the day when I can retire and enjoy them again was never going to happen. It doesn't really matter anyway, because what you do have are the memories of these fine machines and it costs nothing to lock those memories away in your grey matter recalling them as often as you like. If you kept pictures, even better. No maintenance fees associated with such memories either. Then we have the internet. There are just thousands of videos, pictures, write ups and all sorts of stuff on the bikes I have owned and of course the hundreds of bikes I never owned but remember them from days gone by. However, if I could have kept any of my bikes forever then...

The Yamaha FS 1E would be the first in my collection, my first (legal) motorcycle and the bike I think I rode every day I owned it. Next would be the Yamaha DT 175, the bike that got me through the worst weather I have ever ridden through. Then the RD 400, the bike that taught me how to respect motorcycles and allow me to hone my riding and wheelie skills. Now I could add the trusted and reliable XJ 600. The CX 500 E just failed to make the cut due to the maintenance costs and the XS 500 for the same reason, but both were great looking bikes and I have extremely fond memories of both the 500s. More bikes would be added to the inventory down the line. In fact, my next bike would be my all-time favourite road bike. Having said that, I would get another bike in 10 years' time that would be the best all round bike I have ever owned, but that bike was not a pure road bike like the one I was about to get.

I had done some detailed research and I had decided that I wanted to step up in the engine size, *'go naked'* again in terms of body design but try out a different brand. I had read the incredible story of the re-birth of Triumph Motorcycles, and the only memory of Triumph I had up until that point was riding

pillion into London from Aylesbury on my mates old 650 cc Triumph T 120 back in 1977. When we got back to Aylesbury, we had to replace several nuts and screws that had fallen off

My 1994 Triumph Speed Triple (seat hump fitted), RAF Cranwell, England, 1996

the bike along with a few of my fillings in my teeth. It was a fun trip, but boy, did those bikes shake! The new Triumphs were nothing like the old ones - it said in all the reviews. The days of carrying around spare engine parts had been left in the 70s. I had studied the bikes carefully and had set my mind on the beautiful 900 cc Triumph Speed Triple.

Not only did I find the bike I was looking for, I found it in the only colour I wanted. Bright yellow. They only made the bike in three colours; black, orange and yellow. This really was my dream bike (at that time, because you can have more than one dream). It also came with a seat hump to cover the back of the seat when riding solo which just made a beautiful bike look absolutely gorgeous. The Triumph Speed Triple was a pure a motorcycle as could be. It was bloody awesome!

The sad thing of course was I had to trade my Yamaha XJ 600 for the Triumph so there was a changing of the guard in July 1996 whilst we were living in North Yorkshire, England. If ever there was a bike that was designed to do exactly what it says it is going to do, it was the Triumph Speed Triple. As you walked towards the bike, its naked engine sitting high and leaning forward in the frame with upswept exhausts, exposed cockpit and engine componentry just gave it attitude and those looks blended effortlessly into the lines of the tank and side panels that just added class to the attitude. It's hard and aggressive personality traits immediately become apparent the moment you swing your leg over the saddle and grab the bars. A quick press of the starter button immediately brings the triple cylinder engine to life. With its characteristic firing order, the bikes heart beat produces a distinctive off beat burbling note from the exhaust, a sound that had become the hallmark of the Speed Triple. Once you had moved off from a standstill your

My 1994 Triumph Speed Triple, RAF Cranwell, England,

legs naturally swung inwards and your knees would hug the tank, just like the undercarriage retracting on an aircraft. a broad grin would suddenly appear on your face and then you just had to hold on and enjoy the ride. It felt fantastic and so natural to be at one with this bike. This was the fastest bike I have ever owned. With almost 100 horses on tap and a top speed of over 130 mph, you really don't need any more than that being transmitted through a few inches of rotating vulcanised rubber on UK roads. It only had five gears compared with six fitted to the other Triumph models with the same engine, but five was enough as the motor had a sack full of torque that would pull you like a tractor with linear acceleration at any speed above 35 mph in top gear. The handling was phenomenal too, it didn't feel heavy once you got going and it had brakes that really did slow you down. The bike should have been fitted with an accelerometer or 'G' meter because you could feel the lateral acceleration and deceleration on your whole body under rapid throttle openings or heavy braking.

I have never been into pure sports bikes and this was not a sports bike, but it performed like one. The brochures and reviews at the time classed it as a naked café racer. Triumph had upped their game considerably since they re-invented themselves and this was the first of the new generation of Triumphs with better quality parts and finish. They were introduced in 1994 and mine was one of the first out the door. Although it was second hand, the previous owner never really got used to the beast and ended up selling it back to the dealer as it was too much for him to handle. The bike really did go like the preverbal *'bat out of hell'*.

The roads around where we lived at Linton-on-Ouse, North Yorkshire were perfect for this naked café racer - I just loved riding this bike. However, it was like riding a high-performance jet ski, fantastic fun but extremely tiring. If you rode this bike as it was meant to be ridden after just an hour or so you really needed to rest. I also had to be very careful changing gear on this bike, or rather pick my time to change gear. I could literally throw this bike into corners quite aggressively and lean it right over, but if I needed to change up as I was accelerating through the turn, I had to wait until I was out of the bend and the bike was upright as I could easily trap my foot under the bike. It happened just a few times and scared me shitless, badly scraping my boots each time. We (the bike and I) got the technique sorted eventually.

How I never got any speeding tickets on this bike is still a mystery to me. I am not a fast rider per se, but I do like to ride the bikes I have as they were designed and built to be ridden. The Speed Triple was made for North Yorkshire's twisty roads and the name said it all. Having a bright yellow bike in summer and living in a rural area, both the bike and I were magnets for flies, bugs, bees and just about any insect around as it clearly looked like a flower to them. Albeit a very fast flower. Even stopping at traffic lights for a few seconds would attract a swarm of insects. It was a pain in the arse, and the bloody bugs would get everywhere; in my helmet, up my nose, in my eyes and all over my body and the bike. There was no fairing on the bike either - nothing to stop or even slow the little critters down before they hit me, so I used to get plenty of protein in the summer from eating these damn insects.

I never knew the top speed on the Speed Triple as I was always focussed on the road ahead, you had to be. On the few occasions I did look down when ripping through the rubber on the back roads, I would often be travelling over 100 mph. The quarter mile could be covered in 11 seconds on this bike and you would be doing around 115 mph by then, so it was quick; damn quick. The good news was it could also stop very quickly too, that though would be determined by how hard you could hang on when you slammed on the brakes. There was no ABS (Anti-lock Braking System) on this bike it was all about the feel and feedback from the brakes. I never got the rear wheel airborne even during the heaviest of braking, so I guess I was operating the bike within its limits.

The whole bike was a testament to Triumph's engineering and design team. The Speed Triple ended up having a class of its own on the race track too. The Triumph Speed Triple Challenge. The Speed Triple design has changed over the years from the model I had to the T509, then 955i, and finally the 1050, but in my opinion, Triumph got it spot on first time with their 1994 design. To me this is the best of the Speed Triples. It was an awesome bike with an aggressive character. To consolidate my relationship with the brand I joined the only motorcycle club I have ever been associated with, the Riders Association of Triumph - RAT and Triumphs Owners Motorcycle Club.

I enjoy spending time just admiring and looking after my bikes as much as I love riding them. When I looked at my yellow Speed Triple, I would smile and think this bike is a true reflection of me. Sounds a little pretentious I know, but I really felt that I had a close affinity to this bike. The bikes reliability was faultless, and I never took a tumble even after all the aggressive riding I did on

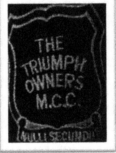

My RAT Patches, Fairfax, USA, 2018

this bike. Including the unconventional gear changes during cornering. The only irritating thing about the whole bike was the farty little indicator light on the dashboard telling me my right or left flasher was on. It was really hard to see unless it was totally dark, and I was for ever leaving my indicator on. I fitted a small buzzer soon after I got the bike so had an audible warning as well, but the buzzer was quite loud and bloody irritating when sat at traffic lights, so it ended up being just a temporary modification before I ripped it off.

The Story of Triumph is an interesting one that spans, bicycles, motorcycles and cars. Originally started in 1886 by Siegfried Bettmann, a German entrepreneur who moved to Coventry, England and started his own business importing bicycles and selling them under his own brand called the Triumph Cycle Company. A year later he was registered as the New Triumph Company Ltd. In 1894 Triumph started to make its own bicycles and then in 1902, Triumph made its first motorcycle. Back in Germany in 1896, in his home town of Nuremberg, Bettmann had set up a second factory producing bicycles under the Triumph-Werke Nürnberg AG or TWN (TWN differentiated the German bikes from the British ones). In 1903, TWN also started to produce the same motorcycle as Coventry which was a Triumph bike with a Belgian Minerva engine. Just two years later in 1905 Triumph had designed and made its own motorcycle and by the end of that year, had made over 250 of them. Two years after that in 1907, Triumph opened a larger plant and were knocking out almost three bikes a day. By 1913 the British and the German Triumph factories had decided to go their separate ways. The German factory finally ceased production of motorcycles under the Triumph (TWN) name in 1956.

After the First World War effort, in 1921 Triumph bought out the Dawson Car Company and produced the Triumph 10/20 car. The company was renamed the Triumph Motor Company in 1930 and by that time had already become one of Britain's main motorcycle and car makers.

Triumph did not do that well in the car industry and was struggling. In 1932, it sold off its bicycle manufacturing to Raleigh Bicycle Company and in 1936 Triumph cars and motorcycles became separate companies. That was the beginning of the (first) end. Triumph went bankrupt and the car factory was bought out by Standard Cars whilst the bikes were bought by Ariel (who also made a number of classic motorcycles). Ariel kept the name and formed the Triumph Engineering Company Ltd. In 1937, the 500cc speed twin engine was developed under this Company name which would feature in all Triumph twins until they ceased production in 1982. The Coventry factory was forced to move to the Meriden plant in Solihull in 1942 because the Germans had bombed the shit out of Coventry during the Second World War. The bombing campaign had just about flattened the city and most of the factory (and it wasn't the team from TWN either). Bikes were made at the Meriden plant right up until Triumph Engineering went into receivership in 1983.

Mr John Bloor bought the Triumph name and manufacturing rights from the official receiver and had plans to compete against the Japanese motorcycles which had dominated the market place. John knew the old Triumph models and manufacturing techniques were dated so held off relaunching Triumph straight away. However, production of the old Bonneville continued under licence by Les Harris of Racing Spares, in Newton Abbot, Devon, just to keep the Triumph name out on the streets until the new Triumphs were ready to be launched in 1991 from their new plant in Hinckley, Leicestershire. Using manufacturing mass production techniques and design ideas learnt from the Japanese, common parts across the range of bikes and the utilization of old Triumph model names and numbers the new Triumph venture was launched and became an outstanding success. A real British phoenix from the ashes story. I am so glad John Bloor had the vision and determination to do that.

I only had the Speed Triple for two years and we were about to move the family again. However, this next move would be a focused family move as we had decided that we needed to put down some roots for the children and stabilise their education. Irrespective of where we would buy a home, this next move meant that I would need to commute to work. I really didn't mind doing the commuting thing, but my job turned out to be a daily commute of 61 miles (100 kilometres) each way.

Doing high mileage everyday all year round, for three years or more on a Triumph Speed Triple was not what I wanted to do. The Speed Triple was not a bike for commuting. The Speed Triple was always my Sunday afternoon thrash around North Yorkshire then clean and admire kind of bike. You have to adopt a different mindset and ride a suitable commuter bike if you are going to commute on two wheels. Riding because you want to, when you want to, is a very different type of riding to when you have to ride to get to work. It was time to consider some additional wheels and a metal cage. We were also building our own house so could not afford to keep the bike and buy a second car to commute. No side dish options for Nigel at this restaurant. So, my gorgeous yellow Triumph had to go. To say I was gutted and upset would be an understatement, but in the back of my mind I always believed that those days of the Speed Triple would return.

So, at the beginning of 1998, the 900 cc Triumph Speed Triple was converted (via cash) into a French Citroen ZX two door commuter car. I would spend a huge part of my life sat in this Citroen over the next six years. The good news about this Citroen was its frugal use of petrol and, at this time, the military in the UK would subsidise my commuting costs. I drove economically on the commute and managed to save enough money over the first four years to be able to......buy another bike. YES!

I really missed not having a motorcycle, but family life was pretty full on and to be honest although I missed not having a bike, even if I did have one, I wouldn't have been able to ride it much. I loved my Speed Triple and I was hell bent on getting another one, but they only made the model I had for two years over 1994/5 and it was really hard to find a good one second hand in 2002. Even harder to find one in yellow. Also, many of the Speed Triples had been modified or raced, some never had the seat hump, but most were just not good enough for me - period.

So, it was back to the drawing board, for deciding on my next bike. I was not sat in front of the drawing board for long. I was going to get another Triumph - period. I had not been bored with the Speed Triple at all. I really believed that I had found Nigel's kindred spirit in a Triumph motorcycle. I really wanted the same 900 cc Triple engine because I loved the motor and the exhaust sound was awesome. Black was my other colour of choice if yellow was not available, but very quickly I realised that I had to consider other models too because finding a Speed Triple in the condition I wanted was next to impossible. What I did find was a 1994 Triumph 900 cc Daytona in jet black. This bike was almost identical to the Speed Triple, but with a plastic jacket (fairing) and an additional sixth gear. This was a real sports bike. I know, I know...... I said I didn't want a sports bike, but this thing was low mileage, affordable and in superb condition. Also, this would be a great bike for commuting on some of the warmer, nicer or even not so nice days as the fairing offered me quite a bit of weather protection.

Isn't it funny how your select criteria - that was never going to be compromised - can change in a heartbeat to fit the bike that's in front of you. I was sold. I would get the Daytona. This bike would accelerate me from 0-60 mph in four seconds and because it was faired you could hardly feel the speed. I had to be very careful, the Speed Triple gave you feedback in terms of wind noise and buffet. The Daytona had none of that. Happy (but be careful) days were here again.

I picked up the Daytona in November 2002, not the best time of year to get a new bike, but a new bike any day of the year is a good day. The Daytona did indeed give me a bit more protection but still posed a bit of a challenge during gear changes. What the fairing could not protect me from, but the indicators could, was a snapped drive chain. I had the bike

Me & My 1995 Triumph Daytona, Caythorpe, England, 2004

about six months and was commuting into work down the A1 cruising along at 80 mph with about eight miles (12 kilometres) to run, I was within a half mile of my exit off the A1. When all of a sudden, the engine screamed out loud, the revs peaked momentarily to the rev limiter before everything fell silent, I mean deadly silent - nothing. This was immediately followed by all the dashboard lights coming on and the bike freewheeling. I don't know why, but I immediately held my breath. It happened so quickly, certainly less than a second, and I had no clue what had just happened. I am still not sure what holding my breath did to help. I could do nothing else other than steer the bike to a safe stop on the side of the very busy A1 road.

A quick glance down to the left side of the bike as I was freewheeling revealed hot black stuff flowing out of the side of the engine crankcase. The hot engine oil had blown all over my leg, the frame of the bike and the road. After a few seconds, I could feel the heat of the oil on my skin as it soaked through my jeans, and as I was slowing, I got a whiff of the synthetic lubricant which just confirmed to me that today's ride was over.

My 1995 Triumph Daytona, Caythorpe, England, 2004

I gracefully came to a stop at my normal exit and wondered how the hell the bike didn't react differently and throw me off. I was so lucky that I was not killed or seriously injured either by a high velocity heavy duty chain ripping me apart at 80 mph or hot oil being squirted over the rear tyre causing me to lose traction.

The chain had clearly snapped. One end had whipped up around the rear of the bike and got itself caught on the left rear indicator lamp arm (thank goodness) and subsequently wrapped itself around the stalk itself which was a much better outcome than wrapping itself around my arm. The other end of the chain had swiftly bundled up and then wrapped itself around the engine driven sprocket and had smashed through the gearbox casing. The subsequent release of hot engine oil from the side of the engine helped waterproof the left side of my motorcycle gear and coat the rear of the bike in a film of hot oil. Engine oil is a little like blood. When you cut yourself, even a small amount of blood seems a lot and it goes everywhere, engine oil is the same; a small amount can make a hell of a mess and when you are travelling at speed the spray from the air flow over the leak seems to make it 10 times worse.

I was a member of the Automobile Association and they eventually picked me and the bike up and took us home. It wasn't until I was sat in the van with the recovery driver going home that the seriousness of the incident hit me. It really was a miracle that I managed to stay on the bike and not crash. The rear of the bike on the left side was smothered in engine oil, including the tyre. Perhaps my guardian angel had looked after me again? This was not the best nor was it the cheapest way to negotiate a day off work. The all up cost of the repair was just over 500 GBP and the only damage done (other than the chain and engine casing) was a bent gear change spindle. The bike was back on the road in two weeks with no long-term damage to the engine or the bike. Nevertheless, riding it again after such an incident did make me a little weary for a while, causing me to be very gentle on gear changing, a little conservative on the right wrist action and always trying my best to keep my speed within the posted legal limit.

Chapter 9
Dual Citizen, Dual Sport

The Triumph Daytona was a great bike and certainly rekindled the Speed Triple days and I was very happy to keep it for as long as I didn't fancy anything else on the menu. Indeed, I considered myself very lucky at this stage of my life (aged 42) because we now had two cars and a bike. That had never happened before with a family. Then out of nowhere we had this crazy idea in 2004 to move to New Zealand (as you do when you are in your 40s). There was a bit more to this story than what I am explaining here, but this is a book about bikes not family life and immigration. The *'flash to bang'* on the timing to move across to the other side of the world was extremely quick; just four months. If you have never emigrated to a new country, believe me when I say there is quite a bit to sort out for a family of five living in their own house with two cars, a motorcycle and lots of stuff.

So, what should I do with the Triumph? We were going to sell the house and both cars, down size as much as we could, but the bike was different. I really didn't want to sell it. I wanted it to be the sixth member of our family. Also, by taking it to New Zealand it was one less thing to worry about. After all, New Zealand drove on the left-hand side of the road, so my bike would be just fine - no change there. It also had mph and kilometres on the speedo so no problem there either. The only expense in taking the bike was that we didn't have room for our dining room furniture and display cabinet in the 40ft container.

To be fair, we didn't know this fact until the day of the move and the bike was already loaded onto the container by then. To protect the bike and everything else, they built a protective frame around the bike which resulted in some head scratching when trying to fit the dining room stuff in around it, but it was never going to work and to change the logistics plan at this stage was not really an option. Bollocks! So, a quick decision was made and a promise to the family that we would buy a new dining room suite in New Zealand rather than leave the beautiful Triumph Daytona behind. I blame the movers for a piss poor assessment of what size container we needed to move us to New Zealand. After all, that was their only job. Turns out that they also underestimated an additional 12 boxes of house pack that had to make its own way to New Zealand because there was no room in the container for these either. These additional boxes arrived in New Zealand sometime after the 40ft container had arrived having had their own mini adventure crossing the globe as part of someone else's house pack.

We had settled into a rental property when the container arrived just three months after we had arrived in New Zealand. As we opened the rear doors of the 40ft container, it felt like we were having an early Christmas. First off, was the Triumph. Whoo Hoo! It was great to be reunited with the bike again and there was not a mark on it. However, the bike was now an imported motor vehicle and it needed to be registered as a New Zealand vehicle before it could be ridden on the road. In New Zealand vehicle insurance is optional, not mandatory. So, I could ride the bike, but as it was an import, my first ride had to be to the NZTA (New Zealand Transport Agency) Inspection station for checking and registering onto the New Zealand vehicle database.

I put some fresh petrol in the bike, connected the battery, hit the starter button and the bike roared into life almost immediately. Another Whoo Hoo moment. Three months in a sealed container and the bike fired up like it had only been on a long weekend. Bloody marvellous. That was the good news. Unfortunately, the removals people, the very same company who failed to calculate the amount of stuff we had, also failed to declare the bike as a legally imported vehicle on the container manifest to the friendly customs people in New Zealand. Therefore, nobody in New Zealand knew anything about a motorcycle.

When I pitched up at the inspection station and presented the bike to the inspector, their first action was to look up the VIN (Vehicle Identification Number) on the national database and confirm that the bike they have in front of them is the same bike that was notified as an import by customs. However, nobody had told customs of course, so the VIN wasn't listed. On finding out this key piece of information or rather lack of, the inspector informed me that he had no choice other than to declare my beloved Triumph an illegal import and immediately impounded the bike. He wouldn't even let me go near the bike again. It was gone. Bollocks! Really?

Not a great start to my motorcycling experience in New Zealand and now I needed alternative transport to get myself back home. It took over a week before all the paperwork was corrected and I got my Triumph back. Other than checking the VIN and ownership details from the country of import, the only other thing New Zealand do is check the brakes. They remove the brake callipers and check the brake pads for some reason. Why it took a week, God only knows, but now I had my bike back with a New Zealand number plate and could legally ride in New Zealand.

I believe that the roads in New Zealand were designed by a motorcyclist for motorcycles. It is just a fantastic country to ride. The traffic density outside the main centres is much lower

Me & My 1995 Triumph Daytona, Number Plate Change, Cambourne, New Zealand, 2004

than the UK and the scenery is spectacular wherever you go. Many of the tarmac road surfaces are much rougher than what's found in the UK partly due to the recycled elements contained in the *'black top'*. This is particularly harsh on

your tyres for wear, but it does give you great traction and you need that traction on the twisties (of which there are many) when you are throwing the big Triumph around.

We were managing with one car at home and it was always my intention to use public transport or the Daytona to get back and forth to work. Unfortunately, the Triumph was a bit of a monster for commuting to my work place in Wellington City. The ride for the last couple of miles as you enter the Wellington harbour area is a sight I never ever got bored of seeing. It is just a spectacular ending to a short 15-mile (24 kilometres) commute. However, I would be lucky if I got out of third gear some days due to the volume of traffic. This was not how I thought it would be. After just a few weeks of usage the Triumph broke down - just stopped (it was nothing to do with the commuting). The diagnostics at the Triumph garage was showing an Engine Control Unit (ECU) malfunction. This is the sealed electronic box that is at the heart of managing the engine. It was over $800 NZD new, but I managed to source a second-hand unit from the UK and got it shipped to New Zealand for less than a third of the price of a new one.

Whilst the Triumph was in the bike hospital awaiting the new ECU, I had already made up my mind to replace the bike with something more fitting for my commute and the harsh New Zealand roads. The Daytona was a great bike for sure, and I would have kept it as a second bike, but it really didn't like the short and often slow commute. Indeed, the commute was not doing me nor the bike much good being stuck in traffic. After a while the 470lb monster gets heavy and it got tiring just stopping and starting all the time. When you use a big bike for commuting like this, I really didn't feel like riding it on the weekends for fun. I needed something completely different. Something lighter and nimbler for an effortless commute and a bike I also wanted to go riding on during the weekend when I could take advantage of the New Zealand roads. Recognising that some of the adventure roads were either unsealed in sections or just dirt tracks.

I wasn't regretting taking the Triumph to New Zealand as it was doing the job, but this new riding environment was very different to the UK and, in my defence, I had no experience of riding in New Zealand until now. On reflection, I should have done a little more research, but on the other hand, I was moving a family of five to New Zealand. Taking the bike with us was a much easier decision. In the showroom at the Triumph hospital was the New Zealand equivalent to my old Speed Triple; a two-year-old Suzuki DR 650.

Let me explain…The Suzuki DR 650 was in my favourite colour, bright yellow just like the Speed Triple and the bike was designed for New Zealand roads. Akin to my Speed Triple being designed for the roads in North Yorkshire. I really believed from my limited experience in New Zealand that a dual sport bike like the DR 650 was the best kind of bike to own here. A bike that was light and powerful enough that could eat the commute in its stride whilst also being a bike I could take advantage of all the different types of roads New Zealand had to offer. Including all the off-road tracks that are scattered throughout New Zealand. I also felt that this bike took me back to my old Yamaha DT 175 enduro days with the power and torque of the Speed Triple. It was the perfect bike for right here, right now, and I wanted it.

The deal with the salesman was that he would give me full second-hand value for the Triumph providing I supplied him with a replacement ECU. It just so happens that the second-hand value of a Triumph Daytona in New Zealand was roughly the same price I paid for the bike two years ago in the UK. Whilst the knockdown price on the Suzuki DR 650 effectively made the deal a bike swap. It was a no brainer. The deal was done.

December in New Zealand is summer time, so my Christmas present from the whole family for our first Christmas in New Zealand was a 2002 Suzuki DR650 motorcycle. I was very happy. I didn't know it at the time, but this bike would be my trusted steed and serve me well for the next five years and I would have a pathetic excuse to change it out down the line.

This was my first Suzuki motorcycle. I mentioned earlier in the book that maybe one day I might own a GT 750 'Water Buffalo' or 'Kettle' two-stroke triple, one day maybe I will. I was happy owning my 2002 Suzuki DR 650, this bike was a great introduction into Suzuki motorcycles.

The story of the Suzuki brand is not to dissimilar to many of the modern-day motorcycle manufacturers in that they never started out making motorcycles, it was something they got into to diversify the business either through the founder's passion, a national demand for a cheap form of transportation or a natural progression from what they were making before the war. In 1909, Michio Suzuki founded the Suzuki Loom Works and built weaving looms for the Japanese silk industry and then made looms for the cotton boom. Suzuki believed that diversification was the key to further success and in 1937 decided on building a small car for the people of Japan.

World War II put the manufacturing of cars on hold as the focus went on the war effort and after the war Suzuki went back to making looms until 1951 when the arse fell out of the cotton market. Like most countries after the war, Japan also needed affordable and reliable personal transportation and Suzuki's experience in building cars was nurtured into motorising bicycles. In 1952 he built his first one horsepower 36 cc two-stroker engine called the *'Power Free'*. His design allowed the rider to either self-pedal, have pedal assist with the engine or let the engine do all the work. Quite a clever concept in Japan at that time. The Japanese government was impressed and subsidised Suzuki's research into motorcycles. By 1954 the newly branded Suzuki Motor Company had gone from making motorised bicycles to real motorcycles, knocking them out at a rate of 200 a day.

There is nothing flashy about the Suzuki DR 650 SE (SE was the signifier for the 1996 major upgrade). The DR 650 has been around since 1990 when it replaced the DR 600 and was still going strong in 2019. The big single cylinder 644 cc engine produces an arse kicking 46 horses and delivers them all with a fist full of torque. In untrained hands this combination can make the bike act a little like an RD 400 by pulling wheelies in first gear if you are clumsy with the throttle and not sitting forward on the bench seat. It will easily take off without you too if you don't have good clutch control and are not in command of the handlebars. In that respect the bike is unforgiving, but once you know how to respect the bike, it's an absolute shit load of fun to ride. My 2002 model had Suzuki's widely recognized yellow off-road racing colours and graphics which was only in production for that year and looked so cool. It was perfect for me.

The DR 650 is a simple bike overall and cost next to nothing to maintain. Other than tyres, oil and filter, I never replaced anything else in the five years I had it. I never modified it either; even the chain would go months before it needed adjustment. There was no complicated fuel injection, a simple carburettor with a choke for cold starts, no tachometer just a speedo, but thank goodness it did have an electric starter. That thing would have been a bugger to kickstart in the cold. The only niggly part of the bike was a pathetic 2.9-gallon fuel tank. Every 120 miles (200 kilometres) I had to fill up. The good news on that front was that after riding 120 miles straight you really needed to stop anyway because the vibration on a single cylinder motor takes its toll and you need your body to recover from the tingling sensation in your extremities.

The DR 650 really didn't need a speedo either as after a while I could guess my speed quite accurately by the amount of vibration I was feeling in the handlebars and foot pegs. Cruising at 60-to-70 mph was easy and it would do the (indicated) ton too, but you really didn't want to hold the bike very long at that speed. Concentration levels above 80 mph on a big single is quite intense particularly if you are on knobbly and not road tyres. The small tank, although a pain in the arse for regular refuels, was unobtrusive and made the bike lighter overall which made it fun to take off road, weighing in at just 324 lbs. Although, when you drop a 324 lbs motorcycle in the soft ground, after a slow speed tumble, as I had done on several occasions, 324 lbs can be bloody heavy and awkward to pick up when you don't have firm footing.

The Suzuki DR 650 like its competition the Kawasaki KLR 650 and Honda XR 650 haven't really changed that much over the years. Every ride is an adventure on any bike, but the DR 650 just seemed to be in a class of its own here and I always had a smile on my face as soon as I climbed aboard. It didn't matter if it was a quick commute into work or an extended weekend ride. The vibration coupled with the massive amount of torque on tap with the big single cylinder engine is as addictive as it is fun. You just knew that every ride on the DR 650 was going to be a mini adventure. Indeed, in New Zealand in 2015, the DR 650 was the best-selling bike over 500 cc and is often in the top five bestselling bikes overall. So, in 2004, after just a few months living in the country, I had correctly assessed the best bike to own in New Zealand and now I had one myself.

In fact, the Suzuki DR model still hold the record for the largest single cylinder engine in production. Suzuki produced the DR 750S which had a displacement of 779 cc (only available in Europe) up until late 1990s when it was replaced it with the Suzuki V-Strom.

The commute on the DR 650 was a breeze. Lane splitting (riding between two separate lanes of traffic travelling in the same direction) is legal in New Zealand and on this very thin and nimble machine it was far easier to manoeuvre than the Daytona. Indeed, lane splitting had become fun. Only once did I hit a car that was switching lanes. It was a sixth sense that indicated to me that the car was about to pull out in front of me - and it didn't disappoint. In what must have been a Nano second, I just lowered my left shoulder and glanced my whole left side (arm, leg and hip) into the side of the car.

This did two things. Firstly, it prevented my handlebars from hitting the car. That impact alone would have caused me to lose control of the steering which would have resulted in a very untidy outcome. Secondly, it allowed me to maintain my momentum and retain control of the bike, so I could quickly get out of the way. I was not going that fast, probably about 25-30 mph and the car was doing a little less, but my

My 2002 Suzuki DR650, Cambourne, New Zealand, 2004

glancing blow just pushed me to the right allowing me to take up the free space in the other lane the car was clearly heading toward. The driver was spooked by my impact and immediately turned back into his lane, I was still upright and moving forward so we both continued on our way. I was not even shook up, my sixth sense Nano second moment prepared me well. My takeaway from this little skirmish was I had probably become a little complacent with my riding in commuter traffic. I was going too fast and probably didn't even appear in his mirror until it was too late. It never happened to me again because I never lane split in fast moving traffic.

One of the fun facts of Wellington, New Zealand is its affectionately called *'Windy Wellington'* because it is the windiest capitol city in the world. It is renowned for its frequent strong and gusty northerlies that can deliver winds gusts of over 40 mph, which is officially a gale force wind and it does this on average for 178 days a year. So, if you ever get to visit Wellington for a few days, the chances are it will be windy at some point in time. What this means for a quick and nimble motorcycle like the DR 650, is you learn to adopt the *'Wellington lean'*. You literally have to ride with a permanent lean into the wind as you ride into Wellington and then be prepared to put the bike upright as you pass another vehicle or just pass a large structure that can block or just interfere with the wind. Like everything you do regularly you get used to it, but on a bad day and in rain it can be quite scary, and the lean can be significant, so you have to be on your 'A' game and be prepared to wrestle with this unseen danger that is the Wellington wind.

Although I never modified the DR 650, there was one change I wanted to make; the number plate. The number plates in New Zealand are just five digits for a motorcycle (six for a car) and for a small fee you can have what you like (providing no one

Me & My TESCO - Plate, Cambourne, New Zealand, 2005

else has it of course, and it's not rude or offensive). I had decided that it was time to get pretentious and make the bike my own, so I changed the number plate from its registered '18UWK' to 'TESCO' (noting my surname Sainsbury is associated with a UK Supermarket and my nickname in the RAF for the first few years was Tesco).

I took the DR 650 off road on numerous occasions, often taking the long way home from work on a nice day. It was so much fun riding on forest tracks, well-trodden dirt tracks and unsealed roads. However, when it came to complicated tracks with obstacles to go over or tight slow speed handling in soft ground, the bikes weight, its immediate on-tap power and my piss-poor balance were not good combinations and I often found myself *'rubber side up'* followed by weight lifting practice returning the bike to *'shiny side up'*. What I learnt from these experiences was it was no lightweight, low geared Yamaha DT 175. It was a dual sport bike for sure, but perhaps it wasn't as good off road in soft ground and slow speed as it was on the faster unsealed but well-trodden tracks and tarmac. I did less and less off-road riding preferring to stick to the solid tarmac wherever possible.

Shit happens in everyone's life at some stage and I am no different. It happened to me in 2006 which, amongst many things resulted in my re-evaluating what bike or bikes I rode. Suddenly, I found myself as a single man again and no longer had to consult a wife if I wanted to change my bike or indeed if I wanted to buy a second bike; I could do that too. So, that's exactly what I did. I bought a second bike. Because, well, I could.

I loved the Suzuki DR 650, it was my work bike and fun machine. I loved the openness and exposure of the upright riding position where I could feel the breeze, smell the air and just enjoy the ride. I felt elevated above the cars and had great all-round vision. The bike handled like a dream both in traffic and at speed and I could throw it around the bends just like I did back in the days of the Speed Triple. The big single 650 cc *'thumper'* engine was phenomenal and for short journeys of less than a couple of hours the Suzuki was perfect.

I wanted something that would do more of the same but had the legs to go longer distances with the ability to take stuff for staying overnight. I was not interested in a naked café racer or any other type of bike, I was sold and committed to dual sport bike riding in New Zealand. I did my research and found a beautiful bike that ticked all my boxes and this bike would take me the length and breadth of both the south and north islands of New Zealand - not once, but twice and so much more in between. It was a second-hand 1997 BMW R 1100 GS. This would be the perfect addition to my motorcycle stable.

The BMW series of 'GS' bikes have been around since 1980 when BMW launched the R 80 GS. The 'GS' not surprisingly is German for Gelände/Straße meaning off-road/road or off-road/sport in its modern term. In 2004, the R 1150 GS Adventure model became famous in the motorcycle adventure

My 1997 BMW R1100GS, Trentham, New Zealand, 2007

'*The Long Way Round*' with Ewan McGregor and Charley Boorman. That single adventure spurred a whole generation of motorcyclist onto the dual sport scene and in particular the BMW GS family. My 1997 R 1100 GS was the model just prior to the famous R 1150 GS and was made for five years (1994-1999).

The Germans certainly know how to build motorcycles because this thing was built like a brick shithouse and it did

142

everything the DR 650 could do plus some. The large 1,085 cc, flat-twin, 4-valve air and oil cooled head (boxer) engine was a first for me and it was a perfect match for the shaft final drive. The economic big twin was fed by a very large 5.5 imperial gallon fuel tank, which would keep you trucking continuously for well over 200 miles (320 kilometres) at a time. Not only that, you never felt fatigued afterwards either. The hand grips were made of soft slotted rubber and the handlebars were mounted on rubber shock absorbers. I would need to replace a number of my teeth fillings after riding the DR 650 for 200 miles in one go.

The boxer engine pushed out 80 horses and with 73lbft of torque on hand, there was enough low down power in the bike to tow a car if it had too. Braking was interesting and different. The bike had ABS (active full time) and was fitted with a telelever front end (central shock absorber attached to the forks) which dampened the dip you experience on a bike when you brake hard using the front brake. The effect was that the bike slowed in a linear fashion - just like a car, the front of the bike hardly dipped at all. It felt strange at first, but you soon got used to it and it felt quite reassuring. However, at 536lb it was no lightweight off-roader, so I didn't take it on anything more challenging than an unsealed road. I also needed to refine my weight lifting techniques because this thing was a real beast to pick up when it is lying on its side. I know this because I dropped it several times. Notice the word dropped not crashed, there is a difference; only one involves speed. You couldn't just lean over and pick it up like the Suzuki, you had to use a proper 'get your back into it' technique otherwise you would simply bust a blood vessel.

I found the bike on the New Zealand website 'Trade Me' a sort of 'e-bay' for New Zealanders. The bike was in Auckland some 400 miles (640 kilometres) away. Easily done in one go. I decided that I would hire a car, drive up to Auckland, drop off the car, buy the bike and ride it back in a day. Easy, what could go wrong with that plan? Actually, nothing. In fact, it was an awesome trip over 800 miles (1,280 kilometres) all up and the first of many adventures I would have on the Beemer. I gave the bike a bit of a thrashing on the way back from Auckland just to see how the bike handled and performed - I was not disappointed. I was tired but not fatigued, the DR 650 would have worn me out and I would have been unlikely to do that sort of trip in one day. This bike also came with proper BMW side cases too, so it was (overnight) adventure ready and after I fitted a large top box, it became a multi-overnighter bike.

My favourite colour for a bike has always been yellow and this bike was Dakar Yellow so it ticked that box for me. However, some of my mates thought the colour was called 'Dakar Puke'. I really liked the colour, but I understood exactly where my mates were coming from. It was more a watery stomach bile than puke. In my defence, it was dark when I picked the bike up, all I had seen was pictures on the web site before I picked it up and I didn't really appreciate the colour until the following morning, but I still loved the bike. It certainly stood out as being different and I like being different.

In July 2007, when I bought my BMW R 1100 GS, the newest model in production was the BMW R 1200 GS which had come to the market place in 2004 in New Zealand. In May 2009 BMW had made half a million GS's (all models), which was impressive. In fact, I was so impressed, I would check out one of these 2004 models for myself in a few years' time.

The R 1100 GS was clearly more potent that the DR 650 and it wasn't long before the New Zealand police were also interested in my Beemer when they clocked me speeding on the twisties on my way to see my lad play football. That's the thing with twisties, you can't see around all the corners and the police know that. However, they are always very friendly in New Zealand and on this occasion the policeman apologized for giving me a ticket, then informed me there were no other policeman around for the next 100 kilometres, so I could *'make up some time'*, his words not mine. The policeman was genuinely concerned that I would miss my boy's game. I didn't know whether to kiss him or hit him. I opted for neither, just smiled and went on my way a few dollars lighter.

It was my left leg that identified the other main difference between the DR 650 and the R 1100 GS. I really struggled to hold up the 536lb monster once it had moved more than a few degrees left of centre. The first time I dropped it was at a petrol station when I failed to deploy the side stand correctly. My gammy left foot was scrambling to find traction on the garage forecourt and as the weight increased with the lean angle, I could no longer support the bike and over we both went. Nobody ran across to assist me, people just looked at the event unfolding in front of them. I guess it was amusing to see this bike topple over in slow motion. They would not have known I had a gammy leg, so would not have even bothered to run over to try to save my arse. I had a couple of these mishaps over the years but the only thing that really got hurt was my pride. Nothing more than a mere scratch on the heavy German engineering.

I took the mighty BMW on several motorcycle rallies in the time I had it, perhaps the most memorable one was the 28th Brass-Monkey Rally on 3rd June 2008. This motorcycle extravaganza is held annually, usually over the Queen's birthday weekend, in the middle of the New Zealand Winter at one of the coldest recorded places in New Zealand; Idaburn

145

Dam, Oturehua in Central Otago on the South Island. Oddly, it is one of New Zealand's best known and longest running Motorcycle Rallies. Around 1500 to 2000 motorcyclists gather to enjoy a large bonfire, live band and various events and displays. Just getting there can be treacherous with frost, ice, snow, as well as grit and salt being scattered over most of the roads in this neck of the woods.

Why would anyone want to go on this? Well, because it's there and you can. This was my first (and only time) at the rally

and although it was very cold, it was not freezing with snow and ice, but we did get lots of rain which made it just wet and miserable - and cold. There were people there who

Brass Monkey Rally, Central Otago, New Zealand, 2008

had been attending this rally for over 20 years. Crazy!

There was a very relaxed atmosphere at the rally with lots of drinking and eating of course, but the field got totally waterlogged over the weekend and so did much of my stuff, although the tent held up well. I dropped my bike twice trying to get out of the place on the Sunday. In fact, there were a couple of recovery teams wondering around the paddock whose sole job was to help people pull their bikes out of the mud and help them get to the main road. It was like trying to ride a bike with jelly tyres, it was awful. How people never got injured from falling over or being hit by out of control bikes, God only knows. There were bikes and bodies everywhere in the mud. Luckily, I had a bit of experience with this kind of riding and only dropped the Beemer twice, once I had found just a little bit of traction on the more solid terra firma under the mud, I just kept the power on and simply weaved and skidded between solid patches until I got out of the field. Luckily all I suffered was mud ingestion on the engine cylinders which was easily removed once the stuff had caked itself on with the engine heat.

My everlasting thought as I was making my way home was why would anyone want to do this shit every year. Kiwi bikers must be crazy. Still, I was glad that I did it once and got some credit (not that I was seeking credit) from biker mates at work – some of whom had never done a Brass Monkey but had always promised themselves they would one day – yeah right! When people say, *'one day'* they normally mean they have no intention of doing it, and now I know why.

My only other significant faux pas on the R 1100 GS would not be a failing of my legs, rather a brain/hand co-ordination problem. To this day I can't believe this happened to me. It was a beautiful normal New Zealand Summer day in February 2008, the weather forecast was great, and I had decided to take the Beemer rather than the DR 650 thinking I would go for a nice long ride after work and enjoy the sunshine. In hindsight, I really should have stayed in bed.

Access to car, motorcycle and pushbike parking at my work place was via three roller doors. The first roller door was at street level and was a slow heavy-duty corrugated steel door that was operated by a chain and electric motor and would take between 15 to 20 seconds to open. After about 10 seconds it would be open enough for you to ride through onto the steep 30 metre (100 feet) access ramp that would lead you down into the basement. To get access into the basement you had to navigate through a couple of pneumatically operated high speed semi rigid roller doors. Easy enough, I had done this procedure daily either in the car or on the DR 650. The knack was to move slowly down the steep ramp on the brakes and on reaching the first high speed door, simply stop and present your access pass to the swipe pillar on the right which would activate the first high-speed door. The door would fly open in less than 5 seconds. Once the door had opened, you simply rolled forward to the second door. Once there, the first high speed door would automatically close behind you thereby trapping you in the void between the two doors before the second high-speed roller door would open and then you simply drive forward into the basement car park area. Simple. This was the first time I had taken the Beemer and clearly my subconscious wanted to make this a special occasion for everyone by complicating a very simple operating procedure.

My approach to the first steel roller door was text book riding. I had stopped, swiped my access card and waited. The door slowly began to lift whilst I prepared myself for the next phase of the entry process - the ramp to the first high speed roller door. To get momentum to start my decent on the ramp I selected first gear and pulled off. The slope on the ramp was severe enough that it required quite a forceful application of the brakes or some extremely strong legs to slow a 530lb motorcycle to a complete stop. For some reason (maybe it was too early in the morning), I had decided to alter my well-rehearsed bike approach routine which resulted in my attempting to go through the first high speed roller door without swiping my access card. With the bike in gear and engine running I needed to slow the bike on the brakes and then pull in the clutch as I approached the swipe card pillar. Brake, Clutch and Swipe, three actions and I only had two hands. I had put my swipe card in the wrong (left) hand rather than the throttle hand as was my usual routine. I clearly had a brain fart. I failed to pull in the clutch at the appropriate time, physics took over and it was clear that the momentum of a 530lb motorbike with the engine running, in gear and going down a slope with me on board was always going to produce more horizontal impact forces than a plastic semi-rigid door could handle. Indeed, the door was no match for this German built battering ram and once contact had been made, the sheer momentum of the bike forced the roller door into submission, ripping it out of its runners, creasing the semi-rigid slats making the door look very sorry for itself and of course now totally dysfunctional.

The door was all but new, having only been fitted a few months earlier – now it had been trashed. To add to the embarrassment the first person on the scene was our company lawyer (who was on a push bike). I thought it unlikely that he could be bribed to keep quiet. However, he did have two good legs and a spare pair of hands so between the two of us we pulled the Beemer out of the door and back up the slope a little. The door had folded itself around the front of the bike and as soon as we pulled the bike back, the door took back a little of it shape, but it was still fucked. I parked the bike in gear on the slope and then laid on my back and started kicking the shit out of the high-speed door from the inside to try and get it back into some kind of operational shape. There was a queue starting to form on the ramp as it was the start of the work day. When the chief of security reviewed the security video footage, I was the first to admit that it didn't look good for me. It looked very aggressive and was perceived as my taking out my anger and frustration on the roller door. I was of course simply trying to straighten the creased slats and push them back into the high-speed runners. There was no sound on the video fortunately, so no-one could hear me cursing at the door.

Luckily, I had the lawyer as a witness who could back me up that it was just an accident. I was quietly informed that I wouldn't be the last person to have this mishap, then in the same breath found out that I was in fact the first. The building administrators tried to charge me for the damage, but it got too difficult and political; mixing building (employer) and motor (employee) insurance claims was just too hard so I was let off the hook. The good news was the bike was just fine - just a small scratch on the front mudguard. That's German engineering for you. The moral of the story. When riding a motorcycle, the first priority must always be to ride the motorcycle. Don't try and get clever by doing two things at once, particularly when the environment is working against you. Secondly, don't do tricks you have never practiced in front of surveillance cameras; there is always someone watching and

judging you. I never felt the urge to go for that long ride after work, the roller door episode sort of killed my enthusiasm. I had an uneventful and slow ride home instead.

Me, Bev & My BMWR1100GS, Trentham, New Zealand, 2009

The R 1100 GS was a great bike all round and all my memories of owning this bike were fond ones, even the silly mishaps. There were however, two real emotional memories I had with this bike. The first involved Bev, the lady that lived in the house behind mine. She was a biker lady back in the 60s and 70s, but she had not been on a bike for decades. Bev was not very well, and I asked if she would like to go for a ride with me one day, and she was absolutely thrilled that I had even asked her. She really enjoyed the ride out for about an hour or so and was so thankful for me taking her - she never forgot it and we became really good neighbour's. It was no big deal for me, it was fun, but never underestimate how powerful a small gesture like this can be on others. Sadly, our ride out on the Beemer was the last time she rode on the back of a motorcycle. Bev died a few months later.

Bev's son was also a biker and had arranged her funeral to be led by a group of local bikers. I felt privileged to have given her the opportunity to ride and feel the wind blow in her face for one last time. I didn't even think when I took her out it would be her last time, but that's the thing, we never know if our next ride is going to be our last so that's why it is important to enjoy them all.

The second emotional memory I had with the bike involved

taking a stuffed Welsh Dragon around New Zealand. The Dragon was a gift given to me from a terminally ill school friend in South Wales. The full story of the Red Dragon is in

Red Dragon Tour, BMW R1100GS, New Zealand, 2010

Chapter 16, but basically, I took the Dragon everywhere I went on the Beemer taking photographs of the Dragon to send back to the UK. Again, I felt privileged to be able to do this for someone who couldn't do it for themselves.

The big Beemer was also the bike I learnt some new riding skills. I had never done a dedicated rider skills course, but I did do a weekend riding skill with the New Zealand Police to improve slow speed handling skills and braking techniques. I had done this course before the roller door incident as well. So not sure what this says about my ability to learn from training. I guess in the back of my mind I had this thought that by doing any training with the New Zealand Police, such experience may work in mitigation and get me off future speeding tickets if I could drop that into the conversation. Then again, maybe not. There were about a dozen of us on the course with a real mix of bikes including Harleys, Beemer's (dual sports), sports bikes, commuters and everything in between. I felt more than a little proud when it was announced that I was the best rider on a dual sports and large bore bike. I won a tyre foot pump for my efforts (I think they thought it was good physiotherapy for my gammy left foot but were too embarrassed to say). To be fair, it was a huge confidence booster for me as my balance is poor at best so to do better on two wheels and get recognized for it was a very pleasant surprise and an accolade to BMW for making a well-balanced bike.

I must admit I did learn a lot about slow speed handling (roller doors aside) and weight distribution when riding slow and at speed. I put some of those handling skills to the test at a track day at Taupo, where I rode the Beemer as fast as I could around Taupo Race Track with about another 30 bikers. High speed cornering, late breaking and accelerating when you are leaning over is a great experience to practice in a safe environment. An environment that does not have any police pointing a speed gun at you around the corner and a road that doesn't have traffic coming the other way. If you were unlucky to take a tumble you could fall with confidence and just skid to a stop rather than into something. Track days are popular in

New Zealand and I am a big fan. Doesn't matter what bike you ride, riding on a race track to your and the bike's limits, without being in a competitive race is a great way to upskill.

Me & My BMW R1100GS, Taupo Race Track, New Zealand, 2008

Chapter 10
What was I Thinking?

The Suzuki DR650 had been my trusted steed since Christmas 2004, but one cold morning in June 2008 it failed to start. This was the first time anything had gone wrong with the bike and I had used it almost daily. I don't know why, but it seemed to be a great excuse to think about a replacement. I guess I considered it time for a change, to try something different on the menu. Crazy really because the bike had been brilliant. It turns out that the fault was simply a flat battery - actually the battery was completely buggered. No big deal, just a

My Yamaha Scorpio, Trentham, New Zealand, 2008

battery and it was the original one that came with the bike, so it had given six years of service. Much cheaper than the bike to replace. There is no kick start on the DR650 and you really couldn't bump start a big single on your own on a level road. I pushed the bike back into the garage and I used the car that day contemplating my options on the drive into work.

The battery was not the only thing affecting my thinking. My girlfriend wanted to learn to ride, so I thought I could kill two birds with one stone and get a smaller bike for her whilst it could also be a new commuter bike for me. On 23rd October 2008 I got a great deal on a brand new 225 cc Yamaha Scorpio in exchange for the DR650 and a bit of cash. I almost immediately regretted that decision on my first ride into work. This new (smaller) bike was cheaper to run and was OK for commuting, but the commute was no longer fun. I had to wring this little Yamaha out to make the same time I used to do the commute on the Suzuki, and of course I could no longer ride off road. I still had the Beemer of course, but that had become my Sunday best bike and was no impromptu off-road bike like the Suzuki. The good news was that this Yamaha was a great bike for me to teach my girlfriend how to ride. After she had learnt and passed her test, I really wanted to flick it on quickly and get something else.

The Yamaha Scorpio was designed with commuting in mind and it looked like it too. It was not that pleasing to the eye

My Yamaha Scorpio, Trentham, New Zealand, 2008

overall and it looked like a bike that had been used for commuting to work for ages even when it was brand new. It was a bike that was more functional than a thing of beauty. The quality of the finish all round was poor with many items being made of plastic and the metal finishes and coatings were poor for the Yamaha brand. It looked cheap and to be fair it was cheap. Not up to the standard of the Yamaha's that were exported to the UK. The engine had a very average 18 horses on tap and all of them had to be fit and active every commute trip because I was wringing that little 223 cc engine out all the time. To be fair, it would cruise at 60-70 mph which is not bad for its size, but it would always let you know it was going that fast with the vibration. It was no DR650, but that was my issue and not the Yamaha's. I sold the bike on the New Zealand e-bay site Trade Me. I had owned the bike for a little over six months and had done just under 6,500 kilometres (around 4,000 miles) on it. It had served its purpose and I was about to move home again, so it was a perfect opportunity for us to part company. This bike would not have made my hall of fame. Even if I could have afforded to keep it.

There were lots of other changes going on in my life over this period and I think swapping bikes was all part of those life changes. Rational thinking was not one of my strengths during this stage of being a grown up. I had regretted selling the Suzuki DR 650 and the Yamaha Scorpio was a disappointment. So, what next? I still had the BMW R 1100 GS and that was my go-to bike for anything over a few miles, but I missed the fun of the DR 650. I wanted something that was fun but not necessarily something that would compete with the Beemer. I was thinking something I could look after and also ride back and forth to work that had an engine size bigger than 500 cc. It had to look different and have plenty of grunt (torque).

Both my sons were studying down at Otago University on the bottom of the South Island and I used to take them back to university after the Christmas break. In early 2009, I took a bit of time to look around the town of Dunedin including of course the motorcycle showrooms. I had been smitten by a 2006 Harley Davidson XL 883 Sportster that I had spotted in the Harley

Davidson Dealership. The bike had a big bore 1200 cc kit fitted and it came with a full complement of Screaming Eagle accessories. This amounted to an additional 14 horses up from 53 to 67 and a massive increase in torque of almost 50% from 51 to 72ftlb. I love bikes with plenty of torque. I like the feel of a bike trying to pull my arms out of their sockets when I whack open the throttle. The immediate lunge followed by a constant linear acceleration and increasing noise never gets boring. It's just one of those simple pleasures of motorcycling that is a sure way to widen my already broad grin.

I took the Harley out for a test ride, and on my return asked the mechanic to look at the front brake as it seemed to require

Me & My 2006 Harley Davidson 1200 Sportster, Dunedin, New Zealand, 2009

an excessive amount of pressure to slow the bike down. Apparently, that bike had one of the better front brakes. They would say that wouldn't they. It did make me smile - after all it was a Harley and I did want something different. The more I looked at it the more I fell in love with the bike, including the dodgy Harley brakes. My plan was to return home and then fly back down to Dunedin a few weeks later to pick it up. I became a Harley owner/rider for the first time on 18th March 2009.

Most modern-day motorcycle manufactures had not started out making motorcycles, they been involved in other heavy industries like ships, trains, trucks and cars. Harley Davidson were different. Harley Davidson set out to build motorcycles from the get-go. The iconic American motorcycle manufacturer has its roots back in a small shed located out the back of the Davidson family home in Milwaukee, Wisconsin in 1903. It was here that William S. Harley and his mate Arthur Davidson decided that they wanted to capitalise on the craze of motorising a bicycle as a cheap and reliable way for people to get around without expending too much physical effort peddling. However, they lacked real manufacturing expertise and roped in Arthur's brother Walter Davidson who was a machinist. Big brother William Davidson soon joined the team as well, making it four. The production run wasn't huge. In fact, they only made three bikes in 1903 and another three in 1904. Then they got their shit together and in 1906, moved out of the garden shed into a purpose-built factory knocking out 50 bikes that same year.

William Harley was the 'bike brains' of the outfit and in 1909 developed the Harley-Davidson '45-degree, Air Cooled, V Twin' engine which has become synonymous with the brand. This engine could take a rider up to a brain numbing 60 mph. By 1910 Harley Davidson were knocking out over 3,000 bikes a year. The Sportster model has always been a little different to the other Harley's in that the engine is combined in one unit with the transmission. Introduced initially in 1952 as the 'K' model it took on the Sportster nametag in 1957. The bike was developed in part to be a real alternative to the big British bike manufactures like Triumph and Norton and to be fair, it was. The Americans just loved it. The look of my 2006 Sportster had not changed that much from the 1957 model. Who would have thought that some 50 years later the same bike would be as popular as ever, even on the other side of the world.

The ride back to the North Island was awesome, although I think I was a little deafer once I had arrived home. These Screaming Eagle pipes were so, so loud. I loved the noise – for a little while until I didn't love it anymore. The exhausts were competition for my tinnitus. The thing was, the engine was so noisy it attracted attention whenever I accelerated hard. It was like the engine was broadcasting to the world that Nigel was opening the fuel taps and was gunning for it. The speed certainly seemed to match the noise and it was a great bike for people watching me to experience the doppler effect. The local police loved the bike too and were always keen to stop and talk

My 2006 Harley Davidson Sportster (Modified), Renwick, New Zealand, 2010

to me and give me a special certificate that required me to hand over some money to the government. I got my first certificate in the first week I had the bike. I needed to be careful, I already had one of these special certificates from a policeman who had been admiring my very nice Beemer.

I needed to do one of two things; either slow down or get a radar deflector/warning for my bike – which by the way, are very popular in New Zealand and although they are illegal to use, they are not illegal to buy or sell for some stupid reason. The traffic police are shit hot in New Zealand for any motoring offence and if you get pulled over, you are almost guaranteed to get yourself a ticket. If they find a radar deflector/detector, you are in big shit. The police are always very nice to you, but you will be issued a ticket. I had quite a collection of tickets at this stage from the bikes and my sporty Subaru WRX car, but luckily for me, an upcoming overseas appointment to the USA for three years would give me some respite and allow the time penalty of the infringements to expire. I managed to collect five certificates in five years. A pretty good average I thought. One to watch in New Zealand is the yellow light infringement. If you can stop safely at a yellow light, then you must stop – it's the law. It is treated like a red light in that respect. Apparently, if you accelerate to get through a yellow light that is an unsafe act. If you cruise through its OK, stopping though is the best policy. The nice policeman heard my exhaust note change, so he believed that I had accelerated through the yellow light which, as we all know now is not allowed.

The Harley Sportster, like all the other Harleys are by design made for the individual. Meaning that there are a shit load of

My Bike Stable, Renwick, New Zealand, 2010

add-on's and accessories for the bike. Mine already had the engine bored and modified intakes and pipes, wider handlebars and a larger fuel tank, I bought a bigger seat and sissy bar for my girlfriend to ride on the back and I could have spent thousands more on little odds and sods to make the bike my own. The bike was naked (which I liked) and pretty comfortable to ride. It would pull like an ox with its low-down torque and in a straight line it was awesome, but I was not that confident throwing it around some of the twisties like I could do with the Beemer or the DR 650. The brakes were, well, they were Harley Davidson - nuff said.

What I really liked about the Harley was it was the perfect bike to clean and admire. Once again, making the point that bikes are an extension of you and therefore it's nice to take pride in the machine. There were plenty of things to clean and polish on the Harley, and to be fair the quality of the parts was 1000% better than the Yamaha Scorpio, but then again that is reflected in the price and the all up weight of the Harley - which at over 550 lbs is quite a beast for a naked bike. Because the seating position is low down and the engine is also slung low to the ground it does not feel heavy at all. I never dropped the Harley in the time I had it and my left leg never once complained about holding the bike up at a stop.

This was also the first bike I had with a belt drive which kept the rear of the bike nice and clean. The belt drive is very low maintenance and extremely smooth, but it was prone to picking up shit off the road. I avoided unsealed roads and dirt tracks as much as I was able because of the belt drive. The Harley seemed to be the perfect complement to the BMW R 1100 GS. My bike stable was complete. Or was it...

In June 2009, I had moved from the North Island and was now living on the South Island. Close to where I lived were a couple of rivers which, depending on the time of year, were either in full flow or were pretty much dried up. When they were drying up there was some great off-road riding to be had on the river bed as well as the riding that was available through the woods and backroads close to the river banks. The R 1100 GS was too big and heavy for this kind of riding and I didn't trust myself riding this terrain on my own with such a big bike - just in case I took a tumble. I didn't go anywhere near it on the Harley. What I needed was a lightweight, dual sport stroker like my old Yamaha DT 175 or even another Suzuki DR 650 perhaps. I eventually found what I thought would be the perfect bike on Trade Me. A 1979 Suzuki TS 250 ER Trail bike.

The Suzuki TS 250 ER was an impromptu buy to satisfy this need to ride the river beds, and if I am honest, it was a real waste of time and money. However, it was indicative of the crazy thinking that was going on in my mind at this particular juncture of my life. I would have been better off hiring a bike to do the riding on the river bed rather than investing (and wasting) both my time and money on this bike which in the end, had very limited use.

The bike was a piece of shit from the start and I should have left it with the previous owner. I had nothing but trouble every time I went out on it. Electrics mainly but fuel and engine problems also plagued me in the few months I had this piece of crap. The irony of having a shit bike at a shit time in my life was not lost on me. However, it was pretty good to ride up and down the river beds and was light enough to handle all sorts of obstacles; trees, rocks, shopping carts and everything else you find on river beds. Dropping the Suzuki wasn't a worry or rather picking it up, as it was half the weight of the Beemer and because it was old, I didn't mind picking up a few battle scars along the way. On the few occasions the bike was running properly, I really did put it through its paces, and it seemed to lap up the hard work and just loved being ridden off-road. It reminded me of my old Yamaha DT 175 days. Also, it was much better than the DR 650 on this terrain as the power to weight ratio was perfect for soft ground including getting over large obstacles. The smaller 250 cc air cooled two-stroke motor seemed very much at home in this environment.

On the open road the bike didn't seem as comfortable as my Yamaha DT 175 from the same era, but it did share the same high-speed buzz vibration you get from most single cylinder bikes when they get into a certain RPM range and you either have to go faster or slow down to get rid of it. My Suzuki ER vibrated most of the time, but I think it was more a worn-out age thing, than anything generated by design. The TS 250 ER was capable on paper of doing 75 mph plus, but the one I had never went anywhere near that speed only because I didn't feel comfortable riding it at that speed. The bike handled poorly on

the road (never noticed it too much off road) and clearly its best days were behind it. The drum brakes were also shitty which was another reason not to push my luck with the

My 1979 Suzuki TS250ER, Renwick, New Zealand, 2010

speed but worked ok at slow speed riding on the river bed and off road where you didn't really need super effective brakes.

The Suzuki was never going to be a long-term addition to the stable but, with a jet ski and three motorcycles in the garage things were getting a little crowded in there.

For two of the five years I had the Suzuki DR 650, I also had another interest; Mopeds. Racing mopeds. The Mopedathon was an annual event that consisted of a team of three or four people riding a modified motorcycle (moped) of no more than 50 cc around a race track for six hours. The team with the most laps at the end of the six hours were the winners. It was simply a race of endurance and attrition. You could swap riders as often as you like and carry out any necessary maintenance throughout the race. These magnificent machines would be continually modified throughout the event just to keep them going as there was no reserve bike or riders allowed once the race was underway. It was the equivalent of the 24hour Le Mans race. It even had a run to the bikes for the start.

The Mopedathon seem to get more popular every year but the organisers had to limit team numbers for safety reasons. Nevertheless, there were about 20 teams competing in all. Most teams had unique names like; *'50 cc's of Fury'* and *'Hells Grannies*. Many of the teams had taken the race very seriously and entered highly-modified mopeds that had seen a significant investment in both time and money. Most of the effort had gone into the little 50 cc engine. The rest of the teams just took a standard moped, stripped it naked and run it on high octane petrol hoping it would last the six hours.

Fancy dress for the riders was optional. Although it was fun, it was also serious. Racing is racing after all and there is no point in racing if you are not doing your best and pushing yourself and the moped to the limits. It's funny how competitive you become when you are part of a team. You are no longer racing for yourself, the effort is a team effort. As with any type of amateur racing there is usually carnage, and this was no different. There was carnage both on and off the track over the six hours as the bikes broke down and blocked the racing lines or just fell apart leaving debris everywhere and of course there were the inevitable crashes.

It was so much fun. My first year in November 2008 I fell and broke my thumb. No big deal, we went on to finish the race - I think we were 10th overall. Notice I said fell and not crashed. I have never found a definitive speed that turns a fall/tumble into a crash - particularly on a moped. Although, 25 to 30 mph is fast to fall off anything. I guess one of the criteria for a crash could be if you hit something, which was not the case on the moped as we were on a made-up track with traffic cones and old car tyres. Nevertheless, a broken thumb bloody hurts however you do it.

The second year I was part of the *Just in Time Racing* team and we were doing really well, then about two thirds into the race, I was making my way through the field of competitors

Me Mopedathon Racing, Ohakea, New Zealand, 2008

when I ran over some loose gravel with the front wheel on a tight right-hand bend and the bike just slipped away from under me. I must have been doing less than 20 mph, it didn't matter. I fell hard onto the track and whacked my head. I was winded, hurting and concussed. The bike was fine. Luckily, I was not wearing fancy dress but rather opted for a full-face crash helmet and leathers. Unfortunately, my injury was a little more serious than scuffs and grazes.

I was taken to the local hospital where they discovered I had a broken scapula and a fractured rib. This was upgraded to fractured and chipped scapula and five fractured ribs after a CT scan. It bloody hurt! My helmet, gloves, jacket and boots were either written off or badly damaged. So, I was lucky to limp away with one broken scapula, oh yes, and a mild concussion. Not bad for a slow speed moped tumble. I classed this more a crash than a fall as the thing I hit hard, in this case was the track. I had come off worse than the frozen chicken did when it was catapulted off the back of my Yamaha Fizzie across the icy supermarket car park back in 1976.

I remember the male nurse at the hospital telling me that he also raced motorcycles, so he was very sympathetic to my injuries and after we had been chatting a little while he asked me *'what kind of bikes do you race, mate?'* I told him I raced superbikes then made a joke of telling him that wasn't true, I had actually fallen off a bloody moped. Not sure to this day what part of the story he believed. After all, who would be riding a moped in full bike leathers. I had now crashed twice in two years and had gone from a broken thumb to a broken shoulder and half my rib cage. I had decided that would be my second and last mopedathon. I was all for the fun, but clearly my competitiveness

Me & Pit Bike Hack, Long Island, New York, USA, 2013

was greater than my ability to ride the moped, so it was time to stop racing.

The next time I would ride a moped would be in 2013, some four years later and it would be on a small pit bike hack at a

166

flying club in Long Island, New York. I would be hard pressed to fall off that and break anything.

Chapter 11
Three, Two, One

Two's company, three's a crowd. Classic cliché that can also be applicable to motorcycles. This period in my life was the first and (most likely) the last time I have owned three legal ridable bikes. Why on earth do you need three of anything? I have already declared that I would have kept several of my bikes if I could have, but that was for nostalgia and to ride in my retirement years when I have the time to just ride for the pure love of it or just simply keep them to polish and admire. Even if that were to happen in the future, the motorcycles I own right here, right now, have a practical use. I need them to get me from A to B as well as riding them in my spare time for pleasure.

Looking critically at the bikes I had, two of them, the BMW R 1100 GS and the Suzuki 250 ER did the same thing. They were both dual sports, good for on and off road. The Beemer also had luggage and could travel high mileages so was great for camping and overnighting anywhere in New Zealand. I never went further than about 20 miles (32 kilometres) away from home on the Suzuki because I couldn't rely on it getting me home. Then there was the Harley which was, well, a Harley. The Harley was in a class of its own and was neither good off road, nor did it have any luggage for overnighting. It was a fun bike in a straight line and was a great bike to spend money on, polish, look at and say to people *'I gotta Harley - what you got?'*.

It was at this time in my life that I was also considering a big bike adventure. Let's call it a mid-life crisis (I was now in my early 50s and single). I had travelled all over New Zealand and now I was expanding my horizons and had the odd desire to ride around Australia. Why? Well, why not? This idea got some serious traction and I had invested in several books by people who had already done this epic ride and did some research myself on the best way to do it. Buy a bike, rent one or something else? I discovered that hiring anything over 21 days was prohibitively expensive. It was much better to buy, ride and then sell again in Australia if that was what I was going to do. My thinking in the end was to get a bike in New Zealand, transport it to Australia and then ship it back. Heck, I may be able to get the Royal New Zealand Air Force to ship it one way for me. I had received several quotes for shipping, transportation and insurance and I was thinking that the ideal bike would be something like the R 1100 GS but a newer, lighter version. Other than the bike, I needed to negotiate the time off work, which was more challenging than I thought.

I really needed to decide what I was going to do with the three bikes. The Suzuki had satisfied my need for riding the river beds, it was the worse bike I had ever bought, but that was more a reflection on my piss poor buying philosophy than Suzuki as a motorcycle manufacturer. The Harley was such a niche ride I had to be in the mood to ride it. It was not a practical bike like the Beemer. What owning the Harley did though was convince me that I was not a Harley rider deep down. It was fun, but the brand and the bike didn't float my boat as much as the dual sports and the R 1100 GS. The Beemer had been all over New Zealand with me a couple of times and it had travelled over 90,000 kilometres (around 56,000 miles) in its 14 years. I loved the GS brand and, when coupled with my crazy Australian adventure, decided that I would get rid of all three bikes and replace them with just one. A BMW R 1200 GS.

The Suzuki went first, followed by the Harley and then eventually the Beemer. I felt sad selling the R 1100 GS, not so much the Harley. I felt absolutely nothing selling the Suzuki.

In 2004, BMW had begun producing the R 1200 GS to replace

the R 1150 GS which itself had replaced the R 1100 GS. I could not afford a brand-new R 1200 GS, so looked for a well looked after early model. I found

My 2004 BMW R1200GS, Renwick, New Zealand, 2011

one in Auckland that had been owned by a chap in his late 60s who had decided to give up motorcycling. This bike was a beauty. It was in Rock Red and Silver and had been fitted with a number of useful accessories like an oil filler cap lock, a wider side stand for soft ground parking and a side handle for pulling the bike up onto its main stand. It also came with a set of expandable panniers and inner bags and with my large top box from the R 1100 GS would give me some serious luggage capacity.

The bike itself was a fantastic replacement for my R 1100 GS as I knew it would be. I had no real preference for colour, it was more important to get a well looked after bike and this one was immaculate. The chap who owned it knew this and wouldn't budge on the price, but I did try. I believed that this bike would be an investment for me and indeed it was. I didn't know it at the time, but I would own this bike for five years and would still have it today If I could have imported it to the USA.

I bought my 2004 BMW R 1200 GS on 1st October 2011. It was perfect for the trip around Australia and all I needed to do now was get time off work. However, I needn't have worried because the ride around Australia would turn into something much bigger in 2016. Nevertheless, me and the new Beemer made it all over New Zealand following in the footpath of its smaller and older brother the R 1100 GS. The BMW R1200GS was (and still is) a fantastic machine and at the time of writing this book, will go down as the best bike I have ever owned. In fact, I believe that the BMW GS series of bikes have probably been the most influential series of mass-produced bikes in the world, more than any other model of bike. I have never met a biker who hasn't heard of the BMW GS. Also, many of the GS's designs and enhancements have been reflected in other models in the BMW range. BMW really did hit on a winning formula in 1980 with their original R 80 G/S. In 2005 BMW made the R 1200 GS Adventurer (GSA) which was a ruggedized version of the R 1200 GS and a more capable bike overall, but it came at a cost. Both the standard GS and the GSA remain in production today (2019).

The Red Dragon and My 2004 BMW R1200GS, Red Dragon Excursion, New Zealand, 2011

I simply loved my R 1200 GS. It had a bigger engine, was almost 100 lbs lighter than the R 1100 GS (mainly due to the use of plastics and aluminium over steel), had almost 25% more power on tap, one extra gear in the gearbox, was more fuel efficient and the ride was just smooth and superb. BMW had taken a great bike and made it brilliant. They did of course make the R 1150 GS in between, but I didn't feel the need to own one of these and went straight to the new R 1200 GS instead. Although the R 1150 GS was probably the most famous from the epic trip 'The Long Way Round' it was also the heaviest of all the GS's. Furthermore, it only had an additional 5 horses on tap from my R 1100 GS with its torque output being pretty much the same. The R 1200 GS was not just an improvement on the R 1150 GS it was a real game changer because this bike could compete with the best both on and off road. The grunt in the R 1200 GS engine, particularly the low-down torque was addictive as it was impressive and the confidence I had in the superb handling around the New Zealand twisties never failed to put a broad grin on my face. It matched the Triumph Speed Triple in that respect. Indeed, it had the same number of horses in the engine and the torque seemed strong enough to pull you up the side of a house. Once you had started rolling forward and put your feet up on the pegs, suddenly, the bike became an extension of you. It was such a natural ride on any road and in all conditions.

Even off road the R 1200 GS was outstanding. It was clearly heavier than the Suzuki DR650, but it didn't feel that much different riding through the woods, on unsealed roads and even on sandy beaches. Standing up on the pegs the bike behaved well and was sensitive to all command inputs which gave me so much more confidence in the bike. The light handling was akin to riding my old Yamaha DT 175. It was just a shit load of fun every time I climbed aboard. Even the stuffed Red Dragon had a smile on its face because he had a much better view through the clear cockpit windscreen.

I had ridden several extended days on the R 1200 GS, well over 12 hours in the saddle sometimes and although I was tired when I got home, I never felt fatigued from riding. I was very happy with my new Beemer and felt that this would be the bike I would keep for a very long time. It was well suited for the adventure around Australia. After all, that was one of the drivers for buying it in the first place.

The flat twin cylinder boxer engine of the BMW GS models is as synonymous with BMW as the 45-degree, V Twin is to Harley Davidson. However, BMW got their hallmark engine and brand via a very different route. In a former life in the UK, I was fortunate to travel to Munich, Germany at least three times a year over a three year period in the late 90s and had the opportunity to visit many of the museums that house the aviation and motorcycle heritage of BMW (Bavarian Motor Works). It was at these places that I got to understand the making of the famous BMW brand.

BMW was an amalgamation of three separate German engineering companies becoming BMW in 1917 making aircraft engines for the war effort. Indeed, the BMW logo of today is a flat representation of a four bladed propeller from its aviation days. After World War One, BMW was forced to stop its aircraft engine production under the terms of the Versailles Armistice Treaty, so they diversified into making farm equipment, pumps and engines for buses and trucks. BMW eventually got into motorcycle production in 1923 when they produced the R32, a classic looking Bobber motorcycle of its era with a characteristic twin cylinder boxer engine. BMW designed the air cooled flat twin configuration simply to ensure consistent cooling of both cylinders whilst delivering engine power through a shaft drive rather than a chain or belt. A configuration package that remains the backbone of many BMW bikes today.

Part of Germany's surrender from World War Two initially forced BMW to stop making motorcycles until the USA eventually gave permission for them to restart production in Munich in 1948. However, BMW had to start from scratch, reverse engineering surviving motorcycles from the war era as all the design and manufacturing blueprints had been held in the production plant at Eisenach, part of East Germany and now under Soviet control. Not surprisingly then, when the Russians got hold of the design and production information for the BMW R71, their Russian motorcycle production company Ural, produced bikes that looked remarkably like the BMW R71 - and still do today.

In 2012 I had decided to put my TESCO number plate on my Subaru WRX car so now I felt I needed to have another

TESCO & ASDA, Auckland, New Zealand, 2012

special plate for my new Beemer. I came up with the idea of ASDA which means Associated Dairies, another UK supermarket chain like TESCO and the same supermarket chain I worked for

when I had my Fizzie back in 1976. I would have liked Sainsbury but of course it has to many letters and 'SAINS' I believe had been taken by a famous New Zealand, news journalist called Mark Sainsbury. 'BURY' was not an attractive proposition as I didn't want to *'bury'* my bike anywhere, so ASDA was the best I could come up with. I now had a couple of famous supermarkets in my vehicle stable.

Chapter 12
Bellissimo Motociclo

I moved to Washington D.C. USA in November 2012 to take up an appointment in the New Zealand Embassy. Before I left New Zealand, I had entrusted my treasured BMW R 1200 GS to my good mate Sid for safe keeping until 2016 when I was due to return. On returning to New Zealand, I had already negotiated unpaid time off work to ride my Beemer around Australia, just like I had planned to do in 2011. All I had to do in the meantime was to get through living for three years in the USA. Easy.

Not being an American, I thought everyone in the USA who was serious about bikes rode Harley Davidson's. Not true of course, I am generalising a bit here to frame how I was thinking - having said that, there are a hell of a lot of Harley's around. Every city seemed to have a Harley Davidson dealership. I wanted the American motorcycling experience but didn't feel the need to get another Harley to have that experience. I guess I didn't want to become an American, I wanted to show others that I was different and not from around these parts. Remembering that in my mind, the bike you ride is a direct reflection of who you are. This was a great opportunity to promote that difference in the USA.

My criteria were straight forward. First; I didn't want a Harley or anything that looked like a Harley (been there, done that). Second, I didn't want it to be a Dual Sport bike (already got one of those - my BMW R 1200 GS back home). Third, it had to have a big enough engine to eat up huge mileages and have enough luggage capacity to get me through being on the road for a few weeks. I was intending to travel extensively around the United States on this bike, the West Coast, Gulf Coast and Route 66 was a given. I had a bucket list of places I needed to visit so the ability to carry luggage was important. Fourth, it had to be small enough for local jaunts and of course commute into work when the weather was good. Fifth, my budget was $8000USD or less. Finally, at the end of my three years, it would be a bike that I would want to take back to New Zealand as a keep sake and partner for my BMW R 1200 GS. A perfect two-bike stable for entering semi-retirement.

If I could get a red one, even better, then I would have a matching pair, but perhaps dictating the colour I wanted in a second-hand bike might be a step to far. Finding the right bike was far more important. I recognised that I had listed quite a lot of criteria, but I wanted to get this right. I only had three years in the USA, and I didn't want to waste any time switching bikes half way through because I got my initial choice wrong. Also, to take a motorcycle back to New Zealand tax free no questions asked, I had to own it for a minimum of 18 months in the USA prior to my return date.

I arrived in Washington in December 2012 and once I had checked into my apartment, the next thing I did was to search for bikes. The hunt was on and it was literally that quick. I was serious. I used the computer in the apartment complex business centre as my research office. As tight as my criteria were, I found the perfect bike almost immediately, well, within the first week anyway. It was as if it was meant to be. This bike ticked all the boxes and not only that, this bike just looked like sex on wheels. It was a brand I had never owned before and with its clear Italian styling and bright red trim, the whole bike just sprung out of the computer screen and said, *'buy me'* I'm a *'Bellissimo Motociclo'*.

The bike was a 2007, 1100 cc, Air cooled, V-Twin, Moto Guzzi, Griso which also came with a fourpiece luggage set – bloody perfect. It was in a dealership in Boston, Massachusetts.

I very quickly nick named it my *'Pocket Rocket'* because it looked as if it had a couple of rocket boosters sticking out of the engine and it just looked fast. The bike just oozed

My 2007 Moto Guzzi Griso, New Zealand Embassy, Washington DC, USA, 2013

different, looked classy and was screaming out *'Ride Me'*. After some negotiations, I secured the bike for $6000USD on 6th January 2013. I didn't know it at the time, but Moto Guzzi are not that well represented across the USA and that seemed to give me quite a bit of leverage on the negotiations as there was not much push back from the dealership on my discussing the price. The Griso had been a trade-in bike and the garage admitted that they just wanted shot of it. The lack of Moto Guzzi service centres would cause me a few problems down track as my Griso reliability was a few notches down from what I had become accustomed to from riding Japanese and the newer European/British bikes.

It is difficult to categorise the Griso which was one of the reasons that attracted me to the bike. Although the marketing paraphernalia put the bike into the *'Techno Custom'* genre, whatever that means. It looks different and does not naturally fall into any particular bike genre. It is naked (which I liked) but it had a small (after market) nose fairing that offered a little protection and made the bike look sporty, but it's doesn't have real sports bike performance. Just because you could stick a four-piece luggage set on board didn't make it a touring bike either and it was most

Me & My 2007 Motor Guzzi Griso, Fairfax, USA, 2014

definitely not a cruiser. The cockpit was modern with a digital speedo which took some getting used to. It had normal handle bars for an upright riding position and a huge final 'shaft' drive (rear swing arm) assembly, which, in a way made it look a little dual sporty, just like my BMW R 1200 GS. The ride itself was akin to the Triumph Speed Triple, you just slotted into the bike, like you were wearing it, so it felt quite natural to me. Whatever the category, we were a great match for each other. Its 87 internal horses were thoroughbreds and could pull the bike through the ton with ease, without putting any undue strain on the rider. However, weighing in at 500lbs it was no lightweight and would be a monster to pick up off the floor after a misplaced kickstand deployment. The Griso was simply the perfect bike for me during my time in the USA.

The name 'Griso' is taken from the name of a trusted body guard in an Italian novel who betrays his terminally ill master and ends up contracting the same illness as his master and dies too. Sounds like the Italians are running out of model names for their bikes. I have difficulty trying to associate that name with this machine. To me, Griso simply means gutsy and fun which is a much better accolade to this bellissimo motociclo.

This was only the second time I had bought a bike on-line without looking at it in the flesh. The BMW R 1100 GS was the first and that was an outstanding success. Now all I needed to do was go and get it. I had two options; get it trucked to me directly (how boring is that) or go and get it myself (much better idea). It was winter time, but after studying the weather forecast, which was favourable for the time of year, I decided that I would go and get it myself and treat the ride back as my first solo US adventure.

I was working as a New Zealand diplomat so owning vehicles and driving in the USA was a little different to a normal US resident or visitor. I had to get a State Department Drivers Licence as my UK and New Zealand drivers' licence were not valid when you are living in the country as a diplomat. Further, any vehicles you own must be registered with the Office of Foreign Mission (OFM) who then take away the title (log book) of the vehicle from you, in exchange for diplomatic vehicle plates. Driving on diplomatic plates is important as it affords you certain rights. Also, it means that you cannot sell the vehicle without the permission of OFM as they hold the title. The process protects everyone and prevents Diplomats trading in motor vehicles as a secondary occupation as some countries (not New Zealand) have tax benefits for motor vehicles.

This process was new to me so going through it for the first time delayed the purchase of the bike by a few weeks. I eventually got my *'dip plate'* in February. Dip plates in the USA are distinguishable in three ways. Firstly, the number plate numbers and letters are pressed on a light blue aluminium plate. Normal plates are pressed on a white background. Secondly, the second and third digits represent the country you

Moto Guzzi Griso, Dip Plate, Fairfax, USA, 2014

represent. For New Zealand it was 'QT'. The OFM offer no explanation for the allocation of country letters. The prefix letter 'D' represents Diplomat. Other embassy staff and officials have a different letter preceding the country code. Thirdly, and most obvious is the words Diplomat on the top of the plate. In my experience the word Diplomat is important because once you travel outside the bounds of DC, Northern Virginia and Maryland, local law enforcement officers don't really understand the rights afforded to foreign Diplomats so it's a useful talking point when discussing traffic violations.

The idea that I could just nip up to Boston, get the bike and ride back in a day was futile thinking and this mini adventure would turn out to be a bit more than a quick trip. I would learn a major lesson about US travel and a lesson that would change my whole thinking about getting around the continental United States. Here's the thing about the USA compared to New Zealand or the UK. It's not just bigger it's not really comparable. New Zealand is roughly the size of Colorado and you could get 36 New Zealand's into the US (all states) whilst you can fit 40 UK's in the same area. This is useful information to know when you are travelling by road. It should be called the United Countries not the United States, because that's what it is. The place is bloody massive. Of course, I knew the US was big beforehand, I was quite good at Geography at school, but when you are living in the US you realize that distance is not a hurdle for people to go places. People just get in their cars and drive on the comprehensive interstate system or take a local flight. What you forget, coming from a small country, is that these road journeys can take days not hours. As the bike was in Boston, Massachusetts, a quick look on the map showed it was just up the east coast – easy. Checked the flight time, an hour and ten minutes out of DC direct into Boston.

My thinking was, Wellington to Auckland is only an hour flying and I can easily drive from one to the other in a day. Indeed, I drove up to Auckland in a hire car, bought my BMW R 1100 GS and then rode it back to Wellington the same day - easy. I was tired and got home very late, but I did it. I could do the same here except I would fly one way, which would save some time too - maybe even get back early evening. No problem. My flight was booked. I would fly direct into Boston on Saturday morning, get my mates girlfriend (who lived in Boston, luckily) to pick me up from the airport and take me directly to the showroom. On arrival I would quickly sort out the sale (bearing in mind the bike had already been paid for) and then ride back to Washington in the afternoon, and with luck, I would be back having a celebratory beer in my apartment in the evening. Great plan. Nothing to go wrong there then.

I really should have talked in detail about this plan to other people who had lived in the USA a little bit longer than I had.

My plan was ambitious to say the least. The first two parts went well, I got to Boston and arrived at the bike shop late in the morning, but then I had a long wait to get things sorted (they had lost the rear luggage bag and because it was a Saturday they were more than a little busy). I eventually left around mid-afternoon minus the rear bag - that would be posted to me when they eventually found it. The ride back looked to be around 500 miles (800 kilometres). So, at best it would have been 10 hours which meant midnight at the earliest to get back home. I had never ridden the bike before, neither had I ridden through Connecticut, New York State (and through New York City including the Bronx), New Jersey, Pennsylvania, Delaware or the top half of Maryland. My assumption that the roads would be in good condition, wide and clear of traffic was not founded on facts or research, more from watching Hollywood movies; my assumptions turned out to be way, way off mark.

The Moto Guzzi, Griso ('Gutzi' for short - because it looks Gutzi) had an aftermarket 'Quat-D' exhaust fitted, and it sounded absolutely gorgeous. The original exhaust fitted to this model was a monstrous affair and looked totally out of proportion to the rest of the bike. Most Griso owners had quite rightly fitted an aftermarket pipe. In my case the previous owner had also fitted a power commander to match the fuel injection system to the new exhaust. I will never forget the first time I started the bike. Indeed, the starting sequence was always a great warm up act for the ride itself. After rotating the ignition key a quarter to the right you are welcomed by an array of flashing cockpit warning lights, followed by a full-scale deflection of the rev counter needle and a decreasing number of illuminated dashboard warnings. The electronics show would finish off act one by throwing up a massive zero on the digital speedo whilst telling you the time of day. Then, with the slightest touch of the starter button, the starter dog immediately engages with the flywheel with a positive clunk and begins to rotate the engine. When the big V-Twin fires on the first power stroke, the whole bike shudders left-right-left for a second as it wakes up and catches its breath. The steady idle beat heard through the single exhaust is a call for you to mentally prepare yourself and go riding immediately.

The bike had a hydraulically operated dry clutch and when you disengaged the clutch the engine note changed from a welcoming burble exhaust tone to something resembling a farm tractor with a couple of loose parts rattling around a worn-out engine. It was pretty disconcerting at first and I had no option other than to take the salesman's word for it that this was normal for a Gutzi and many Ducati's as well. It didn't sound normal to me, but I went with it. In fact, I had little choice. This was my introduction to the world of Gutzi's and dry clutches. Although everything was noisy and seemed like it was shaking itself to bits, the engine and gearbox was actually very smooth and even with my gammy foot, the gear changing was easy, requiring only a small amount of pressure on my heel to change up. When I finally got going, I discovered that this bike was quick, very quick for something that sounded like a 30 year old John Deere tractor. It even had a red light that came on to tell you to change gear once you hit peak revs (something that I found out later could be set manually). I was loving the brutal acceleration of this big V-twin motor. It may not have been a sports bike, but it would certainly give a sports bike a run for its money.

Riding through New York City and the Bronx was bloody hair raising. Massive potholes everywhere, and debris of all descriptions was being recycled and thrown around many of the high walled roads by the wake turbulence of speeding cars and trucks. This coupled with crazy Mad Max type driving made me feel quite vulnerable on two wheels. I found myself jinking left and right for miles just trying to avoid hitting shit that was either lying on the ground or hovering around the space I was just about to transit through. It was like riding through a giant dumpster and smelled like it too. This sideshow of debris distraction ultimately resulted in my missing my turning on more than one occasion.

I was tracking my progress from a paper map on the top of the Gutzi tank bag and not an automatic redirection from a GPS. I must admit I was shitting myself because I had no fucking idea where I was at times and felt almost panicky when I was clearly heading towards what looked like a dead end. It's not that hard to take a wrong turning in New York and the last thing I wanted to do was stop and ask someone. Those mistakes were costly in terms of consuming the time I had given myself to get home. I found myself getting very tired, very quickly and I was also getting cold. It was February in the Northern Hemisphere, so it was cold and short days and even colder evenings. I was just outside of Philadelphia, Pennsylvania when I realized that I was never going to make it home. I found myself a lodge (and there are plenty of them in the US) about 10:30pm, parked the Gutzi at the lighted entrance to the lodge so I could see it, and got my head down for the night.

Just prior to my finding a lodge, I had stopped in New Jersey just off the main highway for fuel. I went into the service station shop to pay for the fuel and grabbed a coffee at the same time. I had a quick look around the shop for something to eat, warmed up a little and then left only to find my bike had disappeared. Fuck! It's been stolen. My heart was pounding, and I immediately started to shake with shock. The guy on the adjacent pump had not seen anything. Fuck. They must have been watching and waiting for me and moved really fast when I went into pay for the fuel. Fuck! What now? My phone and all my other stuff other than my wallet were in the tank bag, I had lost everything. I couldn't believe it, I was devastated. I had the bike for less than 6 hours and now it was gone. I looked around and ran back into the shop to use the phone and see if the security cameras had captured anything. When I got to the checkout desk, I looked to my left to see that there were fuel pumps on the other side of the shop. Shit. Shit. Shit. I had walked into the shop after fuelling the bike and across the aisle to get a coffee, paid for it all and then walked out the nearest door which just happened to be on the opposite side. Imagine my relief when I realized my mistake. I had to sit down. I didn't know whether to laugh or cry.

I found the bike exactly where I left it at the pump waiting to go. I started to shake even more and decided that I needed a bit of a break from riding whilst I got over this episode. I went back into the shop and warmed myself up a bit whilst I was getting myself mentally prepared to ride again. It had been quite a day. I was both relieved and angry with myself at the same time. How could I make such a stupid mistake? I put it down to being tired, cold and fatigued. It felt right that I should not push on much further. I eventually got home Sunday afternoon after a few hours' sleep at the lodge. There were no surprises in work on the Monday when I told them that I had taken two days to get back from Boston. I did get a few laughs for the disappearing bike trick though.

The Moto Guzzi Griso is all Italian, you can tell that just from looking at its sleek design and stylish lines. Moto Guzzi is the oldest (continuous) European motorcycle manufacturer and was founded in March 1921, in Mandello del Lario, Italy by three guys; Carlo Guzzi, Giovanni Ravelli and Giorgio Parodi who shared a passion for aviation and of course motorcycles. The aviation heritage is reflected in the spread-eagle motif that has become synonymous to the Moto Guzzi company logo.

In 2004 Moto Guzzi was taken over and is now one of the seven brands owned by the Piaggio Group. As a result, Piaggio are now (in 2019) Europe's largest motorcycle manufacturer. Moto Guzzi bikes are quite distinguishable from other bikes by their engine configuration. A 90-degree V-Twin (air cooled) cylinders with a longitudinal crankshaft (runs in-line with the bike) that pushes the cylinder heads out into the airflow from either side of the bike.

Most modern-day V-twins run a transverse crankshaft having the cylinders in line with the bike and not sticking out, like the traditional Harley Davidson engines. The Gutzi then is neither a BMW boxer engine or a Harley V-Twin. No other bike manufacturer makes engines in this configuration. Honda did something similar with the CX 500, but that engine was an 80 degree V-Twin not 90 degree like the Gutzi's. The Honda engine was also water cooled. The final drives are different too, most Gutzi's including the Griso are shaft drive (as was the Honda CX 500), which is more suited to the longitudinal crankshaft configurations. The only down side to this configuration is that you can feel a slight torque reaction, a sort of twisting moment on the bike during acceleration. However, you get used to it quickly and it is no big deal. Moto Guzzi had mitigated a large portion of this torsion by their innovative CARC Drive a compact reactive drive with a cardan shaft. 'Cardano' in Italian means any shaft used to transmit power which has one or more universal joints in it. In essence the CARC drive separates the forces of the engine from the swingarm by allowing the drive shaft to float within the (hollow) swing arm through its universal joints. It works. In fact, the Gutzi torque reaction is only really noticeable when stationary and the engine is revved. When riding you can hardly feel it, unlike the CX500 which reminds you all the time that a shaft is driving the rear wheel.

I certainly learnt a lot about riding in the USA from my little Boston adventure. I would not plan such an ambitious one day adventure again. All things considered, future rides would be based on 250 to 400 miles (400 to 650 kilometres) a day, tops. Notwithstanding this inaugural experience, in my opinion, motorcycling in the USA is awesome (second only to New Zealand). You can do any type of motorcycling; on road, off road, sports, adventure, cruising and everything and anything in between. The US offers it all and is a massive playground for the motorcyclist. Often these adventures and trails are amongst some of the most iconic geographically documented places in the USA. The infrastructure in terms of accommodation and petrol (gas) stations seem like they were made for bikers, they are everywhere, and all are biker friendly. I love all the riding the USA has to offer.

I was the only biker within the small team at work. I had not given much thought about a riding buddy in my early days, more concentrating my efforts on actually getting a bike. I met Alex and his girlfriend Sarah in the pub on Christmas Eve 2012. I had been in the USA just three weeks and found myself in my apartment on my own watching TV, wondering what to do. Christmas can be a lonely time when you don't have the kids and other family members around. I did not want my first Christmas to be a lonely one.

I had not got to know many people, but what I did know was that none of them were bikers. In any case, most had either travelled home to family or had made other arrangements.

Although, I had planned to have Christmas lunch with some embassy people, I was on my own on Christmas Eve. At around 7:30pm, I decided that I was not going to just sit and watch meaningless TV on Christmas Eve in the mighty United States of America. I got myself dressed up and headed out to find a pub. To my surprise there was not much open, it was the opposite to what I would have found in the UK. The first pub I did find open was called the Liberty Tavern. There was a comfortable crowd in there, not too full, and I easily found a seat at the bar and got talking to a nice couple who were on their way (moving) to Italy for work. As is usual during conversations, motorbikes cropped up, and I mentioned that I had a BMW R 1200 GS at home in New Zealand. The words BMW 1200 GS got the attention of a chap to the side of me at the bar who looked across and was taking notice.

A short while afterwards, the couple I was in conversation with left, and the chap who had heard me mention the BMW leaned across the bar and asked me about my bike. He introduced himself as Alex and his girlfriend Sarah. Turns out that Alex also had a BMW R1200 GS, but the slightly bigger Adventurer model. We chatted and exchanged numbers and agreed to meet up sometime when I had a bike. I explained to Alex that I was buying a second-hand 2007 Moto Guzzi, Griso from Boston, Massachusetts, and would just fly up there one Saturday morning and ride back in the afternoon. Alex never said anything about my plans, but he did look surprised. I now know what the surprise look was all about.

I caught up with Alex once I got the Gutzi home in February and for the next three years the two of us would experience motorcycling neither of us would have thought possible from that first meeting in the pub on Christmas Eve. Alex's local knowledge and experience of riding in the USA was invaluable to me. We quickly established a trusting friendship and rider leader/follower relationship style that suited us both. He knew his way around and would lead, allowing me to see and experience much more of the landscape than I would have been able to do otherwise. I know this to be the case because I could hardly remember anything of the scenery during my ride back from Boston. All my concentration effort was being used up remembering to ride on the right-hand side of the road and reading road signs. So, what did Alex get out of this? He got himself a biker mate, someone to go ride with and share the experience. I had also discussed with Alex the things on my bucket list, the main one was to ride Route 66 sometime later in the year along with my mate Sid, from New Zealand (who was looking after my BMW R 1200 GS in his man shed). I had hardly finished the sentence before Alex said, *'Yep, I'm in'*.

I did seem to have this ever-growing bucket list of things I wanted to do whilst in the US because the more I got to learn about the USA, the bigger the list grew. Not everything involved biking, but wherever possible I tried to fit a bike ride in there somewhere. Time Square on New Year's Eve, visit all 50 states, stay in iconic cities like Nashville, Memphis, New Orleans, Vegas and visit sites like the Grand Canyon and Hoover Dam, etc. All were hard wired into me and I would do all that (except I would only get to visit 43 of the 50 states - many of them twice) plus some. A lot of these experiences I got to do on the Gutzi. I also wanted to achieve as much as possible in my first two years, giving myself year three as a back-up/reserve year and prepare for returning to New Zealand. I wanted to go back to New Zealand in 2016 content that I did everything I set out to do and to show off the mighty Gutzi, the motorcycle that took me to many of those places.

In my three years of riding in the USA, most of it was with Alex. The first big adventure we shared was of course riding the iconic Route 66 with my mate Sid and a few other mates from New Zealand. We had a second adventure in 2014 which was a lead in for adventure number three which would take us way outside the USA and beyond anything that we could have dreamed about at the time. Let me explain...

Alex and I attended a BMW motorcycle rally over a weekend in May 2014 at a place called Natural Bridge, Virginia. We were surrounded by hordes of bikes and people who just lived for motorcycling. In the evening, Alex and I were discussing our ideal rides over a few beers, because that's what everyone does at these rallies. Bearing in mind we had ridden Route 66 just seven months before, so we had a lot of confidence about what we could achieve, and it gave us a solid baseline to throw any idea out there for discussion. With no loved ones close by who would object to another motorcycle adventure, there was always a high probability that such a conversation would result in some kind of agreement or commitment; and guess what happened...

Alex explained that he would like to tour Europe and had planned to do so with a few mates in 2010. However, one by one, his mates went cold on the idea and the trip never happened. I explained my desire to ride around Australia having ridden New Zealand a few times. I had already pre-positioned my BMW R 1200 GS in New Zealand with Sid to complete the adventure sometime in 2016 once I had returned home. The beer was working well and then I had an epiphany. I suggested to Alex that we could combine the two rides and connect them with a ride through Asia. There was not a huge amount of thought behind the idea, but it piqued both our consciences and very quickly we were googling all sorts of things on our phones. As we were sobering up over the following days breakfast, we both agreed that our discussion the night before had laid the foundation for an adventure that would be a ride of a lifetime. We would have about 18 months to plan the ride having it coincide with my return to New Zealand in 2016. Perfect. We would ride from Washington DC to New Zealand over a period of around six months.

Ok, lets pull up a bit here. Whenever you come up with a great idea for an adventure over beer there is always going to be a flaw in the plan somewhere. It is never going to be perfect first time. The original idea was to ride our bikes from Washington DC to New Zealand (DC2NZ) going east and then heading southeast down towards New Zealand. We would start the adventure in January 2016 once I had finished my job in the embassy. The flaw did not become apparent until I was discussing the adventure with my Norwegian friend, Helge, a week or so later. I was excited to tell Helge that part of the adventure included the Atlantic Road through Norway and we would be there sometime in February. Helge laughed and politely pointed out that if we wanted to ride the Atlantic Road in Norway, we would have to wait a couple of months as it would be impassable until late April because, guess what, its WINTER TIME! Bugger.

After a very quick moment of reflection, I realised that we would be travelling during shortened days and following the Northern Hemisphere winter. Crossing the equator somewhere in Indonesia around May time would see us enter the southern hemisphere's winter. What we needed to do was to turn it on its head and start in New Zealand in January (summertime) and ride back to the USA arriving June. That was the first of what would be many changes over the coming months. In anticipation of this world tour, Alex and I believed we needed to do a warm up adventure later in the year to help us acclimatise to the conditions we would experience during this once in a lifetime trip. We also needed to sort a few other things like packing essential equipment, managing on a budget and a host of other things we hadn't even thought about.

I was very happy about doing another warm up adventure and the flipping of the start location was meant to be. I had just met my American Fiancée a few months previously and it looked as if I was going to be hanging around the USA for a bit longer. In a way, this change would assist my decision making about returning full time to New Zealand. Also, we could ship the bikes from Washington DC to New Zealand along with all my other possessions that were being sent back to New Zealand after I had finished up my job. However, life has a habit of changing the best laid plans by introducing its own unplanned course of events. This trip was certainly going to be a once in a lifetime experience but not in a way I was expecting.

The acronym for the dream trip was born: DC2NZ2DC and we named it 'Chasing the Summer'. We now had 19 months to make the dream a reality and squeeze in another US based adventure as a warm up ride. This warm up adventure would literally be a 'warm up' as it would be going through the southern united states in August. The trip was more about destinations rather than roads and we called it 'Southern Ride'. Not a particularly thoughtful title for a bike ride, but it worked for us. A ride with a purpose, allowing us to experience hot and humid conditions whilst testing our judgement on what essential equipment and clothing we would need to take for this loop around the world. Southern Ride was also a great opportunity for me to experience some great American culture in several iconic cities I had yet to visit.

Chapter 13
Route 66 & Southern Ride

There are not many English-speaking Baby Boomers who don't know of or have not heard about US Route 66. The iconic route across America is a legend and remains to this day part of the American culture that was cemented during the 1950s and 1960s. It was fitting then, that Route 66 would be my first major bike ride in the USA. After all, being a biker and having the opportunity to live in the States why wouldn't I? Initially there would be three of us; myself, Alex and my mate Sid from New Zealand who was taking care of my New Zealand based BMW R 1200 GS. Once word got out that such a trip was in the planning, a few other mates back in New Zealand started to show interest and before I knew it, there were seven of us. Five of us would go west and four return east, each of us with our own personal objectives of what we wanted to get out of this iconic adventure. Only Alex and I would go west then east.

I am not one for riding in big groups, be them friends or strangers as motorcycling is still an individual activity. The ideal group size for sharing any biking experience (in my humble opinion) is between two and six. Any group bigger than six then the logistics of any road trip get more complicated and, as the organiser, you end up concerning yourself more about others in the group and less about enjoying the adventure yourself. Two is perfect, sharing the adventure with someone gives the ride purpose and of course it's useful to have a mate with you when things go wrong. On a big adventure like this, it's almost guaranteed that something will happen.

The first thing I locked down was the timing, so everyone could sort time off work and book travel. The end of August, beginning of September as a start would give us the best chance of good weather, kids would be back in school, traffic would be less and accommodation easy to find. Working on 300 to 400 miles (480 to 650 kilometres) a day we (Alex and I) anticipated it would take us about three weeks to go from Washington D.C. To Chicago to Los Angeles and back to Washington D.C. We never had a detailed plan, but we had enough to get started. The actual dates for Alex and I turned out to be 29th August through 23rd September 2013. Sid wanted to combine west bound Route 66 with World of Speed at Bonneville, Utah, which was another good reason to select the September timeframe.

Sid also wanted me to buy a motorcycle for him and then sell it again afterwards rather than pick up a massive bill for a rental. The search for Sid's bike started as soon as I had ridden the Gutzi back from Boston. The two other mates from New Zealand who joined the westbound adventure also wanted to purchase bikes vice renting. Neil 'Surts' wanted to buy a Harley, ride it across the states then ship it home to New Zealand and Brent 'Shag' had set his mind on a Honda Valkyrie, which is a monster of a bike weighing in at some 700lb and do much the same thing as Surts. Another Kiwi friend of mine Paul was keen to ride Sid's bike back to Washington D.C. from Los Angeles allowing me to sell it again back in D.C. This would be an extremely cheap way for two people to experience the adventure. Paul convinced his New Zealand friend Ian to join him, Alex and I for the ride back eastbound. Ian was the only one with a rental and had decided to rent a one-way Harley which was perfect as Ian's surname was Davidson. So, that was it. Five of us riding westbound and then four of us riding back east.

The purchasing of three additional bikes, shipping, storage, registration and motor insurance for everyone and then hosting in my little two-bedroom apartment was making the logistics plan a little more complicated, but what the hell, it was going to be quite an adventure for all of us. I was so excited about this trip and especially excited to be able to share it with such great friends.

I had given myself several months to do all the preparation in between trying to do my daytime job as well. My new found diplomatic skills effectively secured storage and some workshop facilities at the New Zealand Embassy, and both storage for the bikes and permission to have additional guests at my apartment.

I bought an old 1986 first generation, 1000cc Kawasaki Concours with about a million miles on it for Sid and Paul. It cost $1200 USD and was the perfect bike for such a big trip. I registered the bike as a diplomatic vehicle and tucked it away in the underground car park of the Embassy. Surts secured a Harley Davidson Road King from a dealer in Tampa, Florida and we got that shipped up by truck to Washington D.C. I got that tucked away in the Embassy too. Shag had bought his Honda Valkyrie privately from a Valkyrie specialist in Tulsa, Oklahoma and we got the monster machine craned up to Washington just a few weeks before the trip started. Now I had three big bikes tucked away in the Embassy. The basement car park had started to look a little like a second-hand bike dealership.

The real planning for the adventure didn't actually take place until the day Sid, Surts and Shag (S3 for short) had arrived from New Zealand and even then nothing was set in concrete, it was just a general outline plan of how we were going to make it across country. The day S3 arrived I introduced them to their bikes, Alex, and American beer and Pizza in that order. The latter was the perfect way to spend three hours in the evening discussing our hopes and expectations for the Route 66 motorcycle adventure.

S3 wanted to explore the southern states of the US before embarking on the Route 66 adventure. Due to work commitments neither Alex or I could join them for this part of their journey, but the plan for all of us was to get to Chicago sometime on Saturday 31st August 2013. Alex and I would set off from Arlington, Virginia on Thursday 29th August and meet up with S3 at Indianapolis sometime on Friday and then travel to Chicago together the following day for the start of Route 66. For some stupid reason, Alex and I had decided that we would do an organized Harley Davidson Factory Tour in York, Pennsylvania the same day we were planning to set off. We thought we could just nip up in the car early in the morning, do the tour, come back, pack up the bikes and leave. This was not such a good idea on the day. In fact, it was a pretty piss poor one. We hit some serious traffic coming back from York because of a major road closure which resulted in Alex putting his Porsche 911 through its paces on the back roads to get us home.

We were 90 minutes late getting back, not a big deal under normal circumstances but were about to set off on a massive three-week bike ride which put us under a bit of pressure even before we got started. We had some serious riding to do if we were going to meet up with S3 in Indianapolis. We had started the day at 06:30am, had driven to York and back a journey of about 220 miles (350 kilometres), packed our bikes from scratch and then rode for almost five and half hours, travelling a further 250 miles (400 kilometres) to Clarksburg, West Virginia, arriving at 9:30pm. It was dark, and we were both exhausted, but managed to get within 50 miles (80 kilometres) of our target destination – so not a bad recovery considering.

The Route 66 adventure was truly underway, all the fine details of the planning and organizing was finally paying off and it felt good. I was excited, and that excitement never wavered for the whole 23-day adventure. I had already gotten into the habit early on (before the Route 66 adventure) of taking some Go-Pro video from the cockpit of the Gutzi and hundreds of photographs from a small digital camera. The idea was to run a blog site for the adventure and have a permanent record of the trip for everyone to share - which of course I did. I was living this bucket list trip and was doing it with a bunch of likeminded mates. That just made a great adventure awesome. Unfortunately, I had paid for the blog site and it was taken down just one year after the trip, but not before I managed to save all the details just in case I wanted to write a book.

Alex and I caught up with S3 at a pub that evening in Indianapolis after riding a little over 400 miles (650 kilometres) from West Virginia. Although we planned to start in Chicago on Saturday and finish in Santa Monica as per the original Route 66, our collective thoughts were to use Route 66 as a guide to take us across country rather than stick rigidly to the Route. The 15-day west bound adventure took us through Colorado, Utah and Nevada, none of which are on Route 66. For Alex and me, the bits of Route 66 we missed going west would be covered on our return journey east with Paul and Ian. As we all set off from Indianapolis, we managed to squeeze in a quick visit to the Motor Speedway, where the Indycar 500 and

NASCAR racing is held. This first port of call would make a perfect (first) group photo opportunity before we headed off towards the Route 66 start point in Chicago.

Start of Route 66, Chicago, USA, 2013

The start of the Route 66 (Mother Road) is not easy to find in downtown Chicago, indeed its bloody hard to navigate to the street corner where it all began. We eventually found it and after a few congratulatory handshakes at the Route 66 Begin signpost, some big smiles and a couple of cheesy photos, we were on our way west. It wasn't apparent to us at the time, but it would be easier on the body clock as we travelled west through the times zones gaining an hour through each zone. The opposite would be true of course coming back east.

Some states allow motorcyclist to ride without wearing a crash helmet. I tried it once in Illinois but rode less than a mile and back down the road to a steak restaurant. It felt quite liberating at first, but I also felt very uncomfortable and vulnerable and I have never done it since. On a naked bike like the Gutzi you feel the full force of insects and dust in your face as well as it being extremely noisy. I found the experience quite a distraction and not much fun. Also, my crash helmet saved my life in 1979 and I didn't know it at the time, but the crash helmet I was wearing during this trip, would save my life in 2016.

There have been many books written about Route 66 and its attractions and I am not going to replicate any of that here. For us Kiwis (and Alex who is now an honorary Kiwi), it was not just about the Route 66 sights, we were looking to experience everything the USA had to offer. The USA is an amazing country and heading west you can physically experience the change in geography, rise in temperature and a sense of what it must have been like in the US back in the day. Many of the small villages have been frozen in time and still remain dependent on passing trade from people like us riding Route 66. Incredible really. Also, being a bit of a music man myself, many of the places reminded me of songs. Gene Pitney *'Only 24hours from Tulsa'* springs to mind along

Taking it Easy, Winslow, Arizona, USA, 2013

with Tony Christie's *'Is this the way to Amarillo'* and of course the classic Eagles song *'Take it Easy'* where I actually got to stand on the corner of Winslow, Arizona.

The further you head out west from Washington D.C. the less interest people have in American politics and the workings of government. We encountered a local law enforcement officer for the first and only time during the adventure in Oklahoma. The encounter reinforced my belief that American politics don't have much air time outside of Washington D.C. Having stopped one of us for passing on a solid yellow line, we all stopped and after examining the passports of the Kiwis, the policeman was fascinated but confused about my driver's license. He wanted to know what State my US license had been issued in. I explained to him that I was a Diplomat and that my license had been issued by the Office of Foreign Mission, State Department in Washington D.C. He could not get his head around the fact that a US driver's license issued by the State Department was not actually a State in the USA, but a government department in Washington D.C. Which of course is not a state either, but it is the US Capital City. I found myself having to explain to this Oklahoma policeman how the US Government works with other countries and how they interact through the US Department of State. Our conversation diverted into other areas and the rapport I was clearly developing with my weird Welsh/Kiwi accent seemed to distract him from the real reason why he had stopped us.

After several more minutes of dialogue, and light-hearted banter he was happy to let us all go and took off like a rocket in his unmarked matte black Dodge Challenger squad car, leaving a cloud of dust in his wake as he snaked the rear wheels through the soft dry dirt on the side of the road. It really was an impressive take-off. It looked as if he was throwing down the gauntlet to race our motorcycles, but we thought better of it than to put that one to the test. Unfortunately, in his enthusiasm to get away, he took off with everyone's passport on his passenger seat. Luckily, he did a U-turn just a short distance up the road and came racing back, not to drop off the passports but to pass us at speed almost showing off how fast his car could go. We took the opportunity to flag him down this time to liberate our passports. We all had a good laugh - including the policeman. I couldn't even imagine anything like this happening in D.C. We were in Smokey and the Bandit country now and it was refreshing. My takeaway from this was that most people don't really care what goes on in Washington D.C. Let alone know how it worked.

After a week on the road the inevitable first technical issue with the bikes showed itself. Alex discovered he had an oil leak on his rear drive shaft which was beyond a rag wipe down and was looking like the bike would need major bike surgery. Although unwanted, it is episodes like this that distinguishes a ride from an adventure and strengthens friendships. We had to change our plan to accommodate his mechanical breakdown (not that we had a concrete plan anyway). A few phone calls later, the new revised plan emerged. We needed to get to Santa Fe, New Mexico before 5pm that day for the BMW mechanic to look at it. It was estimated to take at least a day to fix the bike, so we decided to combine the repair wait time with a much-earned rest day in Santa Fe – great plan, sorted.

On arrival in Santa Fe, the Gutzi came out in a show of sympathy with Alex's BMW and had started to weep Gutzi blood (red engine oil) out of the right-hand side rocker cover. There are lots of BMW dealers in the USA but there are very few Moto Guzzi dealerships. I had to nurse the oil leak all the way to Los Angeles. Once again, these are the events that turn a normal ride into an adventure.

It was also in Santa Fe that both Alex and I decided that we were carrying an excessive load on our bikes and clubbed together to send over 20lbs of unwanted and unused stuff back home. We would learn this lesson a second time in 2014 and again in 2016. It's incredible how your thinking before a trip actually changes once you are on the trip itself. All you really need is a change of clothes and underwear for three consecutive days. A small back pack would have been sufficient. If you need anything at all whilst on tour in the USA, Walmart and Target supermarkets are your friends.

Utah was the one state on the whole adventure where I experienced more *'Whoa'* moments than anywhere else. Whether it was just coming over the brow of a hill or straightening up after a tight corner, being greeted by a straight-line and sharpening horizon set between spectacular jagged mountains was a sight I will remember forever. Feeling the sun in my face, the warm breeze rushing through my vented jacket whilst absorbing the reassuring pulse of the V-twin motor through all points of contact with the bike was just pure pleasure. It is during these brief moments that I really felt alive and in sync with the bike and nature. Sounds corny, but it's true. The whole scene is screaming out to you to love your life and enjoy the ride. One of the highlights of going west was visiting Bonneville Salt Flats, which is also in Utah, this was the very place where New Zealander, Burt Munro, raced his Indian motorcycle and was the inspiration for the 2005 movie *'The World's Fastest Indian'*. On 26th August 1967, Burt Munro claimed the World Speed Record in the category of streamlined motorcycles under 1,000 cc with an average speed of 184.087 mph. Sadly, the salt flats were flooded when we got there so the World of Speed had been cancelled. Nevertheless, standing on the very spot where so much history has been made in the world of speed and motor sport was another fantastic memory.

The diversity of the USA is clearly on show in Wendover, Nevada, which is an interesting town as it sits smack on the border of Utah and Nevada – the Ying and Yang of American lifestyles. There is a wide white line crossing the main road that separate the two states. Utah being a religious Mormon state that does not allow gambling of any sorts and then there is

Nevada, which seems to be showing the middle finger to Utah with its flashing lights, casinos and bars, all of which could not have been located any closer to the border with Utah.

We made it into California through Lake Tahoe and rode the Pacific Coastal Highway (PCH) all the way to the finish. Standing on the Santa Monica pier next to the Route 66 sign was both a happy and sad occasion. On the one hand, we were only half way through, but on the other hand it signaled the end of the westbound adventure. The shared experience of riding across country takes friendships to another level and collectively, our shared experiences bonded the group, but this part was now over, but for Alex and I, we were about to do it all again. We all had stuff to do in Los Angeles over the following couple of days. Sid had to sort tyres for the Kawasaki for the return trip for Paul. I had sourced the only Gutzi dealer on the outskirts of Los Angeles and had pre-planned an appointment with one of the mechanics to sort the oil leak and a really annoying fuel problem the bike had developed. For the last couple of hundred miles, just pulling up sharply at traffic lights would cause the Gutzi to stall. It was really annoying but nothing that $300USD couldn't fix. Surts and Shag had some serious shopping to do for home and complete the paperwork for exporting their bikes. As a departing hurray, we had a final dinner as a westbound crew which turned out to be a bit of a late night, but a great celebration of the Route 66 westward adventure. Job done.

Paul and Ian had arrived from New Zealand and were preparing themselves for the trek east. Paul was working with Sid on the Kawasaki handover/takeover arrangements and Ian had already sourced his Harley Fat Boy rental. I updated the blog site and then we were good to start the eastbound adventure.

Both Alex and I had to reset our minds and our expectations as we had two new members of the team who had just arrived from New Zealand. Paul and Ian were as excited as Alex and I were just two weeks ago. So, we needed to cut them some slack and take it easy over the next few days as we got ourselves into a slightly different routine. Going back east for Alex and I was different to our westbound experience. We were effectively going home. It was still a lot of fun, but the group dynamics were different. For a start, there were only four of us now. It was neither better nor worse, just different. Alex and I were quickly becoming Route 66'd out, going eastbound. For anyone reading this and thinking about doing Route 66, do it one way only – you don't need to do it twice. However, the first half of the eastbound route was on roads we had not travelled because of the diversion we took through Colorado and Utah. I took the opportunity to fly over the Grand Canyon by helicopter with Paul and Ian as they had arranged the flight as part of their eastbound adventure. They had booked the flight for late afternoon rather than us hang around overnight to do an early morning excursion. We recognized that we were a little behind schedule to reach the airport for the arranged flight. The lady at the helicopter booking desk suggested that we should cancel as we would never make it from where we were at. She seriously underestimated what four guys on big bikes with a focused commitment could achieve.

We covered the first 111 miles (178 kilometres) in an hour and a half, averaging 74 mph (120 kilometres/hr). That was a record for us and for me personally. I have never travelled that fast for so long on a motorbike ever. However, travelling at that speed, the Gutzi lived up to its name and was literally guzzling fuel. It was the most expensive 111 miles of the adventure – but was well worth it. The Gutzi seemed to enjoy it too, it purred along nicely, giving me a ride that was as smooth as snake shit the whole time. Riding so fast for so long is awesome but it comes at a price. Your concentration level goes up more than a couple of notches and the constant adrenaline rushes makes for a very tiring, but extremely satisfying ride. The 30-mph urban speed limit around the helipad for the Grand Canyon flight felt like a baby crawl. The lady couldn't believe we had made it and was just minutes away from giving our helicopter seats to other tourists. I have to say that flying over the Grand Canyon in a helicopter was simply an unbelievable experience. It made me realize how incredible Mother Nature really is and I felt privileged to be able to do it.

Alex and I faced our first time-zone mix up in Albuquerque, New Mexico. We had been caught out by the different time zones and had lost an hour as we entered Mountain time. Losing an hour is much harder to deal with than gaining an hour heading west. This was also the first time going east that we had stayed in the same place going west. Here on in, Alex and I would be seeing things for the second time.

I don't think Italian bikes like the Griso were designed for long distances and adverse weather conditions. As were leaving Oklahoma City in the pouring rain, the mighty Gutzi started to show the weaknesses that were in the Italian electrics and their disdain for water ingress. The digital speedometer on the Gutzi is fed by a sensor on the rear wheel, which when wet, seems to turn into a random number generator feeding the speedo with numbers ranging from zero to 156 mph all whilst sitting at a red traffic light. On moving off, it could go from a stationary 5 mph indicated to a staggering 70 mph in first gear and in much less than a second. If only. This continued with some variation for about four miles (six kilometres) and because of the large backlit digital display, was a constant distraction to me. Distractions are not what you want when its pouring down with rain. To make matters worse, the headlight bulb blew shortly afterwards, probably out of sympathy with the speedo sensor. This was not the only time Italian electrics would cause me concern. In fact, the speedo would be an intermittent problem that would show up on several occasions over the years and not just in the wet. The issue would hang around for a few minutes to get my attention and concern and then magically disappear before I could diagnose exactly where the fault was.

The trip east had started to give Alex and I many déjà vu moments and although we were happy to continue onto Chicago with Paul and Ian, there was a perfect opportunity for us to do something a little different. Rather than Alex and I leading Paul and Ian, they could continue north with their own mini adventure towards Chicago whilst Alex and I continue east and across states we had not crossed previously. Also, it would mean that we would get back home a little earlier, although that was never an objective, merely a consequence.

I had mixed feelings about this plan as Paul was a close friend of mine and I wanted to spend more time with him and all four of us were getting along just great. However, the thought of spending the last five days of the adventure covering the same ground as we did with the westbound crew was not very appealing after 22 days on the road. Over dinner in an Irish pub that night, it was decided. We would break into two groups the following day and do two separate mini adventures. Much like S3 had done before embarking on the westbound Route 66 adventure. Paul would ride back to Washington D.C. from Chicago (as previously planned – but solo) and stay with me for a few days so we could hang out together and then he would leave the Kawasaki behind for me to sell. We all agreed that was a great compromise. Ian would fly back to New Zealand from Chicago after dropping off his Fat Boy Harley rental.

Day 24 for Alex and I was a mixed bag. We found one of the best motorcycle roads we had ridden on the whole trip. The M0142 in Missouri. The weather was perfect for these 42 miles (67 kilometres) of biker heaven; smooth roads, undulating hills, loads of high speed twisties and great scenery. We were smiling like Cheshire Cats at the end - that was until I discovered the mighty Gutzi had decided to blow a left-hand rocker cover gasket and it had started to dump dark red-hot engine oil (Gutzi blood) all over my left leg. Bugger, here we go again. Exactly the same problem I had going west, just on the other cylinder. Good job it was only a twin cylinder engine. Not a great advert for Italian engineering; two separate oil leaks, a fuel problem, blown headlight and a spurious speedo problem and we were still a few days from home. What would be next? Still, it was all part of the adventure and was much better than being in the office. A fact I had to keep reminding myself of.

The bike limped through the rest of Missouri into Kentucky and then into Tennessee by my clamping a hotel towel I had borrowed onto the top of the cylinder head, holding it in place with my knee. It was the equivalent of a tourniquet on an open wound. When we stopped, I would simply wipe off the excess oil on the cylinder head to try and prevent the oil dribbling down the engine and onto the exhaust. It must have looked strange to other motorists to see this motorcycle with a towel wrapped around half the engine and blue exhaust smoke coming from the front of the bike and not out the exhaust.

We arrived in Nashville, Tennessee early evening and I had a plan to fix the leak early Sunday morning. It had been a long and difficult day under the circumstances, and we had ridden almost 400 miles (650 kilometres) in just under eight hours. Even finding accommodation was hard. Taylor Swift, the famous US singer songwriter was also in Nashville that night and was performing at one of her local venues. This pushed the hotel rates through the roof and made finding a spare room, let alone one with two beds, very difficult. The only good news was that we ended up staying very close to Broadway, the main center of Nashville, and easy walking distance to the downtown action. The bad news was that it was very expensive, it was three times the cost to what we had paid anywhere else – but, in the end it was well worth it. We had one of the best nights we had experienced anywhere so far on the trip. Nashville has a huge selection of bars, and the friendly party mood of the people and the live music everywhere made it a night to remember, or rather don't remember.

It had been a really rough day for me too, not just the Gutzi, so I took the opportunity to let my hair down and have a good night in the bars. Unfortunately, you would think that a 53-year-old man would know better than to go out drinking without having anything to eat first. No, Nigel was concerned about his bike, was more than a little tired and just wanted a beer. Well, the result of this was that Nigel could only remember part of the evening. I know I had a good time, it was awesome flitting between the music bars, I was loving the music, just didn't think to eat. I am very grateful to Alex for looking after me and deleting all the pictures that didn't show me in a diplomatic light. The other bad news was that I felt like crap in the morning and I had a bike with an oil leak to fix whilst nursing a stinking hangover.

Fixing the oil leak on the Gutzi was the priority and I was doing this under extremely difficult circumstances. I attempted to seal the leak from the outside, slapping lots of brown shitty gooey stuff that would go hard with heat. It worked, for 12 miles (20 kilometres) then the small bleed of dark red and hot engine oil all of a sudden became a major hemorrhage. We could travel no further, even the second hotel towel was getting saturated with oil, it had to be fixed and it was a Sunday. I set about showing Alex a little bit of Kiwi ingenuity.

Fixing up the Gutzi, Tennessee, USA, 2013

I made a replacement gasket from pattern. I took the bike apart and drew around the rocker cover onto some gasket material I had bought from the local AutoZone store. I cut it out using a pair of paper scissors bought from CVS (the pharmacy) and punched the screw holes in the gasket with a paper hole punch, also from CVS. The hole punch was the exact same diameter as the rocker head screws – how lucky was that. I did all this on the workshop floor of the parking lot. Two hours later, I restarted the engine and the oil leak was cured. A high five hand slap and a celebratory coffee in Starbucks concluded the fix. My head was also feeling better at this stage too. The fix was permanent and would last right up until the next service was due.

The final part of the Route 66 trip before we headed for home was to visit the motorcycle resort of Deals Gap, North Carolina where we would ride the *'Tail of the Dragon'*. The Tail is a twisty road that has 318 turns in an 11 mile (17 kilometres) stretch and would take us from Tennessee into North Carolina. There was no way we were going to ride this road with a hangover. We needed a quiet and early night if we were going to slay the Dragon. What we didn't know at the time was that getting a good night's rest would pay big dividends because the next day, would be our last and longest day of the whole trip and would end in a most unusual way.

An early start was required as we would lose another hour as we rode east through Tennessee bringing us back onto Home or Eastern Standard Time. We were up at 6am and we were on the road for 7am - the earliest yet. Our last day would actually be a day of firsts; earliest start, longest day, most miles, first injury and our first four wheeled truck ride. We just didn't know all this yet.

It was also one of the coldest and mistiest start to a day we had experienced the whole trip. You could see your own breath and feel the dense air saturate your lungs, enriching your blood and waking up your whole body. It felt really good to be awake without a hangover and I felt that my energy levels had fully recuperated. The low-lying mist in the valley looked like cirrocumulus clouds had fallen from the sky over night and were just hovering above the middle of the Chilhowee Lake. The clouds faded slightly as they approached the banks of the lake and Route 129. It was a perfect start to be riding such a challenging piece of road.

We were keen to get to the Deals Gap resort in North Carolina by midday. Arriving at the start of the Tail of the Dragon in Tennessee I could feel my heart rate increase and my focus become more intense. I wanted this to be a ride to remember, I would not be doing it twice. I set off at pace leaving Alex to explain to the nice Policeman who unfortunately just intercepted Alex ahead of me to discuss the dangers of Route 129 only moments before Alex was about to cross the start line.

The Tail of the Dragon is extremely popular for bikers and the local police capitalize on that. Although, to be fair, it probably does need to be closely monitored as the road is a Mecca for all sorts of motorcyclists which makes it a potential death trap if two bikes overcook the same corner but are travelling in opposite directions. I have never ridden a public road that requires such high levels of concentration for such a long period of time. To make things interesting, a party of 26 trikes had already started slaying the dragon ahead of me and were spread out over the whole 11 miles (17 kilometres). They obviously could not go as fast as motorcycles, which made the ride even more challenging during overtaking maneuvers. On reflection, they probably did me a few favors by making me slow down at various stages on a road I had never ridden before. The high trees which lined both sides of the road restricted the amount of sunlight breaking through, and at speed simply generated a sort of stroboscopic effect which gave me a bit of a headache by the end.

I set up my Go-Pro camera and captured the whole 11 miles on HD Video. It was a fantastic experience to ride and, thank God, to survive it. Having done it once, I have no desire to repeat the performance. There is a tree of shame at the resort for bits of motorcycles that didn't make it in one piece. The tree tells a story all of its own, its full of various motorcycle parts and from all different genres of motorcycles. The road is in great condition, but it is pretty dangerous overall when its populated with nutters riding trikes, bikes and driving cars. Trucks are prohibited because a number of the turns are so tight and close together, they would never be able to make it around many of the corners without crossing the double yellow centre lines. Facing a truck cab on your side of the road when exiting a sharp corner is not something you want to see welcoming you when you are on a motorcycle.

What was not expected at the end was Alex's back injury. It was either during or shortly after riding the Dragon that Alex started to experience pain in his back. His pain got so bad he could hardly ride his bike, and on reaching Asheville, North Carolina, his pain was so intense we took the decision to stop riding altogether. Alex couldn't ride and concentrate on the pain at the same time, so we set about an alternative plan to get us back to D.C. We had started the adventure together, so we would finish it together. We were so close to the finish. We decided that a one-way self-drive truck hire would be the best solution. The procurement of some strops from the local Home Depot Store to hold the bikes steady in the truck would be all the tools we needed, and of course some kind of ramp to get the bikes into the back of the truck.

Alex really couldn't do that much, so when it came to putting the bikes in the truck, I had to ride them in without assistance. This was not a time for diligently manhandling the bikes slowly into the back of the truck. I just had to go for it. Ride the bikes straight up the steep ramp at a speed that allowed me to retain my balance and then slam on the brakes as soon as the rear wheel had got off the ramp. There was not much distance to stop once both wheels were in the back of the truck. It gave me a few nerve-racking moments as my balance is not the greatest. I had to take the seat off the BMW so I could at least touch the floor flat footed from the start of the run up to the ramp. I managed to get both bikes in without dropping them or hitting the front of the truck. With Alex's pain getting worse, we simply drove nonstop the 485 miles (780 kilometres) arriving home at 04:15am the following day. By the time we off loaded the bikes, which was another nerve-racking moment for me, dropped off the truck we had been up exactly 24 hours. It was not the end of the adventure we thought we were going to have, but absolutely the right one under the circumstances. It was great that we finished the trip together, exactly how we started it 27 days ago.

Both Alex and I were sad that the adventure was over even though he was in pain. I actually shed a few tears. Reflecting on the 27 days was awesome and we both agreed we would do it all again in a heartbeat – even the seven-hour truck drive on the last day. It was an amazing experience on so many fronts; the riding, the friendships, the scenery, the people we met along the way and the shared experiences we had had. No money could substitute such an awesome experience. Riding a motorcycle for 27 consecutive days was the same as having 27 different adventures back-to-back. It had become a lifestyle for almost four weeks. It was inspiring to think about other trips now we had this adventure under our belts. Overall, we had visited 18 states (four of them twice) and had covered 7,024 miles (11,300 kilometres). We finished the adventure with an additional 485 miles in a truck, so that was 7,509 miles (12,0851 kilometres) in total, with an average of 278 miles (447 kilometres) a day. Paul and Ian finished their adventure in Chicago the very same day.

The day after we got back felt really strange. Waking up in my own bed was not normal. No more riding, it was over. I felt sad again. We had gotten into such a routine it had become an alternative way of life and now it was hitting home that it was over. I had calculated that Alex and I had spent 135 hours and 58 Minutes riding our bikes. It was pretty accurate, as the time was taken daily from the Moto Guzzi on-board computer - it was one of the things on the Gutzi that never broke. This made our average speed just over 55 mph (the most common speed limit in the US) for the whole adventure. My blog site had received some 5,385 views. I was pretty pleased with that too.

The sense of achievement and the ticking off a bucket list adventure is a very satisfying experience. We had our ups and downs and breakdowns, but these are all key ingredients of a great motorcycle adventure. Would I do it again? Yes, absolutely. However, I would select a  slightly different route next time as there is so much more to see in the USA. I might even consider a different bike. The Gutzi is a small-town bike at heart, long distances were not its forte. However, it got me there and back in style and was an awesome bike that drew a lot of attention where ever we went; just as I knew it would. Let the good times roll.

Route 66 had been a huge success on so many fronts and gave Alex and I the confidence that we could nail this world tour in 2016. We still had the opportunity in the summer of 2014 to do some more prep work and ride through a number of the US cities on my bucket list. All things considered we decided to ride the southern states which would also give us the opportunity to expose ourselves to some of the conditions we would likely be riding through in Australia and Asia. Also, we did have a bit of a habit of over packing, so we would try and travel on the minimalist payload.

Southern Ride as it became known would be a straight forward 12-day motorcycle adventure in September 2014. The trip would be dominated by famous party destinations like Nashville, Memphis, New Orleans, Key West and Miami rather than being focussed on the journey like Route 66. Afterall, the journey in this adventure was more about experiencing the climate and deciding on the luggage and financial preparations for 2016. Also, neither Alex or I could afford the time off work for another epic Route 66 type adventure, so the timeframe for this trip was workable and an opportunity just to enjoy the destination cities.

Over the 12-day adventure we covered over 4,000 miles (6,400 kilometres) and learnt a lot of valuable lessons along the way, some of which were reinforced several times over. I tried to capture a major learning lesson each day so we could reflect on our experiences and use those experiences for the big one in 2016. It was just a simple quote of the day, but nevertheless it was a really good way to capture what had happened in a few words. It also served as a great memory jogger. Over the course of the 12 days, we believed that we had identified the real essentials that were needed to survive months of riding whilst away from home.

We managed a tight budget too, rode though some precarious weather conditions and did some alternative planning on the fly. All of which was great preparation. Unfortunately, the mighty Gutzi limped back home yet again. I had already decided that the Gutzi was not the bike for 'Chasing the Summer', there was no way it would make it in one piece without emptying my bank balance. I had done some research and recognised that I needed a dual sport bike but was not keen to use my BMW R 1200 GS back in New Zealand, particularly the ride through Asia.

I had invested a lot of money in my BMW. My thinking at the time was that I wanted a cheap, relatively new and reliable dual sport bike that I could leave behind if things went bad and we had to quickly get out of the country we were in at the time, for whatever reason. I would not feel bad leaving behind a cheaper bike. After narrowing down the (not very big) field of options, I kept coming back to the Kawasaki KLR 650. Even a brand new one was a third of the price of my BMW R1200 GS or two Gutzi repair bills. It was a no brainer for me in the end and I bought a brand new one in May 2014. I deliberately didn't take the KLR on Southern Ride as I was preparing and modifying the bike and had hidden it away in the New Zealand Embassy alongside my Kawasaki Jet Ski. In any case, I would have ample opportunity in 2015 to shake down the KLR its modifications and get the bike adventure ready for 2016. Also, I considered Southern Ride a bit of a farewell tour of the USA for the Gutzi. After this trip, I was going to pack it up and ship it back to New Zealand along with the Jetski – well, that was the plan I had at the time.

Southern Ride was a great road trip for me. It had a bit of everything, as with Route 66. I experienced a little bit more of the real America and the recording of the lesson of the day served us well. The first lesson I wrote about was learnt a few times over the trip, but it was a great one and would serve us well in the future; 'Amend your plans as necessary, but always get to your destination before dark'. When you travel through places for the first time with little to no intention of returning, you don't want to be experiencing the place in the dark. Post our Nashville stop over, came the second lesson; 'Don't even think of riding early in the morning after a good night out'. Hangovers are a distraction. Our visit to Graceland, the Gibson guitar factory and the motorcycle museum in Birmingham, Alabama taught us another; 'Make the most of the attractions you pass on you travels – you may not come this way again'. Taking time out from riding to soak up the memory adds great value to the adventure.

Someone had cloned my credit card and tried to buy $800USD worth of stuff from Target in New York City. I don't know what hacked me off the most, cloning and losing my credit card for the rest of the trip, or the fact it was used in

Target for $800 - what on earth were they buying that was worth $800 in Target. The learning point here was; *'Have a financial back up plan in case you lose your main source of money'*.

We wanted to experience hot and humid conditions and Florida didn't disappoint. Humidity was sitting around 90% and it was cloudy. If you study weather, then you will know that this is not a good recipe for fine and dry weather. We experienced several heavy downpours, but one in particular lasted well over an hour. Alex was wearing a half helmet and almost drowned as the water forced its way into his eyes, ears, nose and throat. This was a great, albeit a little scary experience, where we both had the opportunity to master the art of driving in torrential rain. The lesson of the day was: *'wear a full-face helmet with a visor'*.

We rode over the Everglades on Route 41, the original alligator alley. This was good preparation experience for Australia. The only gator we saw (thankfully) was a baby gator living in a tub outside a local Indian village shop where we had stopped for an ice cream. Inside the shop were local photographs highlighting the problem of sustaining the wildlife and eco-systems. I never would have guessed what the main threat was living in the everglades. Pythons. Pythons let loose in the wild seem to kill and eat anything and everything from small birds and fish to alligators and even deer. They had caught many pythons over the years, some of which have been over 17 feet (5 metres) in length. Thankfully we never seen any snakes. They would have been scarier than gators. We did travel through an insect storm which almost blacked out my visor. We didn't know it at the time, but the insect storm would be a warm up act for what we would experience in Australia.

We did learn that it is very tiring riding through heat, humidity and heavy rain. They all take a little bit more of your physical and mental energy and after nine consecutive days riding, we were really knackered and in need of an early night with no end of day beer. The lesson of the day was: *'break the routine and have a light relaxing evening every 5th day. Consider a full rest day every 7th day'*.

After visiting Key West, which was literally the end of the road, we were ready to head back home so we decided to get as far as we could as quickly as we could. Unfortunately, the poor Gutzi was feeling a little sick (again) and had started to bleed engine oil or *"Gutzi Juice"* as it became known, just before we arrived at Key West. The oil leak was not from the rocker covers this time but from the back of the engine. There was also a more sinister problem on the Gutzi coming to light; slipping clutch syndrome. The clutch was a real worry and we considered taking the overnight Auto train to rest up the Gutzi, but there was no room for the bikes and we would have to wait at least 24 hours for the next one. I thought the engine oil leak and clutch slip were somehow connected, but it turned out not to be the case - they were two separate issues. The oil leak was a rear engine crankshaft seal and the clutch slipping was metallic debris in the clutch slave cylinder that prevented the discharge of hydraulic pressure when the clutch lever was released. These little faults cost me just over $2500 USD, but to the bikes credit, it continued to truck on without too much drama. A nine-hour ride and with some 630 miles (1,000 kilometres) under our belt, we finally arrived at our destination. Lesson of the Day: *'look at all your options, all of the time, and be prepared to compromise'*.

The last day was a mere 300-mile (480 kilometres) dash to home, but the clutch on the Gutzi was slipping so badly by then it was behaving like an automatic transmission and I did wonder at times if it would make it back at all. We had learnt some valuable lessons and experienced some extreme conditions (as we knew we would). We also gained a much better appreciation of what stuff to take and equally important what not to take. The daily cost of our motorcycle adventure turned out to be roughly $200 a day. With Route 66 and Southern Ride under our belts, we felt we were prepared for the challenges of riding around the world. A switching of bikes for myself from the Gutzi to my Kawasaki KLR 650 was the only change I needed to make. The Gutzi was done. It had served its purpose and deserved semi-retirement back in New Zealand. The final lesson on the last day was; *'allocate a little time each day for reflection. It's a very powerful tool in recognizing and remembering the experiences you have just had'*.

Chapter 14
Big Single, Big Adventure

There are several makes and models of motorcycles that have come and gone over the years. Some have reinvented themselves with all mod cons but have kept the old look that made them popular in their heyday. Bikes like the Triumph Bonneville and Honda CB series spring to mind. There are other bikes that have stayed in production over the generations and have evolved since their introduction like the Honda Goldwing (introduced in 1974). But there are only a handful of bikes that have been around for generations without major changes. Two of those bikes I have owned. The first is the Honda C50 Cub (introduced in 1958) and the Kawasaki KLR 650 (introduced in 1987). Although the KLR is a mere youngster compared to the Honda C50. In 2019 the KLR 650 turned 32 years old and has pretty much stayed the same bike since its introduction. At time of writing, this was also the last year Kawasaki were going to produce this legend of a bike. The term KLR is manufactures code for K=Kawasaki L=4-stroke R=Dual Sport. Some KLR owners think it's an acronym for Keep Lugging (a)Round. I would suggest K=Kuick L=light R=Robust.

Like most other motorcycle companies, Kawasaki has its roots in other heavy industries. Indeed, Kawasaki has dabbled in just about all transport heavy industries. In 1878, Shozo Kawasaki established the Kawasaki Tsukiji Shipyard in Tokyo and went from building ships and submarines to locomotives in 1911 and then aircraft in 1922. Kawasaki also built Japan's first military plane the Otsu 1, a surveillance aircraft. Automobiles, trucks and buses followed in the 1930s before they finally broke into the motorcycle industry producing their very first motorcycle in 1962, the Kawasaki B8. The B8 was a 125 cc single cylinder, two-stroker.

In 1965 Kawasaki made its W1 motorcycle. A classic British looking 650 cc vertical twin cylinder, four stroker. This was their first serious overseas selling motorcycle. Kawasaki then went on to make what I think are probably two of the most influential motorcycles from my youth. In 1969 Kawasaki rolled out the H1. This was a 60 hp two-stroke, three-cylinder 498 cc engine bike that had terrific acceleration. Unfortunately, the engine performance was far more advanced in development than the other aspects of the bike like the frame, suspension, steering and braking systems. It would easily propel the rider to over 110 mph, but it was a beast in the hands of the inexperienced rider and became known as the Widow Maker. Not a great accolade or selling point, but a huge pull factor for those wanting to try one. The H1 was for a time, the most powerful production motorcycle in the world for its size.

The second influential bike was the Kawasaki Z1-900. The Z1 was the world's first Double Overhead Camshaft (DOHC) four-cylinder, four stroke superbike. It made its inaugural appearance in 1972 with its 903 cc motor kicking out a respectful 82 horses that would catapult you to 130 mph in no time at all. The owner of the motorcycle dealership near where I lived had one of these bikes and I remember drooling over its looks. It was a fantastic piece of engineering and it became my boyhood dream to own one. Sadly (or perhaps luckily), I never even got chance to ride one, let alone own one.

Although for very different reasons, the KLR 650 is another iconic Kawasaki motorcycle. Motorcyclists either love it or loath it, few are in between. I have never met a dual sport biker who has never heard of the KLR 650. I will declare up front that I love the KLR and have owned two of them. At the time of writing I still owned the second one. The first one had its life cut short as you will read about in this chapter.

The KLR has a water cooled 651 cc single cylinder engine that kicks out a modest 42 horses that will push you to the indicated ton should you wish to try it. It also has a large 6-gallon fuel tank which is one of the hallmarks of this long-distance dual-sport class of motorcycle. It has no complicated digital engine controls (apart from an electronic ignition system), a large Keihin CVK-40 constant velocity carburettor and relies on a fuel tap on the bottom of the fuel tank and gravity to feed the engine. There is no fuel gauge to remind you to fill up, but the fuel tank does hold a reserve volume of fuel should you need it in an emergency.

Everything is bolted to the bike, there are no quick release fasteners. The speedo and tachometer are analogue dials both fed by mechanical cables and there is a choke lever on the handlebars for cold engine starts - also operated by a bowden cable. However, the bike does have an electric start (no kick-starter), an onboard tool kit, disc brakes front and rear, a single rear shock absorber and a nice little cockpit nose fairing offering some wind protection. What more do you need from an eighties bike?

One of the main attractions of this bike is its low cost of purchase and through life ownership. In 2018 you could buy a brand new KLR 650 for under $7,000 USD. If you wanted the previous year's model, you could get one for around $5,000 USD if you shopped around the dealerships. The KLR 650 really does offer value for money for those who want to ride a dual sports machine on a budget. You could buy four new

KLR's to one new BMW R 1200 GS. Not really a fair comparison I know, but both bikes do the same thing - well sort of....

Some motorcycling aficionados get a little hung up on the terminology. I would call the KLR and the BMW R 1200 GS Dual Sports bikes, but some describe the big Beemers (and other similar bikes) as Adventure Bikes, so what's the difference? Well, technically there are a few things, but an

Me & My Brand New KLR 650, West Virginia, USA, 2014

Adventure Bike is a type of Dual Sport bike. The term Dual Sports was an evolution of the term '*Enduro*' which described smaller lightweight off-road bikes that had been fitted with lights, indicators, a horn and mirrors to make them street legal. My 1977 Yamaha DT 175 was an enduro bike - it said so on the side panel.

Not to get too hung up on the terms, but some of the Dual Sport bikes are also called Dual Purpose bikes and can effectively be made into Adventure bikes through aftermarket modifications which doesn't help anyone trying to understand the differences. The common denominator for all these terms is the fact that these bikes can all be ridden off or on road; period. The differentiators determine what is the bike best at and therefore its motorcycle genre.

If you think Adventure, think distance and comfort akin to a street bike or tourer that can also go off road. If you think Dual

Sport think a basic but heavier motocross style bike with more agility in the dirt than an Adventure bike, but with gearing for the road. Cosmetically and technically they are a little different too. The Dual Sports machine usually has a single cylinder engine, a small fuel tank, a higher ground clearance with high mudguards and is often fitted with an extremely uncomfortable seat. All good requirements for standing up on the pegs when riding off road. Also, when you fall off them (which you invariably will) these bikes are durable so don't damage easily in the dirt and are much lighter and easier to pick up in softer unstable conditions.

Dual Sport bikes are also pretty nippy for their engine size and will get you up to the national speed limit quickly, and herein lies one of the disadvantages. Its ability to stay there - comfortably. Not just from the unfiltered elements bashing into your face and torso, but the rapidly moving parts of the big single cylinder engine. These big singles like to vibrate - a lot, and they get into the vibration groove cruising at highways speeds doing their best to shake all your fillings out of your teeth and making your fingers tingle. The uncomfortable seat plays its part by making your arse numb, but you get plenty of respite because you have to stop regularly due to the piddly small fuel tank.

Then there is the issue of luggage and passengers. Dual Sports are not set up well for either. This can be both an advantage and disadvantage depending on whether you want to take your partner on the back with you. Then there is the maintenance aspect. Dual Sports tend to be fitted with knobbly tyres for off road work and because of the smaller engine tend to demand more regular maintenance.

Not surprisingly, the advantages and disadvantages of Adventure Bikes are, in the main, the opposite of the Dual Sport equivalent. They have twin cylinder engines (which makes them smoother), are more comfortable, heavier, more expensive, can go longer distances between fill ups, offer protection from the elements, are good for luggage and passengers and can cruise effortlessly at highway speeds making the riding experience a little less fatiguing. However, you don't want to drop them. They can be buggers to pick up in the mud and can be expensive to repair if you damage the protective cosmetics. The first true dedicated Adventure Bike was the BMW R80 G/S which made its debut in 1981. However, over the decades the lines have become a little blurred between the two genres. The KLR 650 is a classic example of this and proof that Kawasaki got it pretty spot on when they rolled it out in 1986. It has not needed to change over the years because it includes some of the technical capabilities and cosmetic features found in both Dual Sport and Adventure bikes.

Due to its single cylinder engine, the KLR 650 has its DNA in Dual Sports motorcycling, but it has two of the standard features that are found on an Adventure Bike; a windscreen and a large (six gallon) fuel tank. There is a plethora of aftermarket products for the KLR that will all but convert the machine into a full-on Adventure Bike, and there are literally thousands of reviews and videos of the KLR on the internet from all over the world where people have modified their KLR's to suit a whole range of local requirements. The flexibility of modifications and global availability of parts was another great reason to choose the KLR 650. But there was more....

Most motorcycle owners know a little about motorcycle maintenance and this bike is simply a breeze to maintain requiring no special tools or skills to keep the thing on the road. The KLR is not fast, fancy or particularly brilliant at anything, but it is a fun bike to ride; period. It's a little tall in the seat for my 5ft 9-inch frame sporting a seat height of 35 inches so I need to be careful balancing a 400lb motorcycle on tippy toes. However, I love the absolute basic setup of the bike. The turning on of the fuel tap and pulling out of the choke lever before engine start is part of the pre-riding routine on the KLR. If I haven't ridden it in a while, I may even open the fuel cap and swish the fuel around in the tank by rocking the bike back and forth to either see or listen to how much fuel I have before I set off. These checks and actions are all part of getting to know the bike and remind me of what motorcycling is all about - fun. The more interaction you have with the bike the better your connection to the bike. It's all part of the motorcycle experience.

I don't need a fuel gauge as the engine will splutter and fart a little when I am about to run out of gas. When this happens, I immediately fiddle with the fuel cock with my left hand and turn it 90 degrees forward to the reserve position. Within a few seconds the engine positively responds and begins running normally once more. Once we are going steady, I immediately reset the trip meter on the dashboard knowing that I have about 40 miles (65 kilometres) before the engine will splutter and fart once more, except next time the engine will go very quiet, very quickly.

Being a large capacity single cylinder engine (for a motorcycle), it does suffer a little more than a smaller single cylinder engine because of its rotating mass from the natural phenomenon called vibration. As mentioned earlier, vibration is not a great trait in a motorcycle as it can cause nuts and bolts to shake themselves loose and fall off. It causes blurred visibility in the rear-view mirrors and can cause rider fatigue through handlebar, seat and foot peg tingling. When you ride a motorcycle all five of your senses are on high alert, the sense of touch is affected most by vibration and if it gets bad, your vision can also be affected. But there are things you can do to reduce the amount of vibration and the effects of the vibration on both the rider and the bike itself.

Any big single cylinder motorcycle engine like the Kawasaki KLR 650 will produce vibration. Manufactures normally reduce the engine vibration by putting counterweights that rotate 180 degrees to the crankshaft which balance out the vibration caused by the rotating mass. Some bikes have the engine mounted on solid rubber blocks to reduce the amount of engine vibration being transmitted through the bike frame. However, there is more than pure rotating mass vibration within the engine, other straight line vibrations caused by the movement of the piston, small end bearings and piston rings moving up and down the cylinder itself all add to the mix. There is no way to counter these in a single cylinder engine. To counter straight line vibration, you would need a counter piston, small end and rings and that's called a twin cylinder which can be found as standard on (much smoother) Adventure Bikes. So, the big single cylinder engine (Dual Sport bike) is always going to vibrate more than its multi cylinder big brother; the Adventure Bike.

The science behind vibration is pretty simple. An object tends to vibrate when it has been hit or disturbed from its static state. Think of what happens to a guitar string when its plucked or strummed or a metal pipe when you hit it with another piece of metal. The corresponding vibration has a frequency. Every object then has a natural frequency when it has been disturbed (think different thickness guitar strings). If the amplitude (size) of the vibrations are large enough and falls within the human hearing range, then you will hear the vibration as well as feel it. This can be good news. As an engineer, I can usually tell if an engine is running badly by the noise and amount of vibration it gives off.

The actual frequency at which an object will vibrate is determined by several factors. In a motorcycle engine there are many moving parts and as frequency = Speed divided by Wavelength, any alteration in either speed or wavelength will result in a change to the frequency of the object. So, in a motorcycle engine the vibration you are feeling is the cumulative effect of all moving parts working together. The frequency that causes the worst vibration is normally limited to a small segment of the overall rpm range available. Why? Because each part of the engine has a slightly different natural frequency. So, when all the parts are closest to their individual natural frequencies then that is the rpm that the engine really wants to shake itself to bits. In knowing this information, it's best to avoid operating the engine at those rpm. In the case of the KLR 650 this is between 4,000 and 4,300 rpm which is around the 50% mark of the available rpm (red line at 7,500 rpm). Anywhere above or below this operating band the engine still vibrates but the frequency of the vibration changes too and it doesn't seem anywhere near as bad.

As I was going to ride the KLR every day for months on end, even the slightest reduction in vibration would have a profound effect on my riding experience and fatigue tolerance. I fitted soft vibration absorbing handgrips to save my hands along with a simple friction bar on the righthand side that acted like a cruise control for hands free throttle. Larger foot pegs spread the load through my boots and a more comfortable aftermarket seat saved my arse. Intermediate rubber mounts for the handlebar mounted rear-view mirrors reduced the blur significantly throughout the rpm range.

I did over 25 modifications to my first KLR 650 in preparation for the big trip. Many were quite minor like an iridium spark plug, magnetic sump plug, larger engine driven sprocket (lowers the RPM for any given speed), a main stand (to assist with tyre changes) and a rear brake cylinder guard but all were well thought through and not all were associated with reducing vibration. I fitted lowering links called Dog Bones to the rear suspension which made the bike much easier to handle when stationary. However, in lowering the bike's seat height

My modified 2014, KLR 650. Fairfax, USA, 2015

the ground clearance is also reduced so the bike sits closer to the ground. Modification (shortening) of the side stand is then necessary for the bike to retain an adequate lean angle when parked on the kick stand. The two most expensive modifications were front crash bars and luggage, both of which are normally a standard fit on Adventure bikes or readily available accessories. Although the cost of all these modifications was around $1,200 USD, the KLR 650 was still the best bet for the trip in my view. However, my rationale for getting one would be put to the test big time in 2016.

The logistics involved for a world tour is immense. It was by far the most exciting and most complex event I had ever been involved with planning and the excitement of doing the trip grew daily. From the outset, responsibilities for the planning fell naturally to our previous experience and abilities. Alex did the overall route planning ensuring we would visit all the places we wanted to see as well as sorting the diverse customs requirements for the bikes. I took control of the advertising, sponsorship, visas, and the start-up logistics of getting the bikes to New Zealand. All the other bits and pieces we picked up and dealt with together as we went along. There was so much shit to do – but we got stuck into it and made everything we did, fun.

The adventure would effectively be split into three phases. Phase One was all the run up preparation, physically getting the bikes and ourselves to New Zealand, completing a tour of both north and south islands followed by an anti-clockwise loop of Australia. A short break would follow where we would fly our partners to Australia for a brief holiday before we moved into Phase Two; Asia and transit through China. Somewhere in between Phase One and the short holiday, there would be a break in the proceedings for me to attend my daughter's graduation from University in New Zealand (we just didn't know the date yet). Phase Three would be Europe and transit back to the USA. That was the plan in a nutshell. But plans change and boy, did this plan change.

Initially, our original idea(s) was to try and travel through countries that not many people travel through like Nepal, India, Pakistan and Iran. I was in the ideal position, I had contacts in all the embassies so could get all the security information and visas. As a Kiwi and ex-brit, it was not much of an issue, but for Alex as an American, it was a little more complicated. My friend in the Pakistani embassy helped us a lot and was facilitating visas for both Pakistan and Iran, but the problem we were coming up against was the entry and exits points into both countries. It was at these border crossing locations that much of the security breaches and violent skirmishes was emanating. Given that it was my Pakistani friend's own family that was going to escort us through Pakistan and up to the Iranian border, neither the Pakistani or Iranian government could ensure our safety and therefore neither country would issue us a visa (Iranian visas were sorted through the Pakistani embassy). If we were flying in and out of the country's capital cities – no problem, but land crossings were a no-no.

Conversely, getting visas for both India and Nepal were a walk in the park. In fact, the Nepalese Embassy immigration chap just talked to me about Sir Edmund Hilary and the fact that his sister had met him on one of his Mt Everest visits. After listening to his story for about half an hour and asking a few questions, I gave him $40 cash and left our passports with him overnight. I picked them up in the morning and listened to a bit more of the story, and that was our visas for Nepal done. India was pretty straight forward too, once again using my embassy contacts.

Once I had told people what we were planning, those country representatives went out their way to help us put our plans together. The personal touch was great. It would have cost us a small fortune to get agents to do this work on our behalf. Getting Chinese visas took a few attempts to break through the multiple requirements of the process, but we got there in the end. Any travel through China must be done with a government approved Chinese tour guide. The Chinese visa requirements were tight as we were intending to travel through Tibet – so we never mentioned that. We were advised by our travel guide not to tell them too much at the visa processing because you can't travel through Tibet on your own, and, as we were on our own motorcycles as well, that would also raise a few alarm bells for the issuance of our visas – so we never told them that bit either. Our tour guide put some words in a very nice letter (written in Chinese of course) supporting our application for the visa. That letter made all the difference.

Taking our own bikes into China would require a whole separate process requiring the bikes to be registered in China and displaying Chinese number plates. The tour guide said we could sort all that out once we get to the Chinese border with Laos. We didn't want to jeopardize our visa application, so we just smiled and nodded at the visa official at the Chinese immigration centre depending on the answers they were looking for. I reckon that nearly all visa applications are from people who were getting into China through a major airport. Nobody would want to enter on German and Japanese motorcycles through Laos, would they.

Other Asian countries like Laos, Thailand and Cambodia were more straight forward and we had decided that for those countries and the block of 'Stans' in Western Asia we would do those as we went along. Several countries issued limited time visas so getting the visas early was no advantage if our arrival date was later than the expiry date of the visa. Once we had made it across the Bosporus Straight in Turkey, transiting from Asia into Europe, it would be all plain sailing for the Kiwi and the American. No visas required.

Visas, medical supplies and vaccinations were all part of the work up as was personal travel insurance and bike insurance. Bike insurance was a real problem. No insurance company anywhere offers insurance for around the world travel and some countries require you to take out their own countries insurance once you get there. Other insurance companies would cover certain countries (Europe in the main) but it was too hard to get it all under one policy, so we decided that we would self-insure the bikes and conform to the third-party country requirements when we came up against them. This was another good reason to do the trip on a cheaper bike.

Personal insurance was something else, and for me not being a US resident, I had to wait until we had arrived in New Zealand before I could get my travel insurance. The decision to use a New Zealand insurance company and declare my home as New Zealand, would turn out to be one of the smartest decisions I had made for this trip. I made sure that I had the best coverage possible thinking of the worst-case scenario of crashing my bike down a ravine in China or being shot in the Iranian desert and needing to be air lifted to the nearest hospital and sent home for treatment. The bike, for me, was always going to be disposable asset for an adventure like this. If shit got really serious – I was getting out of wherever we were at the time. I would simply leave the bike behind.

Alex's thinking was a little different, he was more a risk taker. Alex was a happy to ride with no helmet type of guy. Me, not so much. Our life experiences had been quite different in that respect and I considered all the risks and all the mitigation options. Alex's bike was worth three times the value of mine and being a multiple gun owner at home, he would have fought his way out of a place taking his bike with him. As it turned out my decision on both bike and personal insurance would serve me well.

The excitement of the trip got real around October 2015 when all the mods for the bike were complete and we were practicing fitting out the bikes, preparing them for shipping. I trial fitted the bike several times over the coming weeks, constantly making minor changes to the bike and my inventory, including the number plate; DC2NZ. Unfortunately, not everyone at home was as excited as I was. For my birthday, Carol (my wife to be) had bought me a Delorme Satellite

Tracker, this would be the device that would track our progress and allow everyone to follow us though our Delorme website. The tracker also allowed us to keep in contact with loved ones and friends through text messages when we were out of cell phone coverage. It was our back up communications device and turned out to be an excellent piece of kit. It also had an SOS function – so was our safety net as well - just in case shit happened.

A friend's girlfriend helped us put a website together linking up the Delorme site to our blog page and Facebook account. My graphics friend in the Pentagon helped design the logo. My sponsorship attempts were not a great success, in fact it was a major disappointment despite writing loads of letters and emails. Thousands of people ask for similar sponsorship deals and it turned out to be a bit of a lottery. We were using the American Red Cross as a beneficial charity for our efforts and they were the exception; they were very pro-active asking us (me) for

Chasing the Summer Logo and Website, 2015

money all the time. Realizing that my efforts on sponsorship were not being successful, I turned my focus to the trip itself. After all, the trip was self-funded, so sponsorship was just a nice to have. We did however manage to raise a few hundred dollars for the American Red Cross along the way. Nothing you do is ever a total failure.

Carol was a little shocked by my decision to go through with this adventure. She was worried about my being away for so long on a motorcycle just before our wedding. Also, she was shocked that I was still focused on going through with the trip at all, and I had not considered changing my plans as a result of our growing relationship. Carol thought that getting married was a game changer for me - and indeed it was, but to be honest, the thought of cancelling the trip never really entered my mind. I was excited on both fronts; the motorcycle adventure and our wedding. I had been completely focused on the adventure since Alex and I had decided we were going to do it. That was BC (Before Carol), it was merely an extension of my riding around Australia dream I had had for many years, even before I had arrived in the USA.

I was also focused on returning to the USA to marry Carol. In my mind it was going to be a terrific year and why can't you be excited about two things at the same time? As selfish as it sounds, I was going to do them both; it was a terrific way to finish my 40-year military career and start a new life with Carol.

We officially launched the adventure website over a coffee in Arlington on 12th October 2015. On Sunday 13th December our friend Bill set up a video live stream at our favorite 'Meet-Up' group venue, Starnut Gourmet Café, McLean, VA. This allowed us to discuss the preparation we had done for the adventure. We had quite a turn out. It was great to see so many people interested in what we were doing. It was fun to be asked questions and challenged by people who had done something similar. It was also a great opportunity for us to get several useful tips on a range of subjects from couch surfing to money, to medical supplies. Afterwards, Alex and I thought to ourselves that it will be interesting to see how well our planning worked out and we were looking forward to doing another video once we got back from the trip later in 2016. However, things would change significantly, and as a result, we never felt the need to do a follow up.

December 4th was the day the bikes, along with some of my other personal stuff, was dispatched to New Zealand. The trip had just got real. The next time we would see the bikes would be at Sid's, my mates place in Whakatane, New Zealand. Alex and I had both independently sorted our own flights as I needed to sort a few things out in New Zealand before the bike adventure could begin. For Alex, this was a perfect opportunity to have a bit of a holiday before the start. If I thought the trip had got real when the bikes were packed up, there were three further occasions which would re-enforce that fact.

The first was a leaving function Alex's friends had arranged for both of us in a pub in Arlington, on January 16th which was a great send off. His friends had made several lightweight gifts for me and Alex to take with us on our adventure, so we wouldn't forget the loved ones still at home. The second one was on 20th January, my last day at the New Zealand Embassy in Washington D.C. I walked out the door for the last time as a diplomat and full time military officer. A fantastic way to finish off my last three years in uniform. I felt so privileged to have represented New Zealand and to have worked and met some terrific people. It felt right to be leaving now, taking with me some great memories and with so much more to look forward too. The third one was on 21st January and was the toughest of all. This was an emotional and tearful goodbye at the airport with my Fiancée Carol as I departed for New Zealand.

As it happens both Alex and I arrived in New Zealand within 24hrs of each other. I arrived on the South Island in Blenheim (with a lost bag) and Alex arrived up north in Auckland – also without his bags. The bikes had arrived in

New Zealand on 19th January and we had intended to start the adventure on 1st February 2016. However, the New Zealand Freight Forwarder had failed to release the bikes from customs which resulted in a three-day delay at the start. Three days delay was not the end of the world, but it was the first of many more changes that were about to descend upon us. Being flexible is all part of the adventure - we would just take it all in our stride.

On arriving in New Zealand, I was already thinking about my daughter graduation which had now been confirmed as 1st April in Napier, New Zealand. This took some complicated planning. The logistics involved in my getting there from wherever we were going to be in Australia and back again needed some careful thought. My car was in storage in Blenheim on the South Island and I needed to get it serviced after three years in storage and prepositioned in my old flat mate's rental house in Wellington on the North Island. My plan for the graduation was to fly into Wellington from somewhere in Australia, pick up my car, drive to Napier, do the graduation ceremony, drive back to Wellington, put my car back in storage and then fly back to Australia – easy. What could go wrong with that plan? As it turned out, not much but the circumstances and my ability to get there on the 1st April would pose me a serious challenge.

I took the opportunity at Sid's place to reacquaint myself with my 2004, BMW R 1200 GS that Sid had been looking after for me. Alex thought I would change my mind and switch bikes for the trip, but that was never my plan for all the reasons I mentioned previously in selecting the KLR in the first place. In my mind, this once in a lifetime adventure was much bigger than the trip around Australia and I had already been around New Zealand on the BMW. In my mind, I pictured Nigel's bike stable accommodating the BMW R 1200 GS (my best bike), The Moto Guzzi Griso (Route 66) and the round the world Kawasaki KLR 650. How cool would that be. Nevertheless, I took the opportunity and lived in the moment by climbing aboard the Beemer once again and enjoyed riding the big boxer twin. I did think about how I was going to get the bike stable together after the adventure and once I was married and living in the states, but that was a question for another day.

Knowing the bikes were already in the country, Alex and I made an unscheduled call on the Freight Forwarder and got ourselves reacquainted with the bikes and took the opportunity to apply a little pressure on the staff to get them released. It worked. I am convinced that had we not visited, the

Reunited with the KLR, Auckland, NZ, 2016

bikes would have been there another week or so, nobody seemed to care. Now they cared.

The following day, we caught up with Gareth Morgan, a famous New Zealand businessman, economist, investment manager and motorcycle adventurer. Gareth gave us a great insight to adventure riding from someone who had ridden through North Korea from Russia. Gareth has written numerous books on adventure riding and shares the same enthusiasm for riding as his wife. He also cooks a mean steak.

It was the perfect motivational start we needed for our own adventure. Thanks Gareth.

As per my master sub-logistical plan for my daughter's graduation, I still needed to get my car to Wellington ready for when I returned sometime in March. So, I decided to leave my car with Sid whilst we toured New Zealand, then once the bikes were being prepared for Air Freighting to Australia, I would fly back to Sid from Auckland, pick up my car, drive to Wellington and then fly directly to Sydney from Wellington. Alex would fly out from Auckland to Sydney and we would meet in Sydney International Airport (Freight Dept) to get the bikes out of customs. Simple enough....

The 31st January 2016 was my last paid day in the Air Force and was the end of my full-time military career. I was now Mr Sainsbury. On 18th January 1977, I had joined the Royal Air Force. I would retire with a total of 39 years and 14 days Military Service. I felt proud. Not bad for a lad from the Welsh Valleys. I had no real idea what I was going to do when I got back to Carol after the trip, but it didn't matter. I was as excited about getting back to Carol just as much as I was excited about the adventure I was just about to undertake. I felt that I had earned this once in a lifetime opportunity. The last year and a half of planning was just about to play out for real. It had been a long time coming. I was healthy, had money, kids were all sorted, and I was in a stable relationship and about to get married later in the year. This all added up to making Nigel a very happy man. All the little hiccups along the way like lost luggage, incompetent people and delays are quickly forgotten about because the adventure is much, much bigger than those distractions. We choose only to remember the good times because they are the ones that matter.

Day one had arrived (Friday, February 5th) - just four days later than our original plan. Not the best of starts weather wise but it didn't really matter, the adventure was underway. Sid and his family had been terrific hosts and had looked after Alex and I really well. We were escorted out of Whakatane by Surts (of Route 66 fame) and *"the Captain"* who was a biker friend of Surts. I had not travelled very far before I needed to stop and redistribute the weight on the bike. The front end was so light, it was a little scary to handle and the wet conditions were not

Day 1, Zero Miles & Wet, Whakatane, NZ, 2016

helping. I had too much weight on the back. Several adjustments later and it was better but still not great. I was wondering what had happened to all the trial fits and preparation I had done. It would take me a few days to get the weight distribution correct. Even a small amount of weight in the wrong place on the KLR can make a huge difference to the handling characteristics of the bike.

After a coffee stop and a classic Friday kiwi lunch of Fish and Chips (said *'Fush n Cheps'* in Kiwiland), we said goodbye to our escorts and continued south towards Whitby, Wellington, where we were teaming up with my mate Phil and his family. Phil had taken a few weeks off work and was joining us for the tour of the South Island. Phil had a new KTM 1290

Adventurer and needed to get it out of Wellington, what better way to do it than a tour of the South Island.

For both Alex and I, sharing the experience with mates was as important as our own experience. The more people that could tag along with us for any part of the adventure, the better the adventure would be for us. Phil joining us gave us the opportunity to stay with his family, so a nice meal and a comfy bed before a big ride is always welcome – it's all part of the experience. You don't need to be roughing it all the time, even though this was still only day two.

Any tour of the South Island from the north begins with one of the best and most impressive ferry journeys in the world and a mini sea adventure in itself. Cruising through the Marlborough Sounds on the South Island is a sight to behold and once off the boat you are greeted with well-maintained twisty roads that are sparsely populated with traffic. The roads meander through some of the most spectacular countryside you could ever wish to see. Welcome to the South Island. I had decided that we should go anti-clockwise down the west coast around the bottom and back up the east coast. Alex was normally the navigational lead on our bike adventures, but this was my home, so it was fitting that I took the lead for this part of the adventure. He would get his lead role back in Australia.

I had made the conscious decision not to book any accommodation in advance, convinced that we would find something, just like our travels in the USA. However, this was not the USA and it was summer when accommodation is at a premium. We had our tents as back up, but we never really wanted to use them. They were mostly for show and emergency use only. It was a motorcycle adventure after all not a camping expedition.

Even before we started the adventure, Alex and I considered the tour of New Zealand to be a bit of a warm up for us and shake down of the bikes. We would fine tune our loads and adjust the bikes as we went along. It was just day five of the adventure and the KLR had started to shed a little of the excessive weight I was carrying. A bolt had decided to part company with the bike holding on my left-hand rear pannier. I suspect it was the vibration, but more bits were to fall off as we made it around the South Island. I should have used Loctite on everything, but thank goodness for the emergency plastic tie-wrap. Hell, those things are strong and was holding the pannier together pretty well and better than the nut and bolt had done. It was also the day I realized that I needed to modify my side stand as the bike tipped over at a gas station because of the shallow lean angle. The all up weight had lowered the bike overall so the kick stand needed to be shortened. There was a growing list of jobs to do before we moved onto Australia. Despite these small inconveniences the KLR 650 was loving the New

Bottom of the South, Bluff, NZ, 2016

Zealand roads and although it was not a race, it was having no trouble keeping up and cruising with the BMW and KTM.

Invercargill is the hometown of a famous New Zealander, Burt Munroe, the guy who was the inspiration for the film, the World's Fastest Indian. We visited his record-breaking site at

Bonneville Salt Flats in 2013 during the Route 66 adventure and here we were back in his home town where it all started. We took the opportunity to visit the Hammer Hardware store where the Burt Munroe memorabilia museum is located. This is a must for any motorcycle enthusiast visiting the city. It is very cool and very Kiwi. Makes me proud to be a New Zealander.

We reached Bluff on the bottom of the South Island on day seven which was a landmark day. This would be the furthest south Alex and I would travel for our whole adventure. The KLR celebrated the occasion by shedding a few more fasteners. At this rate, there would be nothing left to shake down by the time we had finished the New Zealand part of the adventure. The KLR was literally vibrating itself to pieces. The plastic tie wraps continued to work well, but I did feel the need to get this sorted sooner rather than later much to the amusement of Alex and Phil. Both of them thought it highly entertaining to warn people that my bike was prone to shedding fasteners by placing a homemade poster on my luggage rack.

My KLR & Warning Sign, South Island, NZ, 2016

Apart from Alex hitting a bird and getting it stuck in his engine and my luck running out booking motel accommodation necessitating us to use our tents for one night, the ride north up the east coast of the South Island was uneventful. I did my best to try and convince Alex and Phil that our camping out for one night was a great opportunity to shake down our emergency sleeping equipment, but they weren't buying it. We had more than a few Guinness's in the bar that night in Kaikora and I thought I would impress them with my rendition of *'Knocking on Heavens Door'* on the electric guitar at an open mic night. At least it lightened the mood and give everyone something else to talk about other than sleeping in a tent and bits falling off the KLR.

The last place we visited on the South Island was the Marlborough wine region. A great opportunity to show Alex my piece of New Zealand (my house) in the little town of Renwick. I also introduced Alex and Phil to my local *'Moa'* brewery. It was here that I had the opportunity to demonstrate to Phil and Alex what usually happens to people after they had consumed too much beer and were riding pushbikes. Yep, even before I had consumed any alcohol, both the KLR and I ended up horizontal on the gravel in the car park. Ummm, that was the second time the bike had gone over in a week. If I had forgotten about adjusting the side stand, this was another reminder to get it done.

It was sad to say goodbye to Phil after we crossed back onto the North Island, we had a fantastic time touring all over the south. We immediately caught up with my other friends Dave and Marion who looked after us that first night back on the North Island. The next day (day 10) was our first rest day and I took the time to catch up with my kids before Alex and I moved on to my other friends Richard and Kay. This is how friendships work in New Zealand and it was a great opportunity for Alex to experience some more kiwi hospitality.

Richard joined Alex and I the next day for a few hours riding as we made our way further north. Once again, it was fantastic to be able to call on great friends to share the adventure. Richard also had a BMW R1200 GS Adventurer and suggested that we take a route that had a few stretches of dirt tracks which was absolutely fine with us. This also afforded Alex and I a great opportunity to see how our luggage laden bikes would perform off road.

DC3 Cafe at Mangaweka, NZ, 2016

Although I am used to riding on unsealed and gravel roads, the weight of the KLR bike and the distribution of the weight was not conducive to off road riding. The light handling took me a little by surprise. Riding a heavy bike that was light at the front took a lot of concentration on a rough road and I was exhausted at the end of it. The longest of the unsealed portions was only about six miles (10 kilometres) long, but it seemed to go on forever. Both myself and Alex were relieved to be reunited with sealed pavement at the end of it. The weight issue, like the side stand would need to be sorted before we moved onto Australia.

A quick coffee at a kiwi bird sanctuary and a little lunch further down the road at the unique DC3 aircraft café at

Mangaweka was where we shook Richard's hand, thanked him for his hospitality and off-road riding experience before going our separate ways.

We were heading back to Sid's place at Whakatane. Surts lived just down the road and I had a big favour to ask him. After dropping the KLR twice due to side stand issues, I asked Surts if he could modify the stand. What would have taken me a few hours, Surts had the side stand off, modified and back on the bike in just over five minutes – seriously! This man does not mess about, he had even sprayed it black for me before he put it back on. The man is a technical genius with an angle grinder and welding torch. It was just perfect.

Modification of the KLR Side Stand, Whakatane. NZ. 2016

Surts had also decided that he would join Alex and I for the tour to the top part of the North Island. On route, Surts was keen to show us the picturesque Coromandel. It was not the best of conditions being wet, windy and slippery. Also, as time went on, the road surface seemed to be getting worse but the weather better, it was a little confusing until I realized that I had gotten a puncture in my rear tyre. This was the first puncture of the trip and there is never a pleasant time to get one, but when you do, you gotta sort it out – where ever you are.

Being an aircraft engineer I had the right tools and was preparing to get it all done nice and neatly when Surts (who is a car mechanic and boat engineer) couldn't bear to stand and watch me methodically remove the rear wheel to change the tube. Thinking it would take me a about an hour or so, he leapt into action and in 25 minutes I was back on the road. The shake down of tools and equipment worked perfectly. The KLR was certainly testing our preparations whilst giving us a good work out in unloading and loading up the bikes.

Dave and Wendy were the penultimate family we were visiting and staying with during our tour of New Zealand, they lived in a place called Kerikeri. Dave was my mentor when I

First Puncture, North Island, NZ, 2016

first arrived in New Zealand in 2004 and the whole family had become a great support network over the years. It was a great place to stop off before reaching the Top of the North Island and Cape Reinga. We arrived absolutely soaked through to the skin. It had been a miserable wet and windy day overall making the riding quite tiring and at times bloody hard work. The scenery (when you could look up and see it) was stunning.

We spent the evening at Dave and Wendy's just relaxing, drying out drinking beer and wine and enjoying some great kiwi hospitality - again. Although the fasteners had stopped falling off the KLR, the riding lamps that I had fitted to the crash bars were becoming the next casualty of the dreaded vibration. The right-hand side had suffered fatigue cracking on the bracket. So, rather than waste more tie-wraps, I made the bike a little lighter (no pun intended) and ripped them both off before they fell off.

We had been on the road for two weeks with just one day off. It was awesome fun, but we were feeling a little bit tired and was looking forward to a short break. The weather forecast heading towards the top of the North Island was not good, and we knew it was going to be a tough ride in such poor conditions. The distance we had intended to travel was going to make the day one of the longest yet. If we thought the weather was shite yesterday getting to Dave and Wendy's, Mother Nature was about to show us something worse.

The first hour was just bloody awful. The rain was constant and with the strong winds, we were getting hammered. However, it had started to clear up a bit as we were reaching the Cape; even the sun had started to make an appearance now and again and seemed to be encouraging

Top of the North, Cape Reinga, NZ, 2016

us to keep going. In fact, when the sun did shine it got warm really quickly and we were almost cooking by the time we reached Cape Reinga.

Witnessing the Tasman Sea meeting the Pacific Ocean at the tip of New Zealand is incredible. Seeing the two different colors of the water coming together and reaching out in the distance,

248

you can fully appreciate why the Maori treat this special place as a spiritual site. Like Bluff on the South Island, the Cape has a world signpost and of course we needed to do the half a mile walk to get the mandatory picture before getting back on the bikes and heading south. Weather stayed good for us until about 30 miles (48 kilometres) out from our destination then the heavens opened up once again and Mother Nature reminded us once more who was in charge. It was the longest day yet having covered 355 miles (570 kilometres) in some 11 hours.

Even though we were all soaked and was struggling to dry our things out, it really didn't bother us, and I would suggest that it wouldn't bother other motorcyclists either. Thinking, if I had been in a car and got soaked, it would have been a real inconvenience and even a little irritating but when you are on the bike these kinds of things are acceptable and even fun. Yes, we would prefer not to get wet, but it didn't matter, we still made it to our destination and the fact we arrived in adverse weather made it a real accomplishment and dare I say, even more memorable – it was another experience to add to the adventure. Our motto of *'Chasing the Summer 2016'* really was playing out in New Zealand. We were literally chasing the good weather, we could see it in front of us, but we seem to be travelling towards it at the same pace it was moving away.

Day 15 was a day of challenges. We needed to get the bikes into Auckland, have them serviced, including tyre replacement, drained of fuel, pressure washed, prepared for flight and delivered to Qantas freight by 4pm ready to be transported (flown) to Sydney, Australia. The weather was sunny and fine and working with us today. We had a leisurely ride to the Devonport Naval Museum for coffee and breakfast which allowed us to shake hands and say goodbye to our companion Surts, who had been with us for whole soaking trek north and of course escorted us on day one of our New Zealand adventure. We had booked both bikes into Experience BMW, Kingsland, Auckland for an 11:00 am appointment and on arrival the team immediately got to work on the bikes knowing that we were against the clock. Alex and I used our time wisely and got haircuts and did some emergency shopping. The Experience BMW team were excellent and even helped sort transportation for us and the bikes to Auckland airport.

We loaded the bikes on the truck and were underway for the airport around 3pm. The truck driver got us to the Qantas courier around 4pm where we met our Qantas agent Jacob. Jacob was superb and got the bikes and all the paperwork sorted for us. The bikes would be ready for collection at the Qantas Freight section in Sydney Airport within the next week. Alex and I walked away thinking what an incredible day and indeed, what a fantastic New Zealand adventure we had just had. My friend Pam picked us up from the airport and took us back to her home where we caught up with the two East Bound Crew members from our 2013 Route 66 adventure, Paul (Pam's husband) and Ian. This was a fantastic way to formally close off the New Zealand leg of Chasing the Summer.

New Zealand had been a real test for the bikes, the equipment we were carrying (tents and tools) and a test of our logistical planning prowess. It was the only part of the adventure that I was effectively the lead player. I was on my home ground, and I had ridden on all the roads we travelled at some point in the last 10 years. Apart from sorting the shipping of the bikes out of New Zealand, this leg had been a holiday for Alex and quite rightly so as it was his first time in New Zealand. It was great that he could literally sit back and enjoy the ride. His expertise in route planning and logistics was about to play out in Australia and beyond. The KLR had performed admirably. The issues I had with the bike were, on reflection, all of my own doing. I was still very happy with the KLR and I had ironed out the niggly snags. However, Alex and I had re-learnt a lesson of the past and decided that we were carrying around too much shit again. We reviewed everything and left behind (in New Zealand) over half the stuff we were carrying. It was an incredible and liberating feeling. We were down to essentials now and loving it - it felt good. All that we needed to do now was look forward to the anticlockwise trek around the not so little continent of Australia.

It was great to receive constant support and encouragement from loved ones and friends back in the USA. Social media is awesome for this kind of thing. We had our Facebook page operational and the Delorme tracking device was working well so people could see where we were all the time on our world map. However, we were travelling to fast and our days were far too full to keep the website blog running so we let that lapse and just updated the Facebook page instead – it was much easier. We had travelled some 3,608 miles (5,800 kilometres) in 15 days around New Zealand and not many of those miles were on straight roads. New Zealand is not just the country of the 'long white cloud', it is also the country of the 'twisty roads' and the 'one lane bridge.' We must have gone over hundreds of these tight single lane bridges. I never get tired of motorcycling in New Zealand – I love it. To me, it is the best country in the world for two wheels, but maybe I am a little biased as it is my home. Can't wait to get back and ride throughout Middle Earth once again.

The day after we left the bikes with our freight forwarder, Qantas in Auckland, Alex and I went our separate ways for the next five days. I needed to get sorted for returning to New Zealand for my daughter's graduation whilst Alex spent a little more time in Auckland before making his way to Sydney and setting up our base ready for the start of the Australian adventure. My logistics plan for nipping back for my daughter's graduation from somewhere in Australia was firming up. The plan was complex with many moving parts that included being dependent on others doing certain things for me at specific times.

On day 21, I flew out from Wellington roughly the same time the bikes flew out from Auckland and we arrived at Sydney International Airport terminal almost at the same time. Alex was already there. The logistical plan for Australia had worked a dream. The freight team at Qantas had the bikes processed by 11:00 am and all was looking great until the bike's carnet-de-passage (bike passports) were being held over by bio-security who would not process the bikes after 3pm in the afternoon; for no reason other than it might take them over two hours and they didn't want to stop the checks half way through to go home. We were told that it was a locally enforced policy and was not negotiable. It certainly smelt a little like bullshit bureaucracy to us and we found it extremely frustrating.

Although the bio security fiasco was annoying, we used the rest of the afternoon to sort compulsory third-party Australian motor insurance. After some twenty plus phone calls over a couple of hours with a commitment to part with a shit load of money, we were eventually covered. It was one of the most painful and frustrating experiences on the phone I have ever had. It pushed dealing with the bio-security obstructionists into second place. The problem was we were foreigners with no permanent address in Australia and were riding bikes that had not been subjected to Australian regulatory motoring standards. So, perhaps it was not surprising that I had to tell a few fibs to get us coverage and even then, I could only get coverage for 30 days. I was thinking to myself, what a piss poor welcome we were having in Australia - and this leg of the adventure was all my idea.

It was not the best start, but the Qantas team were excellent and there was a good old kiwi bro from the Qantas freight team who looked after us. He took us to the local gas station, so we could get some fuel for the bikes when they were eventually released from bio-security. It was a long day sorting the logistics and a frustrating train ride to the hotel (Alex's home for the last week), but we finished the day with a bit of sightseeing on Sydney Harbour and reflecting on the experience over a beer. We were adamant we would get the bikes out of the airport the following morning.

The next day Alex and I were fired up for a fight with the bullshit Australian bureaucracy. Our early arrival at the bio security desk at the airport showed we meant business and actually worked wonders. They recognized us immediately and the bikes were inspected and released within 20 minutes. What the fuck! What was all the grandstanding about timings

Unloading the KLR, Sydney, Australia, 2016

yesterday. They could have inspected the bikes five times over and still got home before 3pm. We decided not to make too much of a fuss just in case they changed their minds, so we just smiled, paid our money and walked away - with the completed paperwork.

The bikes were eventually delivered to us outside the Qantas warehouse for unstrapping and de-palletizing and after putting some fuel in the tanks, it was a great sense of achievement to hear the bikes fire up. The Qantas team were awesome once again. Thinking ahead, we decided that the rest of the day should be focused on the logistics for the next leg out of Australia and into Malaysia – which we duly did. Alex and I felt a great deal of satisfaction riding away from the airport having sorted everything out ourselves. No agents, no lawyers, no advisors. We were now free to complete our planned anti-clockwise lap of this bloody huge and wonderful continent called Australia.

Australia is one hellofa place. Distances between towns are huge, and the scenery in between can be the same for hundreds of miles. The Australian police seemed hell bent on catching speeders as we noticed all sorts of different types of speed cameras had been pre-positioned on what looked to be benign stretches of road. We knew that this part of the adventure would be a very different experience to that of New Zealand or any other part of Chasing the Summer to come. These would be long high mileage days over several weeks and from the amount of speed cameras we were seeing, we needed to be cognizant of our speed. We were left wondering if speed would indeed define our Australian adventure.

The one piece of advice we had been given about riding in Australia was to avoid riding during the period just after dusk and just before dawn – Kangaroos and Wallabies are mostly active then, along with all the other bush type creatures who unintentionally could kill you. There were plenty of other bush creatures who, on finding a dead body, could subsequently eat you too. So, Australia was a place where we could literally disappear without a trace. If we needed to understand that we were in a different country - knowing that information did it.

We got into a routine straight away and were quickly knocking out high mileage days. Riding 600 miles in 12 hours is pretty impressive and the KLR and the Beemer were on song and eating up the miles. Our music gizmos were a godsend for entertainment as were our camel baks for refreshments and throttle dampers for preventing right wrist cramps.

We would regularly hit temperatures of over 100 degrees F (38 degrees C) and for prolonged periods which is a great way to lose weight by sweating, but the heat doesn't do much for your concentration levels on boring straight roads. The challenges of riding around Australia were both mental and physical and in equal proportions. I already knew that this was going to be a very different motorcycling experience to New Zealand. Afterall, I had done my homework on this country a few years ago and I knew it would be challenging in a very different way to anything I had done before - that was one of the drivers for doing it in the first place. However, the cumulative effect of these temperatures day after day was draining and the unchanging and generally flat landscapes just added to the overall fatigue.

We could have spent a lot more time taking diversions to break up the day, but we had given ourselves a finite amount of time to get around Australia. As big as it is, it was still only part of Phase One of the overall trip and even the boring parts were still better than sitting at a desk in an office. As we made progress north the road surfaces had started to deteriorate so avoiding potholes became a welcome distraction to break up the monotony. Other than that, all we had to look at was what seemed like the world's supply of sugar cane and bananas.

These crops hugged the road on both sides up the east coast and seemed to go on forever.

To reduce the amount of time we spent in the heat, we figured that the best times to ride was very early in the morning - just before light, and then again after 5pm. This really went against the advice we had been given by the locals about animals that live in the outback. So, it was a tossup between being hit by a wild animal or being worn down by the bloody heat index. Everything in Australia is out to get you – including the heat. How that phrase would ring true in just a few days' time.

Accommodation was a little different from New Zealand. Essentially, you paid more for less. The further you went into the outback and away from civilization the accommodation star rating system plummeted into the minus numbers along with your chances of availability. Both these factors were then proportional to the additional dollar cost the motel would charge if you just pitched up on the day. Afterall, just nipping a hundred miles (160 kilometres) down the road to the next motel (which could be worse) at the end of a tiring day was not really a viable option. We could of course camp out in the outback in our nylon tents with all the creatures that come alive at night to look for food, but that was not a popular consideration either. What we ended up doing was planning a few days ride ahead and then making a call the day before on the preferred destination and the accommodation. That also gave us a bit of a target destination to aim for and took the uncertainty out of finding available accommodation.

Even the wildlife stayed at some of the motels. I was greeted by a very large frog (about the size of a size 7 shoe) outside our motel room deep in the heart of Queensland. I was making my way to the shower; the frog was on his way out. It was going to be another scorcher of a day with temperatures reaching 107 degrees F (40 degrees C) with very high humidity. The frog never told me that because Aussie frogs cannot talk, but the frog was an omen. The day would be dominated by wildlife, mainly suicidal creatures trying to get themselves killed or cause themselves enough harm to claim off our insurance policies. They would either throw themselves into the path of our motorcycles or just hold their ground in the road causing us to take evasive action. We faced cattle, kangaroos, snakes, birds, bats and a few other living creatures that we couldn't really identify. Rather than try to confirm what creature we had just missed by stopping or turning around, we kept on trucking in the direction we were going, thinking it was safer to keep going than to simply satisfy our curiosity on what could have potentially killed us.

The heat index seemed to continue to rise as we headed west into the Northern Territory from Queensland, it was unrelenting. We had to keep dousing ourselves regularly with water just to keep ourselves cool to hold our concentration. I did feel that every day we were getting a little better acclimatized to the conditions. But as soon as I had one of those thoughts, the heat seemed to increase and would be absolutely brutal for a time afterwards just to prove me wrong.

Other than critters and heat there were a few other things to watch out for on the Australian outback roads; Road Trains, Fire and Flash Flooding. Road trains are trucks that can have multiple trailers fitted and are regularly over 180 feet (54 metres) in length, carrying a mass of up to 125 tonnes, and are capable of travelling at speeds in excess of 60 mph. They carry animals, raw materials and general logistics – all in the same vehicle (train). You had to plan your overtaking maneuver as it could take you a good 20 seconds or more to get passed them on the KLR. That's a long time to be alongside such a massive vehicle on a motorcycle. If they were coming towards you in the opposite direction, you simply slowed down and pulled over as far as you could because if they were travelling at speed the wake turbulence behind these trains could easily catch you off guard and scare the shit out of you.

Bush fires were also common in the Northern Territory and Western Australia and they were often left to burn themselves out. We passed a few bush fires and they were a little scary. The flames could easily stretch into the road - as if it wasn't hot enough. The red dusty earth as a backdrop to the flames made the place we were

Passing a Road Train, Australia, 2016

travelling through look like a real living hell.

The other road hazard was flash flooding. We were in Australia during the rainy season. We had already been advised by the Cairns locals to miss the road that went north due to part of the road already being washed out. Even the more direct route west, was susceptible to flash flooding. I had read about flash flooding and if the locals wouldn't risk it, we would have been stupid not to heed their advice. Due to micro weather systems, the actual downpour that causes the flash flooding could happen many miles from where you were, so being caught in a down pour was not always the pre-curser to experiencing a flash flood. We could get caught in one at any time; it was pretty obvious by the soak channels that had been formed on the side of the road by fast flowing water where the majority of the flash floods had occurred in the past.

Once we had entered the Northern Territory, we could legally cruise at 80 mph (130kph) the legal speed limit. A real sweet spot for the KLR, it just loved that cruising speed. It still vibrated, but not nearly as much as travelling at 60-70 mph. The engine felt as if it could go all day at that speed, so I usually got it there as quickly as possible and kept it there for as long as I could. Indeed, most of the miles in this section were covered at around 80 mph. The gas and food stations/ accommodation (road houses) seemed to get further apart, typically they are around every 100 miles (160 kilometres), so you had to seriously consider overshooting one. What we didn't expect was an unscheduled stop by a local policeman at 11am in a place called Avon Downs just inside the Northern Territory, it was at this routine stop that we were both breathalyzed. This was a first for us. The policeman admitted they had a bit of an alcohol problem there. No shit!

Classic Australian Shop Name, Australia, 2016

On the lighter side of life, Australians have a wicked sense of humour, and you don't have to look very far to witness it. Sometimes its splattered all over a shop front like this little fishing shop titled

Master Bait and Tackle. We also found a small café in the outback called 'Gobble n' Go'.

The flash flooding water often runs through creeks and there are thousands of them. One of the funniest ones was called *'Norainhere Creek'*. The prominent red earth/ground in Australia is everywhere, it is like riding on the surface of Mars (not that I have ever been to Mars, but it looks like it), the oxides turn the soil red and there are few nutrients in the soil which generally makes it very baron. The boredom of the landscape is often only broken up by termite towers some of which have been decorated with tee shirts, hats and bras. Very funny. Again, just gotta love the Australians and their sense of humour. However, these things would be like living creatures out of a Stephen King novel at nighttime – not so funny then perhaps.

Showering Everything after a Month, Australia, 2016

After a month on the road and the last week riding in the stinking and intense heat, everything I had worn was smelling of stale sweat. Even the bugs were refusing to rest on me. The day I noticed I was smelling bad I was so fricking hot, I walked into the motel shower with all my gear on, crash helmet, boots, jacket, gloves – everything! I washed everything as I was taking it off and then washed myself and all my clothing a second time. Drying stuff off was not too much of an issue in Australia.

Constant exposure to the heat was not only wearing us out and shrinking our bodies, it was also destroying our tyres, and playing hell with our electronic equipment. My little Sony Walkman would give up playing songs less than half way through the morning ride. It was clearly not made for the Australian market.

Gone were the banana and sugar cane plantations of the east coast. Our trek west was now dominated by Eucalyptus trees and termite mounds – they were everywhere, and it was beginning to feel a lot like Groundhog Day but resetting itself every hour. Like the east coast ride, we looked forward to diversions, only in this part of Australia it was most often an old washed-out road allowing us to ride on some of the Australian red-rock rough track.

We found a cool pub called Daly Waters, just off one of these diversions. These buildings look completely derelict from the outside but there is always a welcome *'G'day mate'* voice reaching out to you when you walk inside. This watering hole was full of memorabilia from just about anyone who had visited over the last 15 years, so we

Daly Waters Pub, Daly Waters, Australia, 2016

were chuffed that we could leave one of our signed bandana's behind for display. These bandanas made great gifts for people and was the brainchild of Sarah, Alex's Fiancée. They were light and very useful for a whole range of things from cooling you down, to wiping your dirty hands to toilet paper. And of course, perfect to give to people who had helped us along the way – but not the ones we planned to use for toilet paper of course.

We stopped in a place called Birdum for lunch, and they had a fascinating collection of Port, there was one called *'Fucking Good Port'*, also known as *'Good Fucking Port'*. The Studmasters Port had an interesting label of a flaccid penis. And the *'Horny Tawny'* port guaranteed not to let you down. Australians!! Gotta love em. These ports clearly left little to the imagination as to their effects on you. No wonder the Police were out breathalyzing.

We were making great progress west and it was Day 30 of the adventure when we arrived at a place called Katherine, Northern Territory. We had decided to stay at this very neat motel called the Paraway Motel. It also had a cool outside swimming pool which was a welcome end to our day. Our host, Bronwyn made us feel really welcome and it turned out she was also a keen Ducati rider. Bronwyn knew first hand how brutal riding in the Australian sun could be, and in the spirit of true Australian hospitality, kept us supplied with beers whilst we took advantage of the swimming pool.

We had decided on a late start the following day after a very pleasant evening chatting about life and bikes to our host and her sister Chef Louise. The heat was particularly grueling and by the time we were dressed and said our goodbyes, we were already sweating like addicts in a drug store. Unfortunately, the Kawasaki had a different idea and failed to start – no power at all - nothing. I immediately diagnosed the problem and set about pulling out the battery which, to my surprise, was not just low but was all but completely dry. Unbelievable, I have never seen a battery like this. I knew that I would need a new battery, so I just filled it up with tap water – yes, ordinary tap water. I knew it would not do the battery much good, but this

KLR Battery, Katherine, Australia, 2016

battery was knackered anyway, we just needed to get the bike going. After about 30 minutes faffing around and filling a bucket full of sweat, the bike fired up.

The combination of the late start, bike not starting and the fact that I felt I was physically melting, we decided that what we really needed was a swim. As we had not fixed a destination for the day, we decided to stay put, have a day off and stay another night at the Paraway Motel and help Bronwyn with reducing her beer stock. It was a good call. The friendship we built up during our short stay would pay real dividends for me in particular in just three days' time. The whole staff at the Paraway Motel were just awesome and if you ever find yourselves in Katherine, the Paraway Motel is the only place to stay.

In a way the KLR battery running dry was a good thing. We had been on the road for over a month and a complete day's rest really did recharge our batteries (including the KLR's). The following morning, we were up and ready to go and it was still dark. We had intentions of making it well into Western Australia, so we needed to crack on and get the miles under our belt. The KLR fired up no problem with its new tap water filled battery and we were making good time. Around midday we could see the dark clouds forming and we were heading right towards them and into our first major Australian storm.

We were looking forward to a bit of cooling rain and we were not disappointed. We got an awesome wetting although the cooling effect was short lived. These storms literally just dump water, it's not even real rain, it really is like a dumping of water out of the sky. Not surprisingly, flash flooding occurs, and it happens very quickly (in a flash). We came across our first proper washed out road from this storm at a place called Ord River. The water was rushing over the road really quickly and we had no idea how deep it was. We could see across the other side, but we thought we would wait a little. A couple of cars diligently made it through, but it was way up to the sills of the car and the water really was flowing too fast to

Flash Flooding Water Crossing, Ord River, Australia, 2016

risk it on a bike.

A road train approached a few minutes later and didn't even slow down it went straight through it. With such weight and momentum, the train hardly slowed at all. The good news was that the water dies down just as quickly as it rises, so even in the space of 10 minutes, the depth and volume of water had slowed quite a bit. We waited another few minutes before I walked across the road to see how deep the water was and to identify the track we should follow. The water reached about half way up my calf and was flowing quickly but not enough to unbalance me (even on my bad leg) so we thought it would be safe enough to attempt a crossing. We both made it across – no problem. The key to these water crossings is to cross at a diagonal and focus on the other side of the road. Once you have started to cross you have to keep going. Looking down or watching the water flowing at right angles to you on the bike is a recipe for an unsuccessful crossing and a water landing.

Our next challenge was not that far away and was literally just down the road where we found ourselves travelling through a different kind of dark cloud, and it wasn't a weather cloud. It was a huge cloud of locusts. We never even saw them coming until it was too late, they seem to appear out of nowhere. Bloody hell these things were massive and there were literally millions of them. They almost blocked out the sun there were so many of them. It was like riding into a set from an Alfred Hitchcock movie. Like the rain, the locusts went as quickly as they came but boy, it was pretty scary riding through the cloud. It was like being in a free for all paintball game where everyone was shooting at us. Luckily, I had no exposed skin, but if I had they would have caused me some harm. We stopped for fuel in a place called Halls Creek just a few miles from the locust storm and decided to stay there for the night. A couple of cars pulled in for fuel and you could hardly see the front grill and lights there were so many locusts covering them - unbelievable. We had picked up a few hundred hitch hikers ourselves and would spend the next hour cleaning the bikes (and ourselves) with hoses. These things had found refuge in all sorts of strange places on the bike and in our clothing; one had found refuge on the back side of my engine and had begun to cook.

The KLR was going well and was just loving lapping up the high mileage days, but the rest of the bike had started to show additional signs of fatigue from the constant vibration. The left-hand pannier bracket had started to crack and would require welding. A few tie-wraps did the job, but I would need a more permanent solution real soon. Little did I know that I would have a permanent solution for this tomorrow, but that would come at significant cost and would be associated with a few other issues that would demand my attention.

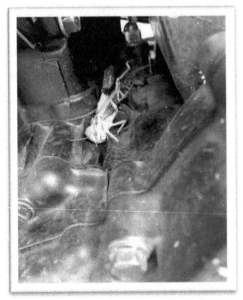

Cooking Locusts, Halls Creek, Australia, 2016

The next day was Day 32 of the adventure, it was Tuesday 8th March. My daughters 22nd Birthday. We had plans to reach the Indian Ocean today at Broome on the west coast. We had set off on yet another early start from Halls Creek, completely free of locust hitchhikers. Again, the weather was hot but the riding good – the riding was always good. In fact, today would see us reach the half way mark around Australia. The terrain had started to look a little like Utah from our Route 66 experience and that had encouraged me to take a few photos along the way. As was normal, I often dropped back behind Alex to take the photos and then speed up again afterwards to catch him up. It was just something that I had done since we had been riding together; it was no big deal. We never let ourselves get too far apart just in case we end up going in different directions. Australia was quite different to anything we had done before, there was often only one road and you could see for miles and the distances between intersections were huge. We had been riding for well over three hours on this particular morning and had clocked up around 180 miles (280 kilometres) without a stop.

For some time, the road surface had not been perfect with some dips in parts and the occasional rut caused by the heavy road trains. This caused the steering to flicker a little every now and again. It was perfectly normal, or rather we had gotten quite used to it. I could see Alex about a mile or so in the distance and I knew we were going to be stopping shortly for fuel as we were about five miles (eight kilometres) out from Fitzroy Crossing. I was clearly catching him up when I started to experience this phenomenon in the steering. I didn't know exactly how fast I was going but it would have been around about my usual speed of 80 mph. Then in what seemed to be a period of a heartbeat, the small steering flicker became a rapid snatching of the handlebars. The bike immediately changed heading and veered off to the right even though I was gripping the handlebars hard and keeping them straight. In a split second the bike had switched lanes and was heading for the bush on the other side of the road. I instinctively knew that the front tyre had blown out, although I choose not to look down to confirm. I could feel the vibration of the unbalanced wheel throughout the whole bike. I immediately backed off the throttle, applied the rear brake and was fighting with the bike to keep it upright and heading straight. Both the tyre and tube had become jelly on the wheel and the tyre had lifted off the rim completely forcing the bike to drift constantly to the right even with the handle bars held straight. Luckily nothing was coming towards me.

There had been nothing on this road for miles other than the odd tree, rocks and scrub but now I was close to a small intersection and had a few obstacles to contend with. Let's call them targets because that's exactly what they had become in that moment. I remember having three choices and none of them were good. I was going to hit something - period. The bike was not going to stay on the sealed road, the drift right was far too strong and even the mere suggestion of a slight counter steer to the left would have thrown the bike horizontal onto the road and me with it. I must have had less than a second or two to decide. The obstacles were also close together and the bike was on a direct trajectory toward them. It was all I could do to hang on and stay upright. The first obstacle was a selection of large rocks, closely followed by two different roads signs which were obstacles two and three – obstacle two, was a road sign that was at head level signifying a junction and was facing me. Obstacle three was a low-down road sign signifying the direction of travel and was running parallel to the road. I decided in a Nano second that hitting the sign facing me was by far the best option. The rocks were huge and would stop me dead in my tracks and, at this speed, the outcome would be very unpleasant for me and the bike. Obstacle three had the potential to cut me in half like a knife, which left the smaller upright sign of obstacle two being my best option.

The sign became my sole focus, my target, for that split second. It might as well have said 'Hit Me'. The steering was becoming harder to control each revolution of the wheel, so I hung on as tight as I could and became totally focused on the sign. I held the bike steady, missed the rocks and hit my target head on at what must have been about 40 mph. The bike and I came to rest about 20 feet (6 metres) from where the sign post had been standing. I had completely leveled the sign – job done.

I stood up and carefully took off my crash helmet as I had banged my head during the tumble. I was hurting - hurting a lot. I knew I had broken several ribs on my right side (it felt very familiar) and my right leg and knee was hurting like hell. Both felt like they were on fire and I was very unstable standing up. The front end of the bike looked exactly how I felt –

Dead KLR and Road Sign, Fitzroy Crossing, Australia, 2016

completely fucked! I knew that this accident was serious. There were people on site within minutes. Alex made it back to me pretty quickly and we knew that this was not something we could fix on the side of the road with a tie-wrap and a Leatherman pocket knife - although I had both.

The adrenaline had started to wear off, so I took a selfie (as you do) before being loaded into the ambulance where I knew I would need to focus on managing my pain. I was taken to the local medical centre for assessment and remained conscious all the time.

I also knew deep in my heart that this was the likely end of my once-in-a-lifetime motorcycle adventure. The smashed front end of the KLR, my leg and chest pain were telling me that this was not going to be something that could be fixed quickly. I wanted to cry but couldn't because I was hurting and aching all over and my whole focus was on coping with the right here, right now and not about some time in the future.

The emergency crew at the medical centre were great and took good care of me, but the facilities were not set up for an accident like mine. Chest injuries and broken legs were a bit beyond their local capabilities. I was, however, very grateful for a facility to be so close by the accident site. For much of the morning we had not been close to anywhere. I clearly needed to be evacuated to a major hospital for treatment. Broome hospital had accepted me but had some technical issue with their CT Scanner as did Kununurra, so the decision was taken to send me to Darwin.

The good news was that all my motorcycling clothing worked. My boots, trousers, and jackets took all the bumps and scrapes and definitely saved my skin. My leg and chest injuries were caused by my going over the bike on impact and from landing on the rocks. My helmet saved my life. I am convinced of that. Although it looked like superficial damage to the helmet, my grazed forehead and massive headache told me something different. That's the thing with a crash helmet, you can't see the real damage caused by the impact, but in my case, there were visible signs of damage on the outside. I will never ride without a crash helmet - ever. This was the second time a helmet had saved my life. I was not wearing any gloves at the time of the crash as I had been operating my camera just a few minutes before the accident, I didn't even have a scratch on my hands. I was very lucky.

The Royal Flying Doctor Service (RFDS) was called into action and they showed up within two hours of the initial call being made for their support, which I thought was quite impressive. Two things happened to me whilst I was waiting for the RFDS, neither of which were very pleasant.

I really didn't want powerful drugs for my pain, I thought I was managing quite well, remembering I had been in a much worse situation back in 1979 and I certainly didn't feel agitated. Nevertheless, the staff recommended I have a shot of morphine just to calm me a little which would also help with the pain I was experiencing. I eventually succumbed to their suggestion only to immediately regret it.

I suffered an adverse reaction to the drug and immediately lost control of my breathing; I thought I was going to die. It was absolutely fucking frightening. I forgot about any pain immediately, so from that respect the morphine was working just great. My breathing was becoming difficult, had slowed right down and I was struggling to do anything about it. It felt like I was dry drowning. I remember

My $25,000 ride to Darwin, Fitzroy Crossing, Australia, 2016

grabbing someone's hand and saying some horrible things I was not proud of, but I was struggling to draw breath. I actually thought to myself this was it, I was about to die. I was immediately given a shot of some anti-morphine stuff (midazolam) which had the desired effect of correcting my foul language, calming me down a little and normalizing my breathing (as much as you can with multiple broken ribs). If that wasn't bad enough, the second thing that happened really did piss me off.

I was being strapped into a cradle so that my body movement would be kept to an absolute minimum once I had been loaded as human cargo onto the RFDS aircraft. Everyone seemed really concerned about my neck and back. Me, not so much. I knew I was ok in those areas, but I can't fault the medical staff for doing what they thought was best for me. I understood that I needed to be secured and immobilized, but I also knew a number of ribs were broken on my right-hand side. In fact, I was to learn from the initial chest x-ray in Darwin that I had broken eight of them, three of them had clearly snapped. I was telling the medics as nicely as I could that the chest straps were too tight for me, but every time someone come close to check, they seemed to ratchet up the tension an additional notch even after asking me the question about how tight they felt. This continued bit by bit putting additional pressure on my chest. Then with the speed of a Mohamad Ali jab, I felt what could only be described as a stabbing pain in my chest. I immediately let everyone know in the room what had just happened by shouting out a few words that even the Australians didn't recognize. These were followed by my repeating my early superlatives as I let out my pain.

The strapping had pushed a broken rib through my lung. I knew this to be the case as when the Flying Doctor arrived, Dr Tom, who just happened to be a Scotsman (made me think about jokes involving a Welshman, Scotsman and an Australian), suspected from my labored breathing that I had suffered a pneumothorax (collapsed lung). The medical staff were not convinced of the diagnosis and simply referred to my vitals on arrival at the medical centre. So that was it. I shared a joke about the term Flying Scotsman as we were heading out to the aircraft in the ambulance and got to build a rapport with the man who would be flying me north to Darwin. When we finally arrived at the aircraft, about 15 Minutes later, Dr Tom, decided to check me out one last time before loading me into the aircraft as excess baggage. During his check, I mentioned to him about the painful strapping incident back in the medical center. Well that was it, I found myself being transported straight back to the medical center for a drain to be stuck into my right lung. Fuck! Fuck! As if I hadn't had enough pain, here was a bit more coming my way. I was immediately reminded of my mother's philosophy in life (God bless her soul) that she used to advocate to me as a kid; mum would say that *'bad things always happen in threes'*. Today, she was spot on. Accident, Morphine, Lung. The good news now was that things can only get better, right?

I had a shot of Ketamine before Dr Tom literally sliced open my chest with what looked like a basic craft knife. The anesthetic injection was much like the ones you get at the dentist – the ones that are only really effective after the tooth job has been done. Dr Tom inserted the chest drain which was a length of plastic tubing, just like the tubing Alex and I had for syphoning fuel out of the bikes. The tube was then simply stuck to my chest with a dozen strips of duct tape of various lengths. I was looking like a piece of abstract art. Once the chest drain had been fitted it was back out to the aircraft where I was secured as human cargo in the cramped cabin around 3pm local time, and that is where I stayed for next umpty, umph hours as we flew low level to Darwin. Dr Tom could not pressurize the cabin with my punctured lung hence the low-level and occasionally bumpy ride north. We also had to fly around a local thunder storm before we finally arrived in Darwin sometime in the evening. I eventually got admitted into Darwin hospital around 10pm.

To say it had been a very long and challenging day would be an understatement. Alex stayed behind, he was not allowed to travel with me, and he needed to sort some shit out now anyway. Not least of course my kit that I had been forced to leave behind, my bike and of course himself. I was only allowed a small carry-on bag of belongings, a bag the size of a plastic supermarket bag. I could only fit in my wallet, Sony Walkman and a pair of clean socks and underpants and a couple of tee shirts. What else was I going to need. Alex did the blog that day telling people that the hospital performed the necessary scans, found no fractures in my neck, spine or head but did manage to find eight broken ribs and a collapsed lung. On the positive side, they did manage to locate my brain. He went on to say *"his right leg - those of you that know Nigel know that's his good leg - also took a beating, well his knee did. On the bright-side his limp is now fixed'*. Humor is your friend at times like this, I appreciated those comments, it humanizes the situation in a positive and healing kind of way. The front end of the bike was so badly damaged I had already written it off in my mind. It had made it exactly half way around Australia. The good news from the crash was that I didn't need to get the pannier bracket fixed anymore or replace the battery. What's that metaphor about clouds and silver linings?

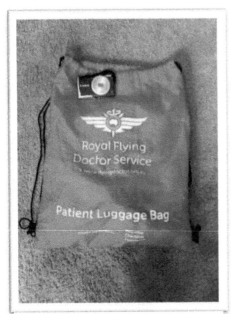

My Allowable Baggage, Fairfax, USA 2018

I was alone in a hospital ward in Darwin hospital the night of my daughter's 22nd birthday. I should have been having a beer in her honour on the West Coast of Australia along with Alex celebrating our crossing the Australian halfway line. The emotional pain took over from the physical pretty quickly and

I cried. I wept quite a bit that first night. I couldn't fucking believe what had just happened to me, and the state I was now in. Here I was lying prone on an uncomfortable single hospital bed, staring through teary eyes at the curling light blue paint peeling off the corners of the wall in my multiple occupancy hospital ward. In that moment, I couldn't have cared less about my pain and my inability to breathe without effort. I had lost my bike and my *'once in a lifetime'* motorcycle dream was over. The word disappointment does not even come close to how I was feeling at that time. I was completely overwhelmed with my loss and grief.

At this point in the proceedings, your mental state is trying to catch up with the reality. The negative thoughts have almost total domination of your thinking, and you have to work hard to start thinking about the positives. And there were lots of positives. I was alive – that was quite a big one for me. And most of my body was still working. If there had been a road train coming at me when the tyre gave out, I would have been killed – period. I had a beautiful Fiancée, Carol, who would be worrying like hell about me at home, but we were getting married later in the year so that was exciting. My kids would have been worried initially, but they knew that motorcycles were an occupational hazard for me and providing I told them I was alright, they would have been fine with that. Life was going to be good once again. I just needed to get through this difficult period.

I then started to think about all the what ifs. What if I had been going slower? What if I had been riding a different bike? What if we had stopped after the first hour to rest? You get the idea. Thinking about anything that could have prevented the accident happening in the first place. These are not helpful thoughts for your wellbeing and does nothing to promote positive thinking, but your mind forces you to logically go through them anyway, which in a way, allows you to come to terms with the decisions that were taken and the set of circumstances you now find yourself in.

One of the ways to mitigate or balance these thoughts is to think about worse outcomes. What if there had been something coming the other way? What if I had been riding my GS, I may have been killed outright or been involved in some different accident at some other time. The physical aspects of healing happen almost immediately, but the mental recovery only starts once you have accepted what has just happened. Sadly, acceptance is never immediate nor is it easy.

As for the accident itself, I knew as soon as the tyre let go through rapid deflation, that I was going to crash. The high speed I was travelling and the way the bike was behaving posed an extremely challenging set of circumstances. At the same time, I also felt that I had some influence on minimizing the outcome and even possibly avoiding a crash altogether if I could slow enough and control the steering. Oddly, I felt that speed did work in my favour at first, as the gyroscopic effect of the turning wheels was keeping me upright. The handling was getting worse as I slowed but I wasn't sure if it was the slowing of the bike or the half set jelly I now had for a front tyre. I never panicked or stressed about what was unfolding, I remained calm and everything was happening in real time – not slow motion. Some people describe accidents occurring in slow motion; I did when I crashed back in 1979. This was different, it was as if my brain said to me 'Nige, we have been here before mate, this is what we need to do, so just do it and let's get it over with'. As the seconds ticked by, I knew that there was going to be a less than an ideal outcome, and I picked my option in a heartbeat and stuck with it. If I had an ejection seat, I would have pulled the handle and ejected without hesitation. I was in control right up until I wasn't capable of control - if that makes sense. They say everything in Australia is trying to kill you. I agree, in my case it was the Australian heat.

All this reflection allowed me to remain focused on the positives as much as I could - it allowed me to accept what had happened. One positive aspect of this accident was that I had already discussed this kind of scenario with Alex, and it was of course one of the main reasons I bought the KLR, although I never thought that I would actually crash. The bike was inexpensive (compared to the total cost of the adventure) and to me was always going to be a disposable asset in a serious accident. I liked the bike a lot but felt that I did not yet have the emotional connection you normally have with a bike through time. This would have been very different if I had taken my New Zealand based BMW R1200 GS because I had a history with that bike over many years. I have no doubt that if I had completed the whole adventure on the Kawasaki, I would feel very different about my emotional connection to the bike by then. Me and the KLR were still in the courting phase of our relationship.

The other aspect to considering serious accidents, was the need to have an inclusive Travel Insurance Plan. I had gone to great lengths in New Zealand to ensure I had the most comprehensive travel insurance I could get. It was not cheap but boy, that was one of the best decisions I made. In fact, it was the complete opposite to what I had in place for my first accident back in 1979. It was a great financial lesson learnt. The insurance cost around $800 NZD, the flight to Darwin with the Flying Doctor had cost $26,307.60 NZD alone. Knowing that those costs were covered made me feel quite a lot better, and those costs were just the beginning.

I would be in Darwin hospital for five days overall. The initial assessment was severe soft tissue damage to my right knee (although I would discover back in the USA after an MRI scan, that I had actually fractured my leg in addition to all the other shit that was going on in the knee) and I had multiple broken ribs. I was a bit of an enigma for the Darwin doctors because physically, my right knee was knackered, so I had to depend on my bad left leg, which of course I have no balance on that side. This resulted in my use of a wheel chair because I had trouble staying upright - *"damaged right leg but can't walk on his left."* The Darwin doctors also had difficulty deciding from a chest x-ray how many ribs were broken because I had broken a number of them before. They thought it was between six and eight. Once again, back in the USA after an MRI the figure was confirmed as eight. It didn't really matter to me what was broken, torn, twisted or bruised, it all hurt like hell.

I was touched by the support I had from family and friends from all over the world. Social media is great for this stuff. The messages were really uplifting and kept me in good spirits. I could thank people and apologize at the same time to everyone in one Facebook post. I felt awful that I had put Carol and the kids through this trauma, they had no idea how bad I was hurting (thank goodness) and I remained upbeat and positive when communicating with them which hopefully helped them as much as it did me. However, in my heart I was absolutely gutted, I felt destroyed that the adventure was over.

I was now totally focused on seeing my loved ones - I couldn't wait. I had the drain removed from my lung on the second day in Darwin and then my thoughts turned to getting back to New Zealand for my daughters' graduation before returning to Sydney to meet with Carol and returning to the USA. What I hadn't catered for was the medical advice that I couldn't fly for at least one month after a collapsed lung, it was too dangerous. Holy Fuck! I had the drain removed on the morning of 10th March and I needed to be in Napier, New Zealand for 1st April. That was just 21 days away. I was adamant that I would not miss my daughter's graduation – no way.

I did the Dr Google thing and researched *'pneumothorax'* and found the advice on flying was between two and six weeks post

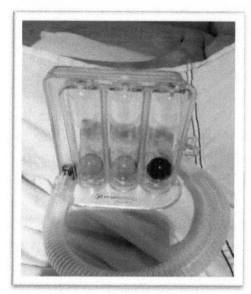

Lung Workout Device, Darwin, Australia, 2016

full inflation of the damaged lung (drain removed), but the wide range in time was dependent on the injury and the person. I now understood why the hospital had said one-month. I shouldn't have challenged the doctors on their assessment, neither should I have told them of my intention to fly back to New Zealand by 1st April, but what I did learn from that conversation was two things.

Firstly, that if I exercised my lungs regularly using this little sucking device with three colored balls, my lung capacity could become stronger, quicker. The test was to suck and hold these balls off the bottom of their columns for as long as I was able. I was still on auxiliary oxygen at this stage and had these little plastic tubes stuck up my nose as my oxygen saturation levels were still well below normal. I was not very good at it at first, and it hurt like hell to expand my chest with all the broken ribs. Nevertheless, I now knew what I needed to do to get my lungs fit again. The leg injury was another issue but that wouldn't stop me from flying.

The second thing I learnt, was that the doctors and hospitals did not have a direct connection to the airlines, so they did not put people on no-fly lists for medical reasons. I took from that information that if I said nothing, no-one would know if I was flying or not. The danger here was that I could cause an in-flight emergency if I did fly with a weak lung in a pressurized cabin. I looked at other means to get myself back to Sydney like trains and cars, but ultimately, I would still need to fly to get to New Zealand. This needed a little more thought.

Seeing Alex again the following day was great. He had sorted all the shit out back in Fitzroy Crossing, including my bike which we had already decided to scrap. Alex had gifted the KLR to one of the nurses who helped me in Fitzroy Crossing. He had packed up my belongings and they had been dispatched to my friends in New Zealand. Alex also made sure that the hospital paperwork and the vehicle accident recovery team at Fitzroy Crossing had been settled. He even bought me some new socks and shirts. I really appreciated everything he had done. It was not easy to do all that when you are in the middle of nowhere and thousands of miles away. He never asked for anything, he just did it. That's a real mate for you. We discussed briefly the future of the trip and I knew he wanted to continue with it, and I was fully supportive of him doing just that. We had put so much time, money and effort into this adventure, it should not go to waste just because of my accident. He had to finish Australia anyway as his bike was in Broome, Western Australia. We would catch up again in Sydney, but I would think differently by then.

Through Facebook, the people we had stayed with at the Paraway Motel in Katherine had been following our adventure and on reading Alex's blog on the accident, immediately reached out offering me somewhere to stay after I had been discharged from hospital. Although they owned and operated the Paraway Motel, some four hours or so south of Darwin, their home was in Darwin, about 20 minutes from the hospital. I was going to be in Darwin for at least the next two to three weeks on my own as I knew Alex needed to get going and ride back to Sydney, so I was most grateful for such a kind offer – it was awesome that they would even think of doing this for a complete stranger whom they met for just two days at their

Crocodile in the Adelaide River, Australia 2016

motel. I will never forget the act of kindness and compassion they showed me over what was a tough time for me both physically and mentally. What a terrific family – thank you so much.

I had a great time getting to know the family, their friends, Darwin City and a few of the tourist attractions – including a river cruise involving feeding crocodiles on the Adelaide River, which was quite spectacular. They were also kind enough to run me back and forth to the hospital and medical center to get my medical treatment and of course to replenish the cocktail of drugs I was now taking.

Carol had already planned to fly out to Sydney after my daughter's graduation in April for a few days, so we could have a mid-adventure holiday together. There was no reason to change those plans except that now I would fly back to the USA with Carol instead of continuing into Asia with Alex. All I had to do now was get myself to New Zealand for 1st April and then back to Sydney for 3rd April to meet Carol. Easy peasy if you are healthy and mobile. Not so much when you are broken.

I handed over responsibility of the Delorme tracker to Alex before he returned to Broome for the beginning of what would now become his solo adventure. The single act of handing over my Delorme Christmas present from Carol to Alex, allowing him to continue an adventure that I should be on, was simply devastating. It reinforced to me (if I had any doubt left), that my once in a lifetime motorcycle adventure was actually over. What should have lasted at least four months, was over in just four weeks. Funny how these little but significant moments stick in your mind in such a big way. It was not lost on Alex either, it was going to be a lonely and reflective few days for him too, until he got used to riding solo and meeting up with other people along the way. I started to cry when he left.

I would write on the Facebook blog every now and again, but it was becoming harder for me to read about Alex's progress on the road. Everything he was experiencing, I should have been experiencing also. It was really upsetting so I had to stop following him for my own wellbeing but felt obliged to keep people informed of my rehabilitation progress every now and again. Although I was making progress, it seemed so, so slow. However, being with my new Australian family rather than being in a hospital or stuck in a hotel room on my own was making all the difference and it stopped me feeling sorry for myself. I was adamant I was going to fly back to New Zealand but wondered how the hell that was going to happen as I could hardly walk, and after a few steps I would get out of breath and my chest pain was crippling.

I needed to be in Napier for 1st April, so I had booked a flight from Darwin to Sydney for Tuesday 29th March. I had been working hard on my breathing and felt that I was fit enough to fly but was extremely anxious. I recalled all the fast jet military flying I had done in the UK, and the strain that flying puts on your body overall. You get to understand what you need to do, and I felt that I had certainly done enough for a passenger aircraft. The first flight was just 19 days after the drain had been removed from my chest. I thought if I could make it to Sydney from Darwin (4 ½ hour flight), I could make in to New Zealand (3-hour flight) easy. My host, Bronwyn and her daughter were also flying out from Darwin the same day I was leaving, so we all hung out in the comfort of the Qantas Lounge. I would like to say I was relaxed and excited, but I wasn't. I was tense and very nervous about what was about to happen, but was glad I was in friendly company, it eased my anxiety a lot. I had taken the support brace off my leg having decided it was best not to draw attention to myself when I boarded the aircraft.

My flight was called, and I said goodbye to my Australian family one last time, thanking them for everything they had done for me. I was sad to be leaving them as we had become great friends. I was now on my own for the first time and was feeling extremely apprehensive about the next few hours. My pulse must have been up around 120 at rest. I was so, so nervous. I boarded the aircraft, strapped myself in and immediately started my breathing exercise. Not sure why I did this, it was too late now to change my mind. If anything went wrong, I would be in such big shit if the airline found out about my condition. I think I was already hyperventilating as the aircraft taxied and when it eventually took off and we climbed out of Darwin, I could feel the cabin pressurize and the strange sensation it was having on my chest. Not painful, just unusual. I am sure a lot of this was pure anxiety. I kept breathing deeply and was expecting my lungs to go kaboom! at any time. They didn't of course, which was a big relief!

I arrived in Sydney after an uneventful flight a little more relaxed than I was before I left Darwin. I had arranged to meet with Alex (who had already arrived in Sydney) before I flew out to New Zealand on 31st March. I would not see Alex again until he had returned to the USA. We discussed the whole experience and I wished him all the best for the remainder of the adventure and a safe trip back to the USA, but it was gut wrenching for me once again. I wanted him to continue, I really did, but another part of me wanted everything to stop right there. This adventure was supposed to be for the both of us, it was not a solo adventure and the thought of Alex continuing on without me didn't seem right. I was not being selfish, I just felt that it was our adventure and the fact that it was now all over for me had made me so upset I was almost physically sick with grief. My injuries were a stark reminder of why I could not continue, and they certainly weren't suppressing my feelings of torment and loss.

The forfeiture of the bike didn't help either, but had I been fit enough to ride, I would have bought another bike and continued in a heartbeat. We said our goodbyes, wished each other luck and looked forward to catching up back in the USA. I was so upset when he left, I was absolutely gutted. I just sat there, reflected for a while, then cried.

My hotel was just 300 feet (less than 100 metres) walking distance to the international airport terminal. I would be flying out to New Zealand first thing in the morning.

The plans I had made for my daughter's graduation were exhausting under the circumstances and how I managed to cram everything in when I could hardly walk and breathe at the same time is still a mystery to me, but it all worked out in the end. I had stopped taking the opioid pain killers the day before I left for New Zealand as I knew I would be driving. That just made the trauma of travelling worse. It was a relief to get back to Australia, get back on the pain killers and wait for Carol to take me back to the USA to start my rehabilitation. The next eight months would be a combination of medical consultations, insurance battles, physiotherapy and sorting a whole load of other life things that would allow me to settle permanently in what would become my third country of residence; the USA.

If giving me serious injuries and taking my bike from me was not bad enough, Australia had another little surprise to piss me off one last time. As Carol and I went to check in for our flight back to the USA, the flight crew wouldn't check me in. I was travelling on the visa waiver (ESTA) program therefore immigration policy stated that I had to produce evidence of my intent to leave the USA before my 90 days ESTA expired. Essentially, I needed a flight ticket out of the USA before I would be allowed back in. And by the way, nipping up to Canada or visiting Mexico doesn't count, it had to be outside continental America. So, I found the airport flight centre and booked the cheapest single ticket back to the UK from the US on the 90th day of my return. I would figure everything else out later. With my next travel adventure ticket in hand, I was finally allowed to check in. Australia was being tough on me right to the end and I was not sad to be leaving this time.

As we flew out from Sydney, I was reflecting not just on the country that had almost killed me, but on the bigger adventure I had been on. Would I do it again? No, I don't think so. This really was a once in a lifetime opportunity and I recognized that. If I had the opportunity to do something similar again, I would plan several shorter adventures and spread them out over a much longer time period. That way I could still get to see all the things I wanted to see but with 'life' happening in between. Also, one of the great things about any adventure is the build-up and the exciting feeling of just looking forward to it. Looking forward to several adventures over a longer period of time seems better than looking forward to one really big one. And finally, in the event that things do go wrong, like they did for me in Australia, the loss and disappointment is not so great because you have the next adventure to look forward too.

Australia Airport Chewing Gum, Sydney, Australia 2016

At the end of the day, all I wanted to do was ride my motorcycle back to the USA via a loop of Australia, but it was not to be. I don't consider it to be a failure even though I only made it half way around. It was challenging riding in a very different way to New Zealand, and I loved every minute of it (until the accident of course- that really wasn't that much fun). It is one hell of a country and I have a huge amount of respect for both the country and its people. I am living proof to the adage that everything in Australia wants to kill you. In my case it was the intense heat, not the wildlife that caused me to crash. Having spent a minimal amount of time lying in the bush on the side of the road post-accident, I am so grateful to the Australian wildlife for not biting, crushing, poisoning or eating me. Perhaps members of the outback wildlife community witnessed my aggressive take out of the road sign and left me alone through respect rather than take the opportunity to have me for lunch.

I looked out the window of the aircraft during takeoff, smiling as the Sydney suburbs shrunk beneath us. I waved goodbye to Australia and thanked it for the life experience, but I would not be back any time soon. I then looked across to Carol who was sat next to me holding my other hand tightly and thought to myself, I am a very, very lucky man. That thought gave me a warm fuzzy feeling inside and made me smile even more. I kicked back with both busted legs, relaxed and enjoyed the flight home.

Chapter 15
Back to my Roots

The road to full rehabilitation was a long one. The medical provisions in the US are second to none but they are costly, and I found the doctors to be more interventionist than New Zealand, Australia or the UK. The injuries to my left leg and knee were much worse than Darwin hospital had suggested, and the orthopaedic surgeon wanted to reconstruct my knee joint. My chest was so badly damaged the thoracic surgeon wondered how I had arrived at his surgery under my own steam and wanted to admit me immediately and reset three of my ribs. I now understood why my recovery was taking so long. Interesting medical term *'reset'*. What that meant was cutting me open, braking the three (already healing) but badly shaped ribs and attaching plates to straighten them up before stitching me back together. I thanked both the surgeons for their suggestions but kindly turned them down for surgery. I know my own body better than anyone else and have adapted to my injuries over the years. I didn't then, and still don't today feel the need to bugger about with my joints and bones unnecessarily. I will heal and work through intense physiotherapy to get myself fit. I had broken my leg before and my ribs have been broken more times than I care to remember, and if a few of them were oddly shaped, I could live with that.

My travel insurance company was playing hard ball with me because I returned to New Zealand from Australia which (under the terms of the policy) made the insurance null and void from that point forward. Luckily, I had paperwork that showed my full itinerary telling them upfront of my intent to return to New Zealand, specifically stating that it was not a return home, merely attending my daughter's graduation before continuing on the adventure. They really did cause me unnecessary grief at a time when I really needed their support, so I responded in kind with slamming in a claim for just about everything I could. It all came good in the end and it didn't cost me a cent, but boy they certainly tried it on, and for a period it was a real battle. Detailed preparation and being up front with everything from the start was the lesson here. There was no wiggle room for them to turn down any of my claims once they realised what we had agreed at the start of the insurance period.

By September 2016, I felt strong enough and ready to get

My Non-Diplomatic (Heritage) Gutzi Tag, Fairfax, USA 2016

back on a motorcycle. The trusted Moto Guzzi Griso had sat patiently in the garage waiting for me to climb aboard once more to go riding. So, I did. Just around the apartment complex at first, then slowly building up my time in the saddle over the autumn when the weather was good. My 500lb Italian pocket rocket was good therapy for me in more ways than one. It made me feel like I was recovering well from the accident and the trauma of loss, it was also good strength building exercises for my leg and it just made me smile to be back on a bike again.

Fast forward another six months, and I had all but fully recovered, accepting that I rarely get back to 100% after a motorcycle accident, but I was certainly sitting around 95%+ and I can usually adapt for the remaining percentage.

I had started to work part time in our local BMW and Triumph dealership, Motorcycles of Dulles. The owners only allow quality 'Trade-Ins' to make it onto the shop floor for resale. They had recently taken a pearl stardust white and ebony, 2014, KLR 650 for a BMW R1200 GS. The KLR was

My 2014 KLR 650, Fairfax, USA, 2018

absolutely immaculate with just a few thousand miles on the clock and was fitted with Tusk hard panniers, a taller protective windscreen and an aftermarket exhaust silencer that made the big single sound awesome.

I was just getting to know my original KLR before I prematurely buried it in Australia, and now felt the overwhelming need to have another one, I had not really given the first one a chance. So, I bought it. I had too. I was admiring this bike every day at work. In my head I had already decided it would be a great stable mate for the Motor Guzzi. Even I would admit that this was a bit of a pathetic excuse to get a second motorcycle, but hey, it worked for me and my (now) wife was very supportive of my getting it. I still have the KLR today and ride it almost daily. It is pure fun, a no-nonsense bike. I have lowered it slightly, put a comfortable seat on it, rubber mounted the mirrors and fitted some nice comfy hand grips. It has made all the difference and were all lessons I had learnt from my first KLR.

I always intended to take the Moto Guzzi back to New Zealand and take my non-diplomatic number plate with me, but that plan had changed a while back when I made the decision not to immediately return to New Zealand. The Italian engineering had not been that reliable in the USA and had started its antics again by developing a rear drive shaft oil leak. The speedo indicator which had been an issue in the past had also resurfaced and seemed to come out in a show of sympathy with the oil leak. I sensed there was another $500 USD bill in the making here and it was forcing me to think seriously about what I should do with the Gutzi. I loved the bike, but it was costing me a fortune to fix all the time. I had spent almost the cost of the bike again on repairs over the four years I had it. Not servicing costs, I did all the servicing myself, this was pure repairs for piss poor aging Italian engineering. My decision to keep the Gutzi or not was influenced by two events that happened in close proximity to each other, both of which indicated it was time for a change.

Saturday 8th April 2017 was a beautiful day in Fairfax, Virginia. Sunny, warm with very little wind. It was a perfect day to go for a ride. As was usual, I had no plan or destination in mind, just ride around the back roads of Northern Virginia until I decided it was time to go home. I had taken a side road and stopped at this tiny old railroad museum that I hadn't seen before to take a photo. I often do this when I am out on my own and my (now) wife, Carol is working. I like to flick her a text just to show her where I am and to tell her how great the day was turning out. It is also a really nice way of sharing the experience with her and for her to know that I am thinking of her. I had taken one photograph and then decided I wanted another with the bike in it. Then I had the mishap.

My right foot slipped as I was reaching for the side stand with my left foot, I lost my balance and over the bike went, and me with it. The left foot peg sunk into my angle, and the 500lb beast crushed my foot and lower left leg before I managed to push the bike and pull my foot out from underneath it. It immediately hurt like shit, and my foot felt like it was connected to my leg by a half empty bag of jelly beans.

Fuel immediately started to spill out of the fuelling cap, and I thought to myself even then, that this was bloody classic Italian engineering. They couldn't even make a spill proof fuel cap. The petrol had quickly formed a damp patch on the gravel and tarmac an there was an overwhelming smell of petrol. I quickly got to my feet and tried to pick up the beast using the correct technique of my back against the bike with one arm on the handlebars and the other on the rear luggage carrier before pushing backwards and lifting at the same time. Unfortunately, I only had one good foot and over strained the lift with the adrenaline rush, doing more damage to my ankle and cracking at least one rib during the lift. I felt the rib go but it didn't hurt at the time. I managed to get the bike shiny side up again on the second attempt.

I couldn't bloody believe that this had happened to me just one year after my Australian outback mishap. I knew a lot more pain was on the way once the adrenaline had worn off. Afterall, I have had some experience in what broken bones feel like. I gave the bike a quick once over and apart from a bent clutch lever it all looked alright. My left leg and foot had saved the day. I immediately got back on the bike and had a quiet an uneventful ride home. Although, changing gear was a bit of a challenge for me with a half set jelly on an already knackered foot. The pain was slowly increasing but not to the extent that it had become a distraction. I was in a shit load of pain that evening and for the next six weeks, I went through my own physiotherapy program for my foot and chest.

I always reflect on my motorcycling after a tumble like this. In fact, I guess I subconsciously reflect a little after every ride. As you get older you become more cautious and regular reflection is a great way of modifying future motorcycling behaviour. What could I have done differently? Was I being stupid? And the $60,000 question, should I stop riding? For those of you who ride, these thoughts are nothing new and you will know the answer. For those who don't ride, well, the body is good at repairing itself and after a few weeks, it was already looking forward to getting back on a bike. Next time I won't be stopping on gravel to put the side stand down. Such events can happen to anyone at any time. What this incident highlighted to me was that even in the most benign set of circumstances things can still go wrong. Low speed or zero speed handling errors can be just as serious as road traffic accidents. Wearing the right clothing (gloves and boots in this instance) reduces the severity.

The second event that tipped my thinking towards selling the Gutzi happened literally days before the gravel mishap, but it didn't seem particularly significant at the time. I had moved from sales into the service department at Motorcycles of Dulles, and a recent customer had purchased a brand new 2017, Triumph Bobber. Triumph policy dictates that before a customer takes ownership of any brand-new Triumph motorcycle, the dealership must put five miles (eight kilometres) on the bike to prove its roadworthiness. A sort of shakedown ride to make sure everything is good for the customer. I was asked to take the Bobber out for a ride to clock up the five miles required by Triumph. I couldn't stop grinning when I got back to the showroom. The bike was bloody awesome, the 1200 cc, High Torque, twin cylinder engine was phenomenal. It had so much grunt over the whole rpm range and the delivery was linear and smooth. I loved the ride and the engine was awesome, but I was not that keen on the Bobber style of bike. However, I had fallen in love with the new 2018, Triumph Bonneville T 120, and that beautiful bike came fitted with the same engine.

So, the Gutzi mechanical problems, the mishap on the gravel and the fact I was falling in love with the Triumph Bonneville T 120 made me realise that perhaps it was time for a changing of the guard. I had in my mind a dollar value for the Gutzi and that was a much bigger number than any trade-in on a new Triumph T 120. I needn't have worried. I could have sold the Gutzi three times over, it was a very popular bike (to my surprise). I sold it in a week and got exactly what I wanted for it. I loved working at Motorcycles of Dulles, but I had spent 15 thousand dollars and earned two. Clearly, I needed to find a different job if I was to survive living in the USA.

At this time in my life, I sense that there is an insidious change going on with my thinking. I am now in my late fifties and motorcycling is definitely becoming more leisurely. I seemed to be enjoying the ride more; I'm slowing down. Although, having a KLR 650 on my inventory would confirm that aspect. The Bonneville T 120 to me is a gentlemen's bike and a true British Classic. The T 120 is the type of bike you ride slowly down the high street, so you can admire your reflection as you flick by the shop windows. The Bonneville T 120 was also the very first big bike I rode pillion on in 1977 when a mate took me into London on his 1973, T 120. That bike was uncomfortable, made a hellofa lot of noise and dispatched a few fasteners along the way due to vibration, but I loved every second of the ride. I now had this overwhelming urge to go back to my roots. I wanted a Triumph Bonneville T 120 to complement the KLR and make my motorcycle family complete for 2019 at least.

The Bonneville T 120 has been produced by three different companies at three different times and in three different locations. The original 649 cc parallel twin was capable of 110 mph when it was released in 1959 and not surprisingly, sold over 250,000 over its 16 years in production. The model name Bonneville was synonymous with speed as a Triumph powered streamliner set an unofficial land speed record of 214 mph for bikes in 1956 at Bonneville Salt Flats, Utah. It was also a T 120 that took Steve McQueen around the fields in the Great Escape.

Me & White Helmets TR7V,Triumph, England, 2011

The Bonneville T 120 was basically a Triumph Tiger with twin carbs and a different paint job. The T 120 was eventually replaced throughout the two-year period 1973/75 by its big brother the 744 cc, T 140.

When Triumph went into liquidation from their Meriden plant in 1983, the bikes had limited production under licence by a chap called Les Harris who made the T 140 for three years between 1985 and 1988 with his company Racing Spares in Devon, England. These bikes were not 100% triumph, they had a few more European parts fitted to them than the original Triumphs. Racing Spares also built the Triumph TR7Vs used by the British Army Royal Signals Motorcycle Display Team, the White Helmets. I was lucky enough to visit their training camp in the UK, in 2011. They let me sit on the bikes but wouldn't let me ride one.

The third relaunch of the Bonneville happened in 2001 when John Bloor who had bought the Triumph license back in 1983 reinvented the model with a new design that had styling that fitted in with the original. A sort of vintage motorcycle with all mod cons. He hit on a winning formula because that is the reason why I own one today and I am sure other Bonneville owners feel much the same way. I loved the look of the original and I can see that reflected in the new modern vintage style. The long classic pea shooter exhausts, flat seat, twin carbs (which are actually throttle bodies for the fuel injection system), wire wheels and

My 2018 Triumph T120, Fairfax, USA, 2018

that classic looking air-cooled twin cylinder motor (which is actually water cooled on the 2017 model and almost twice the cc of the original) are hallmarks of the British Classic.

Triumph have a whole family of bikes now made under the Bonneville banner to cater for a varied motorcycle audience, but the T 120 in its original colour schemes is the most authentic Bonneville of all, in my humble opinion. Riding the T 120 is an absolute dream. In some ways it's as smooth as an electric bike as you don't feel any vibration, being a KLR 650 owner, I know all about vibration. However, its distinctive deep rich classic twin tone from the pea shooter exhaust is something no electric bike could replicate. The 270-degree firing order of the torquey twin delivers the power in a linear fashion when you roll on the ride by wire throttle in any gear with an engine speed of 2000 rpm or higher. If you twist the throttle quickly you can hear the single overhead camshaft rolling up the revs which is met by a seemingly disproportionate increase in speed. It Brings a smile to my face every time I do it and with traction control and ABS, I know I can do it safely. I also have cruise control fitted which can be activated in 3rd gear with an engine speed of 2,000 rpm and over. Auto cruising at 30 mph around country lanes actually fun.

I can put both my feet firmly on the ground which gives me

My Bike Stable, Fairfax, USA, 2018

huge confidence when riding in high volume stop/start traffic. When stationary, the bike feels quite small or rather reassuringly manageable. It has an 18-inch front wheel and the engine sits low in the frame which disguises its 500lbs bulk. The detuned engine thumps out almost as much torque as it has locked up horses and that translates to less gear changes for me. The max running in engine speed of 4000 rpm in sixth gear = 90 mph. I have never had anything that can go that fast when you are running it in. Also, the engine can go 10,000 miles (16,000 kilometres) between servicing, that's almost unheard off and much better mileage than my Korean car.

Other manufactures like BMW with the R nine T, Moto Guzzi with the V7 and even Honda with the CB1100 have capitalised on the retro bandwagon. Then there are the Royal Enfield's of the world who really haven't changed at all other than perhaps fuel injection. Triumph are really hitting the mark and there is a vast array of aftermarket parts available to customise your Triumph to your own taste. They have taken a leaf out of the Harley Davidson book of marketing.

With age comes maturity, and I have become a more traditionalist motorcyclist preferring to keep the original look of the bike from the factory, the *as built* look. Having said that, I have added a small screen to reduce the buffet at highway speeds, a skid plate to protect the catalytic converter and a couple of baggage arms on the back to protect my soft luggage rubbing on the rear suspension. Not customisation, more practical modifications. Other than that, I am very pleased with my Triumph and feel that the bike will be part of my motorcycle stable for many years to come. Alongside the Kawasaki KLR 650, the Triumph is a complimentary ride and between the two, take care of all my motorcycling needs. The only bike missing from the stable is my New Zealand, BMW R 1200 GS (the one on the cover of this book). Sadly, import restrictions prevented me from bringing the GS into the USA. I did try to bring it across as a family member, but Homeland Security was having none of it. In the end, I was forced to sell it in 2016 to a friend whom I knew would look after it. One day perhaps I will own another....

Chapter 16
Final Reflective Thoughts

I was born and bred in the Welsh Valleys in the UK. Although beautiful, valleys have mountains either side and are prone to some interesting (poor) weather patterns. These adverse weather conditions never once deterred me from riding, it was something you just lived with. Indeed, the weather in the UK is not that great wherever you go. Just flick back to Chapter 7 and read about the weather conditions we faced during our Land's End to John O'Groats adventure in September or speak to anyone who has lived in the UK for some time and they will tell you the same thing. You need to have a certain toughness to ride a motorcycle in the UK. I am proud to have come from a country that seen not only the birth of the industrial revolution, but the country that probably started the worldwide motorcycling craze when Edward Butler's three-wheeler invention made an appearance back in 1884 at the Stanley Cycle Show in London.

By the 1930s there were dozens of motorcycle manufacturers in the UK. Triumph, Norton, BSA (Birmingham Small Arms), Ariel, Brough, Vincent, AJS (A.J. Stevens), Scott, Matchless, Royal Enfield to name some of the big ones. This continued well into the 1960s before it all started to fall apart for various reasons, then the Japanese stepped up and began to fill the void - big time. It took the best part of 25 years for a phoenix to rise from the ashes of the British motorcycle industry with Triumph. Norton are coming back, and Royal

Enfield have also made it back in to the mainstream motorcycle fraternity, although to be fair, it never really left, it just went overseas to India. The UK is also the home of famous bike racing tracks like Donnington and Thruxton, and of course, the Isle of Man TT (Tourist Trophy), which is probably the most famous, longest and most dangerous motorcycle race circuit in the world. Tough British motorcycling racing icons like Barry Sheene, Carl Foggerty, Joey Dunlop, Jeff Duke, John Surtees, Phil Read, and Mike Hailwood brought motorcycling into the hearts and homes of millions of aspiring motorcyclists - me included. So why am I telling you all this. Well, I believe that motorcycling is in my British heritage. It wasn't until I moved to New Zealand and then to the USA that I realised many more of my British friends (compared to my New Zealand and USA friends) either rode motorcycles themselves or someone in the family had one. Indeed, it may be a Baby Boomer generation thing, but its uncanny that a large amount of the British people I know as friends ride motorcycles.

So, why do we ride motorcycles? I started off the book declaring my love of motorcycles even before I had even ridden one, and indeed that is true. However, riding for the sheer enjoyment of riding is just one part of what a motorcyclist gets out of motorcycles; any motorcycle. Most recently (last 10 years or so), I personally discovered a much deeper purpose for why motorcycling works for me. But before I discuss that, there are a few common behaviours that bond motorcyclists as a special group of people. They will wave to each other when passing in opposite directions, this is recognition and respect. Doesn't matter if you are male, female, famous, rich or poor. Also, if you have broken down on the side of the road, a passing motorcyclist will stop and lend a hand. In any public place if you are carrying a crash helmet or are in biking gear and you walk past someone who is also a biker you will acknowledge each other. If you are in a café or a pub you might even strike up a conversation. After all, you have something in common. Once again, this just doesn't happen with motorists. All motorcyclists enjoy the freedom and sense of liberation they get from everyday life when they swing their leg over a motorcycle saddle, once underway, the local conditions have unrestricted access to all your senses and the motorcyclist has to deal with all these inputs along with their own ability to handle a mobile mechanical machine, in an environment that they don't have total control over.

The motorcyclist gets a buzz from having their sight and hearing senses immediately raised to a heightened level of alertness. These triggers increase brain activity and any exposed skin gives outside air temperature inputs which collectively allow you to make some judgments on the kind of riding you will be doing and your abilities to ride under such conditions. The smell of unfiltered air and the taste of rain, smoke or whatever else is in the air - including uninvited insects, all feed the heightened level of brain activity. It's an addictive experience.

On top of this the motorcyclist must deal with the 'turbo' brain activity, what most people refer to as the 'adrenaline rush'. Those moments that can be triggered by a positive or negative event. An example of a 'positive turbo' is the selection of the correct riding line as you enter a bend at the right speed, in the right gear knowing that you are at one with the machine. Approaching the exit of the bend, you reward yourself by powering out faster than you entered. A 'negative turbo' example could be taking rapid avoiding action because someone has just pulled out in front of you as they never saw you or were distracted on their phone. Both are adrenaline inducing events. The combination of all this activity makes you totally focussed on the ride. If you are having problems in your life with relationships, money, health or just about anything else, that all disappears when you are at this heightened level of brain activity. This is what makes motorcycling both physically and mentally challenging but very rewarding. It's hard to multitask when you are concentrating on the ride and why would you want to anyway - that's one of the best reasons for riding in the first place.

Motorcycles are also an extension of you. It is a piece of engineering, a work of art for you and others to admire. You feel proud to own it, and when you climb aboard it becomes part of you and you immediately send a signal to others about who you are. You are making a motorcycle fashion statement. Particularly so if your protective clothing matches your motorcycle. After all, you want to look good both on and off the bike.

So, here is the deeper reason why I enjoy riding motorcycles so much. When things are not happening at a hectic pace and I am just cruising along with no distractions, sometimes life issues start to make their way back and begin to compete with the motorcycling activity for brain time. For me, I recognise this is happening and have learnt to make a choice. I can either wrestle with the issues and try and sort them out or use the opportunity to be grateful for what I have and for what I am doing. Both options have benefits and, depending on how I am feeling at the time, I will think one way or the other. I have gone riding sometimes specifically to wrestle with a life issue as I can get myself into the right head space to sort shit out. I am forever grateful to an old school friend who inspired me to be thankful for my life and how, through motorcycling, I can change not just my mood but my attitude and therefore my overall wellbeing. A subset of this ability is being able to sort other things out in my life.

Sian Evans was a '*tomboy*'. The only girl who grew up around a small group of six boys in our village. I was one of the boys. Sian was a year younger than me and although we grew up amongst the same group of people, Sian and I had the closest friendship, we would always be looking out for each other and hang out together, we were like brother and sister.

I left home at age 16 to join the Royal Air Force and we never did keep in touch. We just went our separate ways. Even when I visited home, we never caught up. We took very different paths in life. Then, out of the blue some 35 years later, Sian's mother tracks me down in New Zealand and sends me a letter Sian had written to me. In the letter Sian was doing some serious reflecting on her own mortality informing me that she had Mitochondrial Disease; an incurable and debilitating disease that would eventually kill her. Her health had already deteriorated to the extent that every day was a gift for her. She was wheel chair bound and almost totally deaf. I felt a real need to get back and see Sian and eventually made it back less than a year later in September 2010. I took her a gift, a beautifully groomed New Zealand Paua shell as a reminder of my visit and the place I was now living.

I learnt that Sian had always wanted to visit New Zealand and she was excited to hear my stories about the country, but equally important to her was hearing about the last 35 years and what had become of me once I had left the village. She wanted to share her own life too, not as a comparison, but as a sister would want to share with her brother her own life experiences. She also wanted to recall the good times we had as kids growing up during the 1960s and early 1970s. She knew her life was coming to an end, and she just wanted to recall happy moments and to share those moments with me, her childhood brother, one last time.

We laughed and recalled stories about our childhood days and the games we played as kids which were almost exclusively games played outside. I told her that my own daughter was named Sian and that her name was in part inspired by our own childhood friendship. Sian gave me a gift of a stuffed Welsh Dragon soft toy as a reminder of our childhood friendship and as a constant reminder to me that I was a Welshman. This was important to Sian, she wanted me to remember where I had come from, a Welsh boy from the valleys. That day I really felt like the big brother she never had (Sian had two younger sisters). I promised her the Dragon would be looked after and I would show it around New Zealand on the motorcycle.

I didn't recognize Sian when I visited, she looked so ill. The disease had clearly taken its toll on her. I cried terribly when I left her and knew that I would never see her again.

Sian Evans died 18 months later aged 51 years old. Her funeral was on 14th March 2012 and her ashes were scattered up the dingle (a local wooded area where we played as kids) along with the ashes from her black Labrador companion, Mollie, who had died just a few months beforehand.

I visited the UK once again in August 2012 and paid my respects to Sian up the dingle where her ashes had been scattered. I was accompanied by the Red Dragon. I cried; I wept a lot that day. I felt so sad to be there but privileged to have known her. This was the first time I had lost a childhood friend the same age as me. It made me reflect on how short our mortal lives really are; tomorrow should never be taken for granted. This was the hidden message Sian was telling me when I visited her in 2010, the Red Dragon was gifted as my reminder. Just before she died, Sian asked her mum to give me a book she had had as a child to gift to my own daughter Sian, which, was her way of telling me how much she valued our friendship as kids and her being grateful to me for sharing the memories we had one last time before she passed away.

For all the time after my initial visit until Sian died, I took the Red Dragon everywhere. It was the inspiration for me to ride my motorcycle with a purpose around New Zealand on what I called 'The Red Dragon Tour'. I would photograph the Red Dragon sometimes with me and my motorcycle, sometimes on its own and then send those photos to Sian so she could see that the Red Dragon was experiencing the New Zealand dream on her behalf and was always by my side. I continued to take the Red Dragon with me right up until I had finished Route 66 in September 2013 some 18 months after Sian had died. I also took the dragon to Canada, Singapore and Ireland. The Dragon now sits peacefully on my bookcase. Its travelling days are over.

So, if I am not sorting out my life issues, then I reflect on how lucky I am to be alive and fit enough to ride my motorcycle that day. Such happy thoughts lift the bar on my mood and I immediately start to feel better (even if I was feeling ok before I set off). Passing a cemetery on a motorcycle triggers a reflective thought and I slow down, salute and pay my respects to all those who have passed away. I then lift my head and continue to enjoy the ride as I know they would have wished me to do. I have not found any other activity in life that allows me to feel good about myself and feel alive as much as motorcycling. It is a special activity for sure.

According to the US National Highway Traffic Safety Administration, your chances of dying on a motorcycle are 35 times higher than in a car. Well, I have not died once in a car yet so 35 times Zero = Zero. I am not being flippant, but as a motorcyclist, risk is part of the activity and adds a little something, another dimension, to the ride. After a host of minor mishaps and several serious accidents resulting in hospitalisation and lengthy rehabilitation, why do I still ride a motorcycle? It's a great question and I'm betting that most people who do ride, will have similar responses to my previous comments.

I don't care much for anyone telling me that motorcycles are dangerous. Motorcycles are not dangerous at all. People are dangerous and some situations you find yourself in with a motorcycle can be dangerous. Motorcycles are safe, but they do need to be respected and they are unable to cheat the laws of physics or save you from yourself. I am living proof of that. So, I ride because I can, and will continue to ride until the day I physically can't get my leg over the seat or some other infirmity gets to me and prevents me from riding.

The only negative thing I can think about motorcycling, is that sometimes I do get grumpy when I haven't ridden for a while. The only medicine for that, is to go for a ride. It's a game changer. Motorcycles have enabled me to travel and see parts of the world I would never have seen otherwise. I have met some terrific people through motorcycles and have had some of the best and worse experiences of my life, courtesy of two wheels.

As I have gotten older, I am a little pickier about when I ride. I have a car from getting from A to B but will always consider the bike first. The following are times that I will put a little more thought into my decision to go for a ride.

Rain & Snow & Strong Winds. I don't care for dressing up for wet weather. If I am already out and it rains, that's fair enough, but riding for pleasure in the rain doesn't exist anymore for me and if its windy too it's just bloody miserable. I would stay at home in the snow unless I had a small lightweight dual sport bike like my old Yamaha, DT 175 in the garage, then I would go and have some fun.

Cold & Heat. Providing its dry and not icy - I am happy to go riding but I always make sure I wear the proper protective clothing for the conditions. Sensing the outside temperature is all part of the fun of riding, but I am also conscious of the wind chill factor when the outside air temperature is around freezing. Regular coffee stops, and warm ups are the order of the day. For extreme heat, ventilated jacket and trousers are awesome, just need to keep riding to feel the benefit.

Mental State. Here's the thing about motorcycles, they can be great therapy and they will improve your mood but riding one when you are really pissed off about something, frustrated or just in a bad place and angry can impair your judgement and negative thoughts can become a distraction. That's not good. I consciously leave all that shit behind or go for a walk or do something else before I climb aboard my bike.

Clothing is an essential element of motorcycling. If you can dress in the style of what you are riding, then all the better. Afterall, a motorcycle is an extension of you. There are loads of apparel manufactures out there who cater for the full spectrum of motorcyclist so there is no excuse. I cringe when I see the photograph of myself standing on a moped seat with no protective clothing at all. It is just stupid. Being in my early 20s is no excuse - but I was in my 20s so that was my excuse. My Griffin crash helmet in 1979 and my Shoei helmet in 2016 saved my life. I have no doubt about that. Both helmets were the full-face type, and both suffered damage at the back and on the chin portion. The full face not only saved my life but saved me ripping my face off too. A good quality crash helmet will give

307

you some hearing protection too. Wind noise can cause hearing damage and I am pretty sure it's the major cause of the tinnitus I have today. I wear earplugs now but should have started wearing them much earlier. Had I been wearing my proper motorcycle boots on the Gutzi the day I had failed to deploy the side stand, I would not have damaged my foot as badly. No good having all the right clothing and not wearing it.

The rule of thumb when riding a bike should be no exposed skin. Helmet, gloves, jacket, trousers and boots irrespective of weather. Skin is very thin. Pavement coverings and off-road dirt is much tougher and will always come off better than you during a tumble. I will admit that I don't always dress for the worst-case scenario, but I always dress for a tumble. There are many reasons (excuses) why I don't always dress for the worst case scenario, but it's a conscious decision, a simple risk assessment. At the end of the day, you never know when you are going to need the protection. Any investment in good protective clothing is a wise investment.

Motorcycle Insurance. This is a very simple concept. If you can't afford to purchase the bike outright, make sure you can afford insurance that covers the total loss of the bike either in an accident or through theft. There is nothing worse than continuing to pay for something that you can't use or don't have. If you can't afford the best comprehensive insurance, then you can't afford the bike. Simple.

The future of motorcycling looks electric. There has been an explosion of new manufactures coming to the market over the last couple of years with their designs and that will continue and eventually see the death of the internal combustion engine motorcycle. The riders of tomorrow want machines that are fast, look good, are cheap to run with low to nil maintenance activity. Noise and getting your hands dirty whilst understanding how things work will be less important to future generations. It won't be better or worse, but it will be different. Even hardened historic names like Harley Davidson and BMW are realising that electric bikes are taking up a section of the motorcycle industry that will not be taken back by the internal combustion engine. It will be a change similar to that of the Industrial Revolution where the steam engine replaced horses on land and sails at sea and it will dominate cars and motorcycles in the next 10 to 20 years.

I have ridden a couple of electric bikes and they are extremely fast and very torquey, and they are getting even quicker and faster, but the ride takes some getting used too. Turn on the ignition, twist and go. No starting sequence, no warming up, no noise, no gear changing, no maintenance (not true but significantly less) no worries other than a flat battery. The electric motorcycle is all about the ride. A motorcycle to me is a lot more than just the ride. The noise along with the vibration, smell of fuel and burnt exhaust gases, the gear changing, and routine maintenance is all part of the motorcycling experience.

I bought my Bonneville primarily because it looks good and I feel good on it. The electric bikes seem a little bland in comparison although they are getting much better at the aesthetics and their designs are getting more futuristic as they are not bound by designing around a reciprocating engine, hot exhausts and allowing for a large vacant space to hold liquid carbon fuel. I can't imagine sitting admiring my electric bike as I do the Triumph. I look at the Triumph and see hundreds of parts connected and can imagine them all moving in sync with each other to generate a machine that can take you wherever you want to go.

The science is pure and sophisticated. The engine converts the chemical energy from a hydrocarbon fuel into heat energy in a combustion chamber, transferring that into mechanical energy delivered through the piston which is fed through a transmission that ultimately powers your bike giving it kinetic energy. Electric bikes are just magic. Not as much science and unsophisticated. You can't see or smell the fuel and there are very few moving parts.

One day I won't be able to swing my leg over a saddle. Then what. Well there are trikes. Trikes are becoming very popular for the older generation and offer a real alternative to motorcycles. There are only two configurations for three wheels, two at the front and one at the back (2+1), or one at the front and two at the back (1+2). The former you drive the latter you ride. I have owned both these configurations (see Chapter 4 for 1+2 and Chapter 6 for 2+1) albeit both my vehicles had steering wheels not handlebars. One wheel in the front is by far the best configuration if you want to imagine you are riding a bike. Once again plenty of options out there and it's only a matter of time before they also become electrified. Indeed, if any vehicle was suited for electrification, the trike would seem to be a good choice due to its ability to place a large battery pack literally anywhere in the frame or through the bodywork.

I visited a motorcycle show recently (February 2019) and noticed that there had been a proliferation of motorcycle tour companies. All these companies seem to offer exactly the same service, even the bikes are identical. The difference is their geographical location in the world of where they run their tours. They are all after customers who want the experience of riding a motorcycle in a new place without the hassle of arranging and sorting things themselves. I am not judging, these companies offer some great adventures and experiences, but for me, part of the motorcycle adventure is doing all this stuff myself. Learning about visa applications, sorting logistics, accommodation, researching driving laws and customs and all the other aspects of planning an adventure are extremely satisfying. Combine all this hard work with the ride itself and you have just made your dream come true. That is pretty special, and the rewards speak for themselves, but if you have a busy life, these tour companies can be a great solution to fulfil your motorcycle dreams. I often thought that when I moved to the USA, I would do something like that myself, and run organised tours. However, on reflection I decided it was not for me. Happy to do it for a few mates and join in the adventure, but not for commercial gain. My advice for anyone thinking about doing a self-organised motorcycle adventure is to start small, a long weekend away perhaps and then build on that. Before you know it, you will be planning an adventure that will be fulfilling your once-in-a-lifetime dream. This is a much better option than using a commercial company who may have a different idea on your dream. How rewarding would that be.

Since age 13, I have been the proud owner of 7 Yamahas, 3 Triumphs, 3 Honda's, 2 BMW's, 2 Kawasaki's, 2 Suzuki's, a Harley, a Moto Guzzi, a Vespa, an NSU and a Tomos. I have listed all the bikes in the table at the back and my grading in the far right column is based on nothing more than the fun factor I had with each of the bikes, the learning experience it gave me and the attachment I felt toward it.

The story continues. I can't wait to see what my next bike will be, because there will be a next one. If past ownership is anything to go by, looks like it will be sometime in 2020......

# Year Owned	Bike Details & Months owned	Size/Config/BHP-HP/Gears	Weight lbs /Torque lbft	Top MPH/ & Grade
1: 1973	1959 NSU Quickly - 8	49cc/2stroke/Single/1.4/2	73/ 1.5	25 - 23
2: 1974	1959 Vespa 150GS -5	145cc/2stroke/Single/8.2/4	220/8.5	62 - 21
3: 1975	1969 Honda C50 - 10	49cc/4stroke/Single/4.5/3	158/2.8	43 - 19
4: 1976	1976 Yamaha FS1E -12	49cc/2stroke/Single/4.8/4	154/3.6	48 - 12
5: 1977	1977 Yamaha DT 175 - 10	171cc/2stroke/Single/16.5/5	236/12	70 - 13
6: 1977	1976 Yamaha RD400 - 6	398cc/2stroke/Twin/44/6	364/30	107 - 3
7: 1978	1978 Yamaha XS 500 - 15	498cc/4stroke/Twin/48/5	458/32.5	105 - 15
8: 1979	1979 Yamaha XS 650 Special - 3	653cc/4stroke/Twin/53/5	463/40	105 - 16
9: 1982	1976 Honda CJ 250T - 48	249cc/4stroke/Twin/27/5	384/14.5	84 - 17
10: 1984	1982 Honda CX500 E - 58	497cc/4stroke/V-twin/50/5	458/31	106 - 18
11: 1992	1991 Yamaha XJ 600 - 48	599cc/4stroke/4Cyl/72/6	467/39.8	123 - 10
12: 1993	1982 Tomos A3 - 15	49cc/2stroke/Single/<2/2	80/1.5	20 - 22
13: 1996	1994 Triumph Speed Triple - 18	885cc/4stroke/Triple/98/5	460/58.6	135 - 2
14: 2002	1995 Triumph Daytona - 24	885cc/4stroke/Triple/98/6	470/60	140 - 11
15: 2004	2002 Suzuki DR650 SE - 54	644cc/4stroke/Single/46/5	324/39.8	100 - 4
16: 2006	1997 BMW R1100GS - 51	1084cc/4stroke/Boxer Twin/80/5	536/73	125 - 6

17: 2008	2008 Yamaha Scorpio - 6	223cc/4stroke/Single/18/5	300/12.9	80 - 20
18: 2008	2006 Harley Davidson Sportster - 20	883cc&1200cc/4stroke/V Twin/53 & 67.7/5	555 & 556/51 & 72.9	102 & 118 - 14
19: 2010	1979 Suzuki ER 250 - 5	246cc/2stroke/Single/23/5	262/19.6	75 - 24
20: 2011	2004 BMW R1200GS - 60	1170cc/4stroke/Boxer Twin/98/6	438/85	132 - 1
21: 2012	2007 Moto Guzzi Griso - 62	1064cc/4stroke/V Twin/87/6	500/69.3	125 - 5
22: 2014	2014 Kawasaki KLR650 - 22	652cc/4stroke/Single/42/5	432/34.7	108 - 9
23: 2016	2014 Kawasaki KLR 650 - -	652cc/4stroke/Single/42/5	432/34.7	108 - 8
24: 2018	2018 Triumph T120 - -	1200cc/4stroke/Twin/80/6	494/77	120 - 7

About The Author
Nigel M Sainsbury

Border of Arizona and New Mexico, USA, 2013

Born in Newport, Gwent, UK. Nigel grew up in the coal mining valleys of South Wales, in the United Kingdom during the 1960s and 70s. An avid motorcyclist, musician and aviation professional, Nigel joined the Royal Air Force (RAF) at age 16 and served for twenty-seven years as an Aero Systems Engineer. In 2004 Nigel retired for the first time and emigrated with his family to the other side of the world to join the Royal New Zealand Air Force (RNZAF). Nigel officially became a Kiwi in 2007 and completed twelve years active service in the RNZAF. In 2016 Nigel retired a second time on completion of his tour of duty as the Defence Advisor to Canada and Air Attaché to the United States of America, located in the New Zealand Embassy in Washington D.C. Rather than return to New Zealand, Nigel married his American Fiancée, Carol, and started his own consultancy business ***www.nigelsainsburyconsulting.com*** and now lives in Fairfax, Virginia. A citizen of both the United

Kingdom and New Zealand, Nigel hopes to add the USA to his list of citizenship countries by 2022.

CPSIA information can be obtained
at www.ICGtesting.com
Printed in the USA
BVHW081425021219
565404BV00002B/131/P